D1167673

THE KENYON REVIEW

Readings for Writers

David H. Lynn, Editor

THE KENYON REVIEW
GAMBIER, OHIO

Copyright © *The Kenyon Review*, 2009.

All rights reserved. No part of this book may be reproduced in any form or by any electronic or mechanical means including information storage and retrieval systems—except in the case of brief quotations embodied in critical articles or reviews—without permission in writing from its publisher, *The Kenyon Review*.

Published by *The Kenyon Review*
Finn House, 102 West Wiggin St., Gambier, Ohio 43022
(740) 427-5208
Fax: (740) 427-5417
www.kenyonreview.org

ISBN: 978-0-9840628-0-5

Contents

Introduction

Readings for Writers is a very different creature from your usual anthology. Yes, everything here has appeared in *The Kenyon Review* sometime during the past seventy years. That should establish literary merit, aside from the fame of many of the featured authors. But a different principle of selection comes into play: choosing stories, poems, and essays from across the decades to provoke lively responses from writers today, to inspire and challenge.

In truth, we have been creating a more informal version of this reader each summer for our writing workshops. The Kenyon Review Young Writers program, for example, isn't about force-feeding proper English grammar into high school students, nor perfecting the five-paragraph essay, nor earning a high grade. Although we offer students the chance to write in many different genres, it isn't about genres either. It's about writing in response to something. And the prompts our young writers respond to are literary. With the treasure trove of the *KR* archive at hand, why turn elsewhere for material? For nearly twenty years, then, we have published a special anthology to be used in these workshops.

So now we have decided to publish this larger, handsome volume for a larger, and I'm quite sure equally handsome, audience. I don't imagine most readers sitting down and working their way through, beginning to end, though that would certainly be a treat. Rather, I'd suggest you pick and browse and choose. There's plenty of delight to be had, plenty of ready inspiration.

One of the miracles of great literature, of course, is that it can be both timeless and yet forever fresh. Read Flannery O'Connor's story "The Life You Save May Be Your Own" and see what I mean.

Still, because the volume has been arranged chronologically, it is also an interesting testament to the evolution of *The Kenyon Review*'s aesthetic over seven decades. This reflects and reveals, not just the changing tastes of a series of editors, but also the changing nature of our society. You may notice that authors in the early years were largely white and largely male, and the prosody of the poetry tended, generally, to be formal in structure. Among them we include poems by John Crowe Ransom, the great poet and critic who founded the *Review* in 1939. Though not published in *KR*, his work and presence here seem important.

To be sure, recent issues of *The Kenyon Review* have featured plenty of white males and formal poetry as well, but far less exclusively so. The writing, I warrant, is every bit as masterful. Skeptical? Have a look at "The Clipping" by Dolen Perkins-Valdez.

Because the selections here are intended to inspire active response—pen to paper, fingers to keyboard—we have left out literature that might afford different kinds of pleasure. For example, *The Kenyon Review* was long renowned for its literary criticism, but though many of those articles remain fascinating, they are not featured in this particular volume. Likewise, I have tried to offer a deliberate medley of forms, strategies, and techniques, and the selections tend to be somewhat shorter than might have been the case in an anthology with a different purpose.

Just as the success of our writing programs is the result of inspired teamwork — and an exceptionally great team — so, too, this volume reflects the creative efforts of many souls, among them David Baker, Elizabeth Forman, Loretta Godfrey, W. David Hall, Geeta Kothari, Marlene Landefeld, Sergei Lobanov-Rostovsky, Michael Matros, Tyler Meier, John Pickard, Anna Duke Reach, Abigail Wadsworth Serfass, Thomas Stamp, G. C. Waldrep, and Nancy Zafris. Of them I am proud. To them I am grateful.

—D. H. L.

RANDALL JARRELL

The Winter's Tale

The storm rehearses through the bewildered fields
Its general logic; the contorted or dispassionate
Faces work out their incredulity, or stammer
The mistaking sentences. Night falls. In the lit
Schoolroom the hothouse guests are crammed
With their elaborate ignorance, repeat
The glib and estranged responses of the dead
To the professor's nod. The urgent galleries
Converge in anticipation on the halls
Where at announced hours the beauty,
Able, and Laughable commence patiently
The permanent recital of their aptitudes:
The song of the world. To the wicked and furred,
The naked and curious, the instruments proffer
Their partial and excessive knowledge; here in the suites,
Among the grains, the contraceptives and textiles,
Or inside the board cave lined with newspapers
Where in one thoroughly used room are initiated,
Persevered in, and annihilated, the forbidding ranges
Of the bewildered and extravagant responses of the cell;
Among all the inexhaustible variations — of milieu,
Of compensation and excess — the waltz-theme shudders,
Frivolous, inexorable, the inadequate and conclusive
Sentence of our genius.
Along the advertisements the blisses flicker,
Partial as morphine, the terminal moraine

1

Of sheeted continents, a calendar of woe.

We who have possessed the world
As efficiently as a new virus; who classified the races,
Species, and cultures of the world as scrub
To be cleared, stupidity to be liquidated, matter
To be assimilated into the system of our destruction;
Are finding how quickly the resistance of our hosts
Is built up—can think, "Tomorrow we may be remembered
As a technologist's nightmare, the megalomaniacs
Who presented to posterity as their justification
The best armies that the world ever saw."
Who made virtue and poetry and understanding
The prohibited reserves of the expert, of workers
Specialized as the ant-soldier; and who turned from their difficult
Versions to the degenerate myth, the cruelties
So incredible and habitual they seemed escapes.

Yet, through our night, just as before,
The discharged thief stumbles, nevertheless
Weeps at its crystals, feels at the winter's
Tale the familiar and powerful delight;
The child owns the snow-man; the skier
Hesitant along the stormy crest, or wrenching
His turn from the bluff's crust, to glide
Down the stony hillside past the robbers' hut
To the house of the typhoid-carrier; the understanding
Imperturbable in their neglect, concentrating
In obscure lodgings the impatient genius
That informs all the breasts; the few who keep
By lack or obstinacy scraps of the romantic
And immediately adequate world of the past—the
Strangers with a stranger's inflections, the broken
And unlovely English of the unborn world:

All, all, this winter night
Are weak, are emptying fast. Tomorrow puffs
From its iron centers into the moonlight, men move masked
Through streets abrupt with excavations, the explosive triumphs
Of a new architecture: the twelve-floor dumps
Of smashed stone starred with limbs, the monumental
Tombs of a whole age. A whole economy;
The fiascoes of the metaphysician, a theology's disasters,
The substitutes of the geometer for existence, the observation
Of peas and galaxies—the impatient fictions
Of the interminable and euphuist's metaphor exploding
Into use, into breath, into terror; the millennia
Of patience, of skills, of understanding, the centuries
Of terms crystallizing into weapons, the privative
And endless means, the catastrophic
Magnificence of paranoia; are elaborated into
A few bodies in the torn-up street.
The survivor poking in the ruins with a stick
Finds only portions of his friends. In this universe
Of discourse the shameless and witless facility
Of such a conclusion is normal, and no one thinks:
"What came before this was worse. Expected so long,
Arrived at last, tomorrow is death."

From the disintegrating bomber, the mercenary
Who has sown without hatred or understanding
The shells of the absolute world that flowers
In the confused air of the dying city
Plunges for his instant of incandescence, acquiesces
In our death and his own, and welcomes
The fall of the western hegemonies.

[OLD SERIES VOL. I, NO. 1 / WINTER 1939]

ALLEN TATE

The Trout Map

The Management Area of Cherokee
National Forest, interested in fish,
Has mapped Tellico and Bald Rivers
And North River, with the tributaries
Brookshire Branch and Sugar Cove Creek:
A fishy map for facile fishery.

Now consider it: nicely drawn in two
Colors, blue and red; blue for the hue
Of Europe (Tennessee water is green),
Red lines by blue streams to warn
The fancy-fishmen from protected fish;
Black borders hold the Area in a cracked dish.

Other black lines, the dots and dashes, wire
The fisher's will through classic laurel
Over boar tracks to foamy pot-holes lying
Under Bald falls that thump the buying
Trout: we sold Professor, Brown Hackle, Worms.
Tom Bagley and I were dotted and dashed wills.

Up Green Cove Gap from Preacher Millsaps' cabin
We walked an hour confident of victory,
Went to the west down a trail that led us
To Bald River — here map and scene were one

In scene-identity. Eight trout is the story
In three miles. We came to a rock bridge

On which the road went left around a hill,
The river, right, tumbled into a cove;
But the map dashed the road along the stream
And we dotted man's fishiest enthymeme
With jellied feet upon deductive love
Of what eyes see not, that nourishes the will:

We were fishers, weren't we? And tried to fish
The egoed belly's dry cartograph —
Which made the government fish lie down and laugh;
Tommy and I listened, we heard them shake
Mountains and cove because the map was fake.
After eighteen miles our feet were clownish;

Then darkness took us into wheezing straits
Where coarse Magellan, idling with his fates,
Ran with the gulls for map around the Horn,
Or wheresoever the mind with tidy scorn
Revisits the world to hear an eagle scream
Vertigo! Mapless, the mountains were a dream.

[OLD SERIES VOL. I, NO. 4 / AUTUMN 1939]

Poem

"If my head hurt a hair's foot
Pack back the downed bone. If the unpricked ball of my breath
Bump on a spout let the bubbles jump out.
Sooner drop with the worm of the ropes round my throat
Than bully ill love in the clouted scene.

"All game phrases fit your ring of a cockfight:
I'll comb the snared woods with a glove on a lamp,
Peck, sprint, dance on fountains and duck time
Before I rush in a crouch the ghost with a hammer, air,
Strike light, and bloody a loud room.

"If my bunched, monkey coming is cruel
Rage me back to the making house. My hand unravel
When you sew the deep door. The bed is a cross place.
Bend, if my journey ache, direction like an arc or make
A limp and riderless shape to leap nine thinning months."

"No. Not for Christ's dazzling bed
Or a nacreous sleep among soft particles and charms
My dear would I change my tears or your iron head.
Thrust, my daughter or son, to escape, there is none, none, none,
Nor when all ponderous heaven's host of waters breaks.

"Now to awake husked of gestures and my joy like a cave
To the anguish and carrion, to the infant forever unfree,
O my lost love bounced from a good home;
The grain that hurries this way from the rim of the grave
Has a voice and a house, and there and here you must couch
      and cry.

"Rest beyond choice in the dust-appointed grain,
At the breast stored with seas. No return
Through the waves of the fat streets nor the skeleton's thin ways.
The grave and my calm body are shut to your coming as stone,
And the endless beginning of prodigies suffers open."

[OLD SERIES VOL. I, NO. 3 / SUMMER 1939]

WALLACE STEVENS

Variations on a Summer Day

I

Say of the gulls that they are flying
In light blue air over dark blue sea.

II

A music more than a breath, but less
Than the wind, sub-music like sub-speech,
A repetition of unconscious things,
Letters of rock and water, words
Of the visible elements and of ours.

III

The rocks of the cliffs are the heads of dogs
That turn into fishes and leap
Into the sea.

IV

Star over Monhegan, Atlantic star,
Lantern without a bearer, you drift,
You, too, are drifting, in spite of your course;
Unless in the darkness, brightly-crowned
You are the will, if there is a will,

Or the portent of a will that was,
One of the portents of the will that was.

V

The leaves of the sea are shaken and shaken.
There was a tree that was a father.
We sat beneath it and sang our songs.

VI

It is cold to be forever young,
To come to tragic shores and flow,
In sapphire, round the sun-bleached stones,
Being, for old men, time of their time.

VII

One sparrow is worth a thousand gulls,
When it sings. The gull sits on chimney-tops.
He mocks the guineas, challenges
The crow, inciting various modes.
The sparrow requites one, without intent.

VIII

An exercise in viewing the world.
On the motive! But one looks at the sea
As one improvises, on the piano.

IX

This cloudy world, by aid of land and sea,
Night and day, wind and quiet, produces
More nights, more days, more clouds, more worlds.

X

To change nature, not merely to change ideas,
To escape from the body, so to feel

Those feelings that the body balks,
The feelings of the natures round us here:
As a boat feels when it cuts blue water.

XI

Now, the timothy at Pemaquid
That rolled in heat is silver tipped
And cold. The moon follows the sun like a French
Translation of a Russian poet.

XII

Everywhere the spruce trees bury soldiers:
Hugh March: a sergeant, a red coat, killed,
With his men, beyond the barbican.
Everywhere spruce trees bury spruce trees.

XIII

Cover the sea with the sand rose. Fill
The sky with the radiantiana
Of spray. Let all the salt be gone.

XIV

Words add to the senses. The words for the dazzle
Of mica, the dithering of grass,
The Arachne integument of dead trees,
Are the eye grown larger, more intense.

XV

The last island and its inhabitant,
The two alike, distinguish blues,
Until the difference between air
And sea exists by grace alone,
In objects, as white this, white that.

XVI

Round and round goes the bell of the water
And round and round goes the water itself
And that which is the pitch of its motion,
The bell of its dome, the patron of sound.

XVII

Pass through the door and through the walls,
Those bearing balsam, its field fragrance,
Pine-figures bringing sleep to sleep.

XVIII

Low tide, flat water, sultry sun.
One observes profoundest shadows rolling,
Damariscotta da da doo.

XIX

One boy swims under a tub, one sits
On top. Hurroo! The man-boat comes,
In a man-makenesse, neater than Naples.

XX

You could almost see the brass on her gleaming,
Not quite. The mist was to light what red
Is to fire. And her mainmast tapered to nothing,
Without teetering a millimeter's measure.
The beads on her rails seemed to grasp at transparence.
It was not yet the hour to be dauntlessly leaping.

[OLD SERIES VOL. II, NO. 1 / WINTER 1940]

What Are Years?

What is our innocence,
what is our guilt? All are
        naked, none is safe. And whence
is courage: the unanswered question,
the resolute doubt,—
dumbly calling, deafly listening—that
in misfortune, even death,
        encourages others
        and in its defeat, stirs

        the soul to be strong? He
sees deep and is glad, who
        accedes to mortality
and in his imprisonment, rises
upon himself as
the sea in a chasm, struggling to be
free and unable to be,
        in its surrendering
        finds its continuing.

        So he who strongly feels,
behaves. The very bird,
        grown taller as he sings, steels
his form straight up though he is captive.
His mighty singing
says; satisfaction is a lowly

thing, how pure a thing is joy.
    This is mortality,
    this is eternity.

A Glass-Ribbed Nest

    For authorities whose hopes
are shaped by mercenaries?
    Writers entrapped by
    teatime fame and by
commuters' comforts? Not for these
    the paper nautilus
constructs her thin glass shell.

    Giving her perishable
souvenir of hope, a dull
    white outside and smooth-
    edged inner side as
glossy as the sea, the watchful
    animal takes charge of
    it herself and scarcely

    leaves it till the eggs are hatched.
Buried eight-fold in her eight
    arms, for she is in
    a sense a devil-
fish, her glass ramshorn-cradled freight
    is hid but is not crushed.
    As Hercules, bitten

    by a crab loyal to the hydra,
was hindered to succeed,
    the intensively
    watched eggs coming from

the shell, free it when they are freed,—
   leaving its wasp-nest flaws
   of white on white, and close-

laid Ionic chiton-folds
like the lines in the mane of
   a Parthenon horse,
   round which the arms had
wound themselves as if they knew love
   is the only fortress
   strong enough to trust to.

[OLD SERIES VOL. II, NO. 3 / SUMMER 1940]

JOHN BERRYMAN

The Imaginary Jew

The second summer of the European War I spent in New York.
I lived in a room just below street-level on Lexington above
34th, wrote a good deal, tried not to think about Europe, and
listened to music on a small gramophone, the only thing of my
own, except books, in the room. Haydn's London Symphony,
his last, I heard probably fifty times in two months. One night
when excited I dropped the pickup, creating a series of knocks
at the beginning of the last movement where the oboe joins the
strings which still, when I hear them, bring up for me my low
dark long damp room and I feel the dew of heat and smell the
rented upholstery. I was trying as they say to come back a little,
uncertain and low after an exhausting year. Why I decided to do
this in New York — the enemy in summer equally of soul and
body, as I had known for years — I can't remember; perhaps I
didn't, but was held on merely from week to week by the motive
which presently appeared in the form of a young woman met the
Christmas before and now the occupation of every evening, not
passed in solitary and restless gloom. My friends were away; I saw
few other people. Now and then I went to the zoo in lower Central Park and watched with interest the extraordinary behavior of
a female badger. For a certain time she quickly paced the round
of her cage. Then she would approach the sidewall from an angle
in a determined, hardly perceptible, unhurried trot; suddenly,
when an inch away, point her nose up it, follow her nose up over
her back, turning a deft and easy somersault, from which she
emerged on her feet moving swiftly and unconcernedly away, as

if the action had been no affair of hers, indeed she had scarcely been present. There was another badger in the cage who never did this, and nothing else about her was remarkable; but this competent disinterested somersault she enacted once every five or ten minutes as long as I watched her,—quitting the wall, by the way, always at an angle in fixed relation to the angle at which she arrived at it. It is no longer possible to experience the pleasure I knew each time she lifted her nose and I understood again that she would not fail me, or feel the mystery of her absolute disclaimer,—she has been taken away or died.

The story I have to tell is no further a part of that special summer than a nightmare takes its character, for memory, from the phase of the moon one noticed on going to bed. It could have happened in another year and in another place. No doubt it did, has done, will do. Still, so weak is the talent of the mind for pure relation—immaculate apprehension of K alone—that everything helps us, as when we come to an unknown city: architecture, history, trade-practices, folklore. Even more anxious our approach to a city—like my small story—which we have known and forgotten. Yet how little we can learn! Some of the history is the lonely summer. Part of the folklore, I suppose, is what I now unwillingly rehearse, the character which experience has given to my sense of the Jewish people.

Born in a part of the South where no Jews had come, or none had stayed, and educated thereafter in States where they are numerous, I somehow arrived at a metropolitan university without any clear idea of what in modem life a Jew was,—without even a clear consciousness of having seen one. I am unable now to explain this simplicity or blindness. I had not escaped, of course, a sense that humans somewhat different from ourselves, called "Jews," existed as in the middle distance and were best kept there, but this sense was of the vaguest. From what it was derived I do not know; I do not recall feeling the least curiosity about it, or about Jews; I had, simply, from the atmosphere of an advanced heterogeneous democratic society, ingathered a gently negative attitude towards Jews. This I took with me, untested, to college, where it received neither confirmation nor stimulus for two months. I rowed and danced and cut classes and was political; by mid-November I knew most of the five hundred men in my year. Then the man who rowed Number Three, in the eight of which I was bow, took me aside in the shower one afternoon and warned me not to be so chatty with Rosenblum.

I wondered why not. Rosenblum was stroke, a large handsome amiable fellow, for whose ability in the shell I felt great respect and no doubt envy. Because the fellows in the House wouldn't like it, my friend said. "What have they against him?" "It's only because he's Jewish," explained my friend, a second-generation Middle European.

I hooted at him, making the current noises of disbelief, and went back under the shower. It did not occur to me that he could be right. But next day when I was talking with Herz—the coxswain, whom I found intelligent and pleasant—I remembered the libel with some annoyance, and told Herz about it as a curiosity. Herz looked at me oddly, lowering his head, and said after a pause, "Why, Al *is* Jewish, didn't you know that?" I was amazed. I said it was absurd, he couldn't be! "Why not?" said Herz, who must have been as astonished as I was. "Don't you know I'm Jewish?"

I did not know, of course, and ignorance has seldom cost me such humiliation. Herz did not guy me; he went off. But greater than my shame at not knowing something known, apparently, without effort to everyone else, were my emotions for what I then quickly discovered. Asking careful questions during the next week, I learnt that about a third of the men I spent time with in college were Jewish; that they knew it, and the others knew it; that some of the others disliked them for it, and they knew this also; that certain Houses existed *only* for Jews, who were excluded from the rest; and that what in short I took to be an idiotic state was deeply established, familiar, and acceptable to everyone. This discovery was the beginning of my instruction in social life proper—construing social life as that from which political life issues like a somatic dream.

My attitude toward my friends did not alter on this revelation. I merely discarded the notion that Jews were a proper object for any special attitude; my old sense vanished. This was in 1933. Later, as word of the German persecution filtered into this country, some sentimentality undoubtedly corrupted my no-attitude. I denied the presence of obvious defects in particular Jews, feeling that to admit them would be to side with the sadists and murderers. Accident allotting me close friends who were Jewish, their disadvantages enraged me. Gradually, and against my sense of impartial justice, I became the anomaly which only a partial society can produce, and for which it has no name known to the lexicons. In one area, but not exclusively, "nigger-lover" is cast in a parallel way: but for a special sympathy and liking for Jews—which became my fate, so that I trembled when I heard one abused in talk—we have no term. In this condition I still was during the summer of which I speak. One further circumstance may be mentioned, as a product, I believe, of this curious training. I am spectacularly unable to identify Jews as Jews,—by name, cast of feature, accent, or environment,—and this has been true, not only of course before the college incident, but during my whole life since. Even names to anyone else patently Hebraic rarely suggest to me anything. And when once I learn that So-and-so is Jewish, I am likely to forget it. Now Jewishness may be a fact as striking and informative as someone's past heroism or his Christianity or his understanding of the subtlest human relations, and I feel sure that something operates to prevent my utilizing the plain signs by which such characters—in a Jewish man or woman—may be identified, and prevent my retaining the identification once it is made.

So to the city my summer and a night in August. I used to stop on Fourteenth Street for iced coffee, walking from the Village home (or to my room rather) after leaving my friend, and one night when I came out I wandered across to the island of trees and grass and concrete walks raised in the center of Union Square. Here men—a few women, old—sit in the evenings of summer, looking at papers or staring off or talking, and knots of them stay on, arguing, very late; these the unemployed or unemployable, the sleepless, the malcontent. There are no formal orators, as at Columbus Circle in the Nineteen-thirties and at Hyde Park Corner. Each group is dominated by several articulate and strong-lunged persons who battle each other with prejudices and desires, swaying with intensity, and take on from time to time the interrupters: a forum at the bottom of the pot,—Jefferson's fear, Whitman's hope, the dream of the younger Lenin. It was now about one o'clock, almost hot, and many men were still out. I stared for a little at the equestrian statue, obscure in the night on top of its pedestal, thinking that the misty Rider would sweep again away all these men at his feet, whenever he liked,—what symbol for power yet in a mechanical age rivals the mounted man?—and moved to the nearest group; or I plunged to it.

The dictator to the group was old, with dark cracked skin, fixed eyes in an excited face, leaning forward madly on his bench towards the half-dozen men in semicircle before him. "It's bread! it's bread!" he was saying. "It's bitter-sweet. All the bitter and all the sweetness. Of an overture. What else do you want? When you ask for steak and potatoes, do you want pastry with it? It's bread! It's bread! Help yourself! Help yourself!"

The listeners stood expressionless, except one who was smiling with contempt and interrupted now.

"Never a happy minute, never a happy minute!" the old man cried. "It's good to be dead! Some men should kill themselves."

"Don't you want to live?" said the smiling man.

"Of course I want to live. Everyone wants to live! If death comes suddenly it's better. It's better!"

With pain I turned away. The next group were talking diffusely and angrily about the Mayor, and I passed to a third, where a frantic olive-skinned young man with a fringe of silky beard was exclaiming:

"No restaurant in New York had the Last Supper! No. When people sit down to eat they should think of that!"

"Listen," said a white-shirted student on the rail, glancing around for approbation, "listen, if I open a restaurant and put *The Last Supper* up over the door, how much money do you think I'd lose? Ten thousand dollars ?"

The fourth cluster was larger and appeared more coherent. A savage argument was in progress between a man of fifty with an oily red face, hatted, very determined in manner, and a muscular fellow half his age with heavy eyebrows, coatless, plainly Irish. Fifteen or twenty men were packed around them, and others on a bench near the rail against which the Irishman was lounging were attending also. I listened for a few minutes. The question was whether the President was trying to get us into the War,—or rather, whether this was legitimate, since the Irishman claimed that Roosevelt was a goddamned warmonger whom all the real people in the country hated, and the older man claimed that we should have gone into the f..ing war when France fell a year before, as everybody in the country knew except a few immigrant rats. Redface talked ten times as much as the Irishman, but he was not able to establish any advantage that I could see. He ranted, and then Irish either repeated shortly and fiercely what he had said last, or shifted his ground. The audience were silent—favouring whom I don't know, but evidently much interested. One or two men pushed out of the group, others arrived behind me, and I was eddied forward towards the disputants. The young Irishman broke suddenly into a tirade by the man with the hat:

"You're full of s. Roosevelt even tried to get us in with the communists in the Spanish war. If he could have done it we'd have been burning churches down like the rest of the Reds."

"No, that's not right," I heard my own voice, and pushed forward, feeling blood in my face, beginning to tremble. "No, Roosevelt as a matter of fact helped Franco by non-intervention, at the same time that Italians and German planes were fighting against the Government and arms couldn't get in from France."

"What's that? What are you, a Jew?" He turned to me contemptuously, and was back at the older man before I could speak, "The only reason we weren't over there four years ago is because you can only screw us so much. Then we quit. No New Deal bastard could make us go help the goddamned communists."

"That ain't the question, it's if we want to fight *now* or *later*. Them Nazis ain't gonna sit!" shouted the redfaced man. "They got Egypt practically, and then it's India if it ain't England first. It ain't a question of the communists, the communists are on Hitler's side. I tellya we can wait and wait and chew and spit and the first thing you know they'll be in England, and then who's gonna help us when they start after us? Maybe Brazil? Get wise to the world! Spain don't matter now one way or the other, they ain't gonna help and they can't hurt. It's Germany and Italy and Japan, and if it ain't too late now it's gonna be. Get wise to yourself. We shoulda gone in—"

"What with?" said the Irishman with disdain. "Pop pop. Wooden machine-guns?"

"We were as ready a year ago as we are now. Defence don't mean nothing, you gotta have to fight!"

"No, we're much better off now," I said, "than we were a year ago. When England went in, to keep its word to Poland, what good was it to Poland?" The German Army—"

"Shut up, you Jew," said the Irishman.

"I'm not a Jew," I said to him. "What makes—"

"Listen, Pop," he said to the man in the hat, "it's OK to shoot your mouth off but what the hell have you got to do with it? You aren't gonna do any fighting."

"Listen," I said.

"You sit on your big ass and talk about who's gonna fight who. Nobody's gonna fight anybody. If we feel hot, we ought to clean up some of the sons of bitches here before we go sticking our nuts anywhere to help England. We ought to clean up the sons of bitches in Wall Street and Washington before we take any ocean trips. You want to know something? You know why

Germany's winning everything in this war? Because there ain't no Jews back home. There ain't no more Jews, first shouting war like this one here"—nodding at me—"and then skinning off to the synagogue with the profits. Wake up, Pop! You must have been around in the last war, you ought to know better."

I was too nervous to be angry or resentful. But I began to have a sense of oppression in breathing. I took the Irishman by the arm.

"Listen, I told you I'm not a Jew."

"I don't give a damn what you are," he turned his half-dark eyes to me, wrenching his arm loose. "You talk like a Jew."

"What does that mean?" Some part of me wanted to laugh. "How does a Jew talk?"

"They talk like you, buddy."

"That's a fine argument! But if I'm not a Jew, my talk only—"

"You probably are a Jew. You look like a Jew."

"I *look* like a Jew? Listen," I swung around with despair to a man standing next to me, "do I look like a Jew? It doesn't matter whether I do or not—a Jew is as good as anybody and better than this son of a bitch—" I was not exactly excited, I was trying to adapt my language as my need for the crowd, and my sudden respect for its judgment, possessed me—"but in fact I'm not Jewish and I don't look Jewish. Do I?"

The man looked at me quickly and said, half to me and half to the Irishman, "Hell, I don't know. Sure he does."

A wave of disappointment and outrage swept me almost to tears, I felt like a man betrayed by his brother. The lamps seemed brighter and vaguer, the night large. Looking around I saw sitting on a bench near me a tall, heavy, serious-looking man of thirty, well dressed, whom I had noticed earlier, and appealed to him, "Tell me, do I look Jewish ?"

But he only stared up and waved his head vaguely. I saw with horror that something was wrong with him.

"You look like a Jew. You talk like a Jew. You *are* a Jew," I heard the Irishman say.

I heard murmuring among the men, but I could see nothing very clearly. It seemed very hot. I faced the Irishman again help-lessly, holding my voice from rising.

"I'm *not* a Jew," I told him. "I might be, but I'm not. You have no bloody reason to think so, and you can't make me a Jew by simply repeating like an idiot that I am."

"Don't deny it, son," said the redfaced man, "stand up to him."

"God damn it," suddenly I was furious, whirling like a fool (was I afraid of the Irishman? had he conquered me?) on the redfaced man, "I'm *not* denying it! Or rather I am, but only be-cause I'm not a Jew! I despise renegades, I hate Jews who turn on their people, if I were a Jew I would say so, I would be proud to be: what is the vicious opinion of a man like this to me if I were a Jew? But I'm not. Why the hell should I admit I am if I'm not ?"

"Jesus, the Jew is excited," said the Irishman.

"I have a right to be excited, you son of a bitch. Suppose I call you a Jew. Yes, you're a Jew. Does that mean anything?"

"Not a damn thing." He spat over the rail past a man's head.

"Prove that you're not. I say you are."

"Now listen, you Jew. I'm a Catholic."

"So am I, or I was born one, I'm not one now. I was born a Catholic." I was a little calmer but goaded, obsessed with the need to straighten this out. I felt that everything for everyone there de-pended on my proving him wrong. If *once* this evil for which we have not even a name could be exposed to the rest of the men as empty—if I could *prove* I was not a Jew—it would fall to the ground, neither would anyone else be a Jew to be accused. Then it could be trampled on. Fascist America was at stake. I listened, intensely anxious for our fate.

"Yeah?" said the Irishman. "Say the Apostles' Creed."

Memory went swirling back, I could hear the little bell die as I hushed it and set it on the felt, Father Boniface looked at me tall from the top of the steps and smiled greeting me in the dark-ness before dawn as I came to serve, the men pressed around me under the lamps, and I could remember nothing but *visibilum omnium . . . et invisibilium*?

"I don't remember it."

The Irishman laughed with his certainty.

The papers in my pocket, I thought them over hurriedly. In my wallet. What would they prove? Details of ritual, Church history: anyone could learn them. My piece of Irish blood. Shame, shame: shame for my ruthless people. I will not be his blood. I wish I were a Jew, I would change my blood, to be able to say *Yes* and defy him.

"I'm not a Jew," I felt a fool. "You only say so. You haven't any evidence in the world."

He leaned forward from the rail, close to me. "Are you cut?"

Shock, fear ran through me before I could make any meaning out of his words. Then they ran faster, and I felt confused.

From that point, nothing is clear for me. I stayed a long time—it seemed impossible to leave, showing him victor to them—thinking of possible allies and new plans of proof, but without hope. I was tired to the marrow. The arguments rushed on, and I spoke often now but seldom was heeded except by an old fat woman, very short and dirty, who listened intently to everyone. Heavier and heavier appeared to me to press upon us in the fading night our general guilt.

In the days following, as my resentment died, I saw that I had not been a victim altogether unjustly. My persecutors were right: I was a Jew. The imaginary Jew I was was as real as the imaginary Jew hunted down, on other nights and days, in a real Jew. Every murderer strikes the mirror, the lash of the torturer falls on the mirror and cuts the real image, and the real and the imaginary blood flow down together.

[OLD SERIES VOL. VII, NO. 4 / AUTUMN 1945]

MURIEL RUKEYSER

Eyes of Night-Time

On the roads at night I saw the glitter of eyes:
my dark around me let shine one ray; that black
allowed their eyes: spangles in the cat's, air in the moth's eye shine,
mosaic of the fly, ruby-eyed beetle, the eyes that never weep,
the horned toad sitting and its tear of blood,
fighters and prisoners in the forest, people
aware in this almost total dark, with the difference,
the one broad fact of light.

Eyes on the road at night, sides of a road like rhyme;
the floor of the illumined shadow sea
and shallows with their assembling flash and show
of sight, root, holdfast, eyes of the brittle stars.
And your eyes in the shadowy red room,
scent of the forest entering, various time
calling and the light of wood along the ceiling
and over us birds calling and their circuit eyes.
And in our bodies the eyes of the dead and living
giving us gifts at hand, the glitter of all their eyes.

[OLD SERIES VOL. IX, NO. 2 / SPRING 1947]

The Duet

All winter long the huge sad lady
Sang to her warm house of the heart betrayed: —
   Love lies delirious and a-dying;
The purlieus are shaken by his sharp cry.
   But back across the fret dividing
His wildernesses from her floral side
   All winter long a scrunty beggar
With one glass eye and one hickory leg,
   Stumping about half-drunk through stony
Ravines and over dead volcanic cones,
   Refused her tragic hurt, declaring
A happy passion to the freezing air,
   Turning his barrel-organ, playing
Lanterloo my lovely, my First-of-May.

   Louder on nights when in cold glory
The full moon made its meditative tour,
   To big chords from her black grand piano
She sang the disappointment and the fear
   For all her lawns and orchards: — *Slowly*
The spreading ache bechills the rampant glow
   Of fortune-hunting blood; Time conjures
The moskered ancestral tower to plunge
   From its fastidious cornice down to
The pigsties far below; the oaks turn brown;

The cute little botts of the sailors
Are snapped up by the sea. But to her gale
  Of sorrow from the moonstruck darkness
The ragged runagate opposed his spark,

  For still his scrannel music-making
In tipsy joy across the gliddered lake,
  Praising for all the rocks and craters
The green refreshments of the watered state,
  Cried nonsense to her large repining:
The windows have opened; a royal wine
  Is poured out for the subtle pudding
Light industry is humming in the wood;
  The bluebirds bless us fromn the fences;
We know the time and where to find our friends.

[OLD SERIES VOL. IX, NO. 4 / AUTUMN 1947]

THEODORE ROETHKE

A Light Breather

The spirit moves,
Yet stays:
Stirs as a blossom stirs,
Still wet from its bud-sheath,
Slowly unfolding,
Turning in the light with its tendrils;
Plays as a minnow plays,
Tethered to a limp weed, swinging,
Tail around, nosing in and out of the current,
Its shadow loose, a watery finger;
Moves, like the snail,
Still and inward,
Taking and embracingits surroundings,
Never wishing itself away,
Unafraid of what it is,
A music in a hood,
A small thing,
Singing.

[OLD SERIES VOL. XII, NO. 3 / SUMMER 1950]

Helen Forman

Ophelia

Forlorn Ophelia draggles everywhere,
An ivory tower for polliwogs,
Her feet and her hands and her shattered hair
Weeping undone as peas and pods.
She was marvelous and tall in her dream.
She was, she was, and she spilled in a stream.

Fallow Ophelia waited, flecked with spring,
Glittering to embrace that prince.
He might salve her mouth, the taut bee sting
Where honey bled. Why did he mince?
He would weave her tapestries of ardor.
She wanted a plain bed founded harder.

The old stream holds forever its cold load,
Lopsided lily sprout of grief.
Never deflowered by the colder toad
Whose soggy thighs clamp to her leaf.
Felon, Ophelia! ruined water buoys
Your green inane careening counterpoise.

[OLD SERIES VOL. XIII, NO. 2 / SPRING 1951]

The Black Swan

When the swans turned my sister into a swan
  I would go to the lake, at night, from milking:
The sun would look through the reeds like a swan,
  A swan's red beak; and the beak would open,
And inside there was darkness, the stars and the moon.

Out on the lake a girl would laugh.
  "Sister, here is your porridge, sister,"
I would call; and the reeds would whisper,
  "Go to sleep, go to sleep, little swan."
My legs were all hard and webbed, and the silky

Hairs of my wings sank away like stars
  In the ripples that ran in and out of the reeds:
I heard through the lap and hiss of water
  Someone's "Sister . . . sister," far away on the shore,
And then as I opened my beak to answer

I heard my harsh laugh go out to the shore
  And saw—saw at last, swimming up from the green
Low mounds of the lake, the white stone swans:
  The white, named swans. . . . "It is all a dream,"
I whispered, and reached from the down of the pallet

To the lap and hiss of the floor.
     And "Sleep, little sister," the swans all sang
From the moon and stars and frogs of the floor.
     But the swan my sister called, "Sleep at last, little sister,"
And stroked all night, with a black wing, my wings.

[OLD SERIES VOL. XIII, NO. 2 / SPRING 1951]

The Life You Save May Be Your Own

The old woman and her daughter were sitting on their porch when Mr. Shiftlet came up their road for the first time. The old woman slid to the edge of her chair and leaned forward, shading her eyes from the piercing sunset with her hand. The daughter could not see far in front of her and continued to play with her fingers. Although the old woman lived in this desolate spot with only her daughter and she had never seen Mr. Shiftlet before, she could tell, even from a distance, that he was a tramp and no one to be afraid of. His left coat sleeve was folded up to show there was only half an arm in it and his gaunt figure listed slightly to the side as if the breeze were pushing him. He had on a black town suit and a brown felt hat that was turned up in the front and down in the back and he carried a tin tool box by a handle. He came on, at an amble, up her road, his face turned toward the sun which appeared to be balancing itself on the peak of a small mountain.

The old woman didn't change her position until he was almost into her yard; then she rose with one hand fisted on her hip. The daughter, a large girl in a short blue organdy dress, saw him all at once and jumped up and began to stamp and point and make excited speechless sounds.

Mr. Shiftlet stopped just inside the yard and set his box on the ground and tipped his hat at her as if she were not in the least afflicted; then he turned toward the old woman and swung the hat all the way off. He had long black slick hair that hung flat from a part in the middle to beyond the tips of his ears on either side. His face descended in forehead for more than half its length and ended suddenly with his features just balanced over a jutting steel-trap jaw. He seemed to be a young man but he had a look of composed dissatisfaction as if he understood life thoroughly.

"Good evening," the old woman said. She was about the size of a cedar fence post and she had a man's grey hat pulled down low over her head.

The tramp stood looking at her and didn't answer. He turned his back and faced the sunset. He swung both his whole and his short arm up slowly so that they indicated an expanse of sky and his figure formed a crooked cross. The old woman watched him with her arms folded across her chest as if she were the owner of the sun, and the daughter watched, her head thrust forward and her fat helpless hands hanging at the wrists. She had long pink-gold hair and eyes as blue as a peacock's neck.

He held the pose for almost fifty seconds and then he picked up his box and came on to the porch and dropped down on the bottom step. "Lady," he said in a firm nasal voice, "I'd give a fortune to live where I could see me a sun do that every evening."

"Does it every evening," the old woman said and sat back down. The daughter sat down too and watched him with a cautious sly look as if he were a bird that had come up very close. He leaned to one side, rooting in his pants pocket, and in a second he brought out a package of chewing gum and offered her a piece. She took it and unpeeled it and began to chew without taking her eyes off him. He offered the old woman a piece but she only raised her upper lip to indicate she had no teeth.

Mr. Shiftlet's pale sharp glance had already passed over everything in the yard—the pump near the corner of the house and the big fig tree that three or four chickens were preparing to roost in—and had moved to a shed where he saw the square rusted back of an automobile. "You ladies drive?" he asked.

"That car ain't run in fifteen year," the old woman said. "The day my husband died, it quit running."

"Nothing is like it used to be, Lady," he said. "The world is almost rotten."

"That's right," the old woman said. "You from around here?"

"Name Tom T. Shiftlet," he murmured, looking at the tires.

"I'm pleased to meet you," the old woman said. "Name Lucynell Crater and daughter Lucynell Crater. What you doing around here, Mr. Shiftlet?"

He judged the car to be about a 1928 or '29 Ford. "Lady," he said, and turned and gave her his full attention, "lemme tell you something. There's one of these doctors in Atlanta that's taken a knife and cut the human heart—the human heart," he repeated, leaning forward, "out of a man's chest and held it in his hand," and he held his hand out, palm up, as if it were slightly weighted with the human heart, "and studied it like it was a day-old chicken, and Lady," he said, allowing a long significant pause in which his head slid forward and his clay-colored eyes brightened, "he don't know no more about it than you or me."

"That's right," the old woman said.

"Why, if he was to take that knife and cut into every corner of it, he still wouldn't know no more than you or me. What you want to bet?"

"Nothing," the old woman said wisely. "Where you come from, Mr. Shiftlet?"

He didn't answer. He reached into his pocket and brought out a sack of tobacco and a package of cigarette papers and rolled himself a cigarette, expertly with one hand, and attached it in a hanging position to his upper lip. Then he took a box of wooden matches from his pocket and struck one on his shoe. He held the burning match as if he were studying the mystery of flame while it traveled dangerously toward his skin. The daughter began to make loud noises and to point to his hand and shake her finger at him, but when the flame was just before touching him, he leaned down with his hand cupped over it as if he were going to set fire to his nose and lit the cigarette.

He flipped away the dead match and blew a stream of grey into the evening. A sly look came over his face. "Lady," he said, "nowadays, people'll do anything anyways. I can tell you my name is Tom T. Shiftlet and I come from Tarwater, Tennessee, but you never have seen me before: how you know I ain't lying? How you know my name ain't Aaron Sparks, Lady, and I come from Singleberry, Georgia, or how you know it's not George Speeds and I come from Lucy, Alabama, or how you know I ain't Thompson Bright from Toolafalls, Mississippi?"

"I don't know nothing about you," the old woman muttered, irked.

"Lady," he said, "people don't care how they lie. Maybe the best I can tell you is, I'm a man, but listen, Lady," he said and paused and made his tone more ominous still, "what is a man?"

The old woman began to gum a seed. "What you carry in that tin box, Mr. Shiftlet ?" she asked.

"Tools," he said, put back. "I'm a carpenter."

"Well, if you come out here to work, I'll be able to feed you and give you a place to sleep but I can't pay. I'll tell you that before you begin," she said.

There was no answer at once and no particular expression on his face. He leaned back against the two-by-four that helped support the porch roof. "Lady," he said slowly, "there's some men that some things mean more to them than money." The old woman rocked without comment and the daughter watched the trigger that moved up and down in his neck. He told the old woman then that all most people were interested in was money, but he asked what a man was made for. He asked her if a man was made for money, or what. He asked her what she thought she was made for but she didn't answer, she only sat rocking and wondered if a one-armed man could put a new roof on her garden house. He asked a lot of questions that she didn't answer. He told her that he was twenty-eight years old and had lived a varied life.

He had been a gospel singer, a foreman on the railroad, an assistant in an undertaking parlor, and he had come over the radio for three months with Uncle Roy and his Red Creek Wranglers. He said he had fought and bled in the Arm Service of his country and visited every foreign land and that everywhere he had seen people that didn't care if they did a thing one way or another. He said he hadn't been raised thataway.

A fat yellow moon appeared in the branches of the fig tree as if it were going to roost there with the chickens. He said that a man had to escape to the country to see the world whole and that he wished he lived in a desolate place like this where he could see the sun go down every evening like God made it to do.

"Are you married or are you single?" the old woman asked.

There was a long silence. "Lady," he asked finally, "where would you find you an innocent woman today? I wouldn't have any of this trash I could just pick up."

The daughter was leaning very far down, hanging her head almost between her knees, watching him through a triangular door she had made in her overturned hair; and she suddenly fell in a heap on the floor and began to whimper. Mr. Shiftlet straightened her out and helped her get back in the chair.

"Is she your baby girl?" he asked.

"My only," the old woman said, "and she's the sweetest girl in the world. I wouldn't give her up for nothing on earth. She's smart too. She can sweep the floor, cook, wash, feed the chickens, and hoe. I wouldn't give her up for a casket of jewels."

"No," he said kindly, "don't ever let any man take her away from you."

"Any man come after her," the old woman said, " 'll have to stay around the place."

Mr. Shiftlet's eye in the darkness was focussed on a part of the automobile bumper that glittered in the distance. "Lady," he said, jerking his short arm up as if he could point with it to her house and yard and pump, "there ain't a broken thing on this plantation that I couldn't fix for you, one-arm jackleg or not. I'm a man," he said with a sullen dignity, "even if I ain't a whole one. I got," he said, tapping his knuckles on the floor to emphasize the immensity of what he was going to say, "a moral intelligence!" and his face pierced out of the darkness into a shaft of doorlight and he stared at her as if he were astonished himself at this impossible truth.

The old woman was not impressed with the phrase. "I told you you could hang around and work for food," she said, "if you don't mind sleeping in that car yonder."

"Why listen, Lady," he said with a grin of delight, "the monks of old slept in their coffins!"

"They wasn't as advanced as we are," the old woman said.

· ·

The next morning he began on the roof of the garden house while Lucynell, the daughter, sat on a rock and watched him work. He had not been around a week before the change he had made in the place was apparent. He had patched the front and back steps, built a new hog pen, restored a fence, and taught Lucynell who was completely deaf, and had never said a word in her life, to say the word "bird." The big rosy-faced girl followed him everywhere, saying "Burrttddt ddbirrrttdt," and clapping her hands. The old woman watched from a distance, secretly pleased. She was ravenous for a son-in-law.

Mr. Shiftlet slept on the hard narrow back seat of the car with his feet out the side window. He had his razor and a can of water on a crate that served him as a bedside table and he put up a piece of mirror against the back glass and kept his coat neatly on a hanger that he hung over one of the windows.

In the evenings he sat on the steps and talked while the old woman and Lucynell rocked violently in their chairs on either side of him. The old woman's three mountains were black against the dark blue sky and were visited off and on by various planets and by the moon after it had left the chickens. Mr. Shiftlet pointed out that the reason he had improved this plantation was because he had taken a personal interest in it. He said he was even going to make the automobile run.

He had raised the hood and studied the mechanism and he said he could tell that the car had been built in the days when cars were really built. You take now, he said, one man puts in one bolt and another man puts in another bolt and another man puts in another bolt so that it's a man for a bolt. That's why you have to pay so much for a car: you're paying all those men. Now if you didn't have to pay but one man, you could get you a cheaper car and one that had had a personal interest taken in it, and it would be a better car. The old woman agreed with him that this was so.

Mr. Shiftlet said that the trouble with the world was that nobody cared, or stopped and took any trouble. He said he never would have been able to teach Lucynell to say a word if he hadn't cared and stopped long enough.

"Teach her to say something else," the old woman said.

"What you want her to say next?" Mr. Shiftlet asked.

The old woman's smile was broad and toothless and suggestive. "Teach her to say 'sugarpie,'" she said.

Mr. Shiftlet already knew what was on her mind.

The next day he began to tinker with the automobile and that evening he told her that if she would buy a fan belt, he would be able to make the car run.

The old woman said she would give him the money. "You see that girl yonder?" she asked, pointing to Lucynell who was sitting on the floor a foot away, watching him, her eyes blue even in the dark. "If it was ever a man wanted to take her away, I would say, 'No man on earth is going to take that sweet girl of mine away from me!' but if he was to say, 'Lady, I don't want to take her away, I want her right here,' I would say, 'Mister, I don't blame you none. I wouldn't pass up a chance to live in a permanent place and get the sweetest girl in the world myself. You ain't no fool,' I would say."

"How old is she?" Mr. Shiftlet asked casually.

"Fifteen, sixteen," the old woman said. The girl was nearly

thirty but because of her innocence it was impossible to guess.

"It would be a good idea to paint it too," Mr. Shiftlet remarked. "You don't want it to rust out."

"We'll see about that later," the old woman said.

The next day he walked into town and returned with the parts he needed and a can of gasoline. Late in the afternoon, terrible noises issued from the shed and the old woman rushed out of the house, thinking Lucynell was somewhere having a fit. Lucynell was sitting on a chicken crate, stamping her feet and screaming, "Burrddttt! bddurrddtttt!" but her fuss was drowned out by the car. With a volley of blasts it emerged from the shed, moving in a fierce and stately way. Mr. Shiftlet was in the driver's seat, sitting very erect. He had an expression of serious modesty on his face as if he had just raised the dead.

That night, rocking on the porch, the old woman began her business at once. "You want you an innocent woman, don't you?" she asked sympathetically. "You don't want none of this trash."

"No'm, I don't," Mr. Shiftlet said.

"One that can't talk," she continued, "can't sass you back or use foul language. That's the kind for you to have. Right there," and she pointed to Lucynell sitting cross-legged in her chair, holding both feet in her hands.

"That's right," he admitted. "She wouldn't give me any trouble."

"Saturday," the old woman said, "you and her and me can drive into town and get married."

Mr. Shiftlet eased his position on the steps.

"I can't get married right now," he said. "Everything you want to do takes money and I ain't got any."

"What you need with money?" she asked.

"It takes money," he said. "Some people'll do anything any how these days, but the way I think, I wouldn't marry no woman that I couldn't take on a trip like she was somebody. I mean take her to a hotel and treat her. I wouldn't marry the Duchesser Windsor," he said firmly, "unless I could take her to a hotel and give her something good to eat.

"I was raised thataway and there ain't a thing I can do about it. My old mother taught me how to do."

"Lucynell don't even know what a hotel is," the old woman muttered. "Listen here, Mr. Shiftlet," she said sliding forward in her chair, "you'd be getting a permanent house and a deep well and the most innocent girl in the world. You don't need no money. Lemme tell you something: there ain't any place in the world for a poor disabled friendless drifting man."

The ugly words settled in Mr. Shiftlet's head like a group or buzzards in the top of a tree. He didn't answer at once. He rolled himself a cigarette and lit it and then he said in an even voice, "Lady, a man is divided into two parts, body and spirit."

The old woman clamped her gums together.

"A body and a spirit," he repeated. "The body, Lady, is like a house: it don't go anywhere; but the spirit, Lady, is like a automobile: always on the move, always. . . . "

"Listen, Mr. Shiftlet," she said, "my well never goes dry and my house is always warm in the winter and there's no mortgage on a thing about this place. You can go to the court house and see for yourself. And yonder under that shed is a fine automobile." She laid the bait carefully. "You can have it painted by Saturday. I'll pay for the paint."

In the darkness, Mr. Shiftlet's smile stretched like a weary snake waking up by a fire. "Yes'm," he said softly.

After a second he recalled himself and said, "I'm only saying a man's spirit means more to him than anything else. I would have to take my wife off for the weekend without no regards at all for cost. I got to follow where my spirit says to go."

"I'll give you fifteen dollars for a weekend trip," the old woman said in a crabbed voice. "That's the best I can do."

"That wouldn't hardly pay for more than the gas and the hotel," he said. "It wouldn't feed her."

"Seventeen-fifty," the old woman said. "That's all I got so it isn't any use you trying to milk me. You can take a lunch."

Mr. Shiftlet was deeply hurt by the word "milk." He didn't

doubt that she had more money sewed up in her mattress but he had already told her he was not interested in her money. "I'll make that do," he said and rose and walked off without treating with her further.

On Saturday the three of them drove into town in the car that the paint had barely dried on and Mr. Shiftlet and Lucynell were married in the Ordinary's office while the old woman witnessed. As they came out of the courthouse, Mr. Shiftlet began twisting his neck in his collar. He looked morose and bitter as if he had been insulted while some one held him. "That didn't satisfy me none," he said. "That was just something a woman in an office did, nothing but paper work and blood tests. What do they know about my blood? If they was to take my heart and cut it out," he said, "they wouldn't know a thing about me. It didn't satisfy me at all."

"It satisfied the law," the old woman said sharply.

"The law," Mr. Shiftlet said and spit. "It's the law that don't satisfy me."

He had painted the car dark green with a yellow band around it just under the windows. The three of them climbed in the front seat and the old woman said, "Don't Lucynell look pretty? Looks like a baby doll." Lucynell was dressed up in a white dress that her mother had uprooted from a trunk and there was a panama hat on her head with a bunch of red wooden cherries on the brim. Every now and then her placid expression was changed by a sly isolated little thought like a shoot of green in the desert. "You got a prize!" the old woman said.

Mr. Shiftlet didn't even look at her.

They drove back to the house to let the old woman off and pick up the lunch. When they were ready to leave, she stood staring in the window of the car, with her fingers clenched around the glass. Tears began to seep sideways out of her eyes and run along the dirty creases in her face. "I ain't ever been parted with her for two days before," she said.

Mr. Shiftlet started the motor.

"And I wouldn't let no man have her but you because I seen you would do right. Goodbye, Sugarbaby," she said, clutching at the sleeve of the white dress. Lucynell looked straight at her and didn't seem to see her there at all. Mr. Shiftlet eased the car forward so that she had to move her hands.

The early afternoon was clear and open and surrounded by pale blue sky. The hills flattened under the car one after another and the climb and dip and swerve went entirely to Mr. Shiftlet's head so that he forgot his morning bitterness. He had always wanted an automobile but he had never been able to afford one before. He drove very fast because he wanted to make Mobile by nightfall.

Occasionally he stopped his thoughts long enough to look at Lucynell in the seat beside him. She had eaten the lunch as soon as they were out of the yard and now she was pulling the cherries off the hat one by one and throwing them out the window. He became depressed in spite of the car. He had driven about a hundred miles when he decided that she must be hungry again and at the next small town they came to, he stopped in front of an aluminum-painted eating place called The Hot Spot and took her in and ordered her a plate of ham and grits. The ride had made her sleepy and as soon as she got up on the stool, she rested her head on the counter and shut her eyes. There was no one in the Hot Spot but Mr. Shiftlet and the boy behind the counter, a pale youth with a greasy rag hung over his shoulder. Before he could dish up the food, she was snoring gently.

"Give it to her when she wakes up," Mr. Shiftlet said. "I'll pay for it now."

The boy bent over her and stared at the long pink-gold hair and the half-shut sleeping eyes. Then he looked up and stared at Mr. Shiftlet. "She looks like an angel of Gawd," he murmured.

"Hitch-hiker," Mr. Shiftlet explained. "I can't wait. I got to make Tuscaloosa."

The boy bent over again and very carefully touched his finger to a strand of the golden hair and Mr. Shiftlet left.

He was more depressed than ever as he drove on by himself. The late afternoon had grown hot and sultry and the country had flattened out. Deep in the sky a storm was preparing very slowly and without thunder as if it meant to drain every drop of air from the earth before it broke. There were times when Mr. Shiftlet preferred not to be alone. He felt too that a man with a car had a responsibility to others and he kept his eye out for a hitchhiker. Occasionally he saw a sign that warned: "Drive carefully. The life you save may be your own."

The narrow road dropped off on either side into dry fields and here and there a shack or a filling station stood in a clearing. The sun began to set directly in front of the automobile. It was a reddening ball that through his windshield was slightly flat on the bottom and top. He saw a boy in overalls and a grey hat, standing on the edge of the road and he slowed the car down and stopped in front of him. The boy didn't have his hand raised to thumb the ride, he was only standing there, but he had a small cardboard suitcase and his hat was set on his head in a way to indicate that he had left somewhere for good. "Son," Mr. Shiftlet said, "I see you want a ride."

The boy didn't say he did or he didn't but he opened the door of the car and got in, and Mr. Shiftlet started driving again. The child held the suitcase on his lap and folded his arms on top of it. He turned his head and looked out the window away from Mr. Shiftlet. Mr. Shiftlet felt oppressed. "Son," he said after a minute, "I got the best old mother in the world so I reckon you only got the second best."

The boy gave him a quick dark glance and then turned his face back out the window.

"It's nothing so sweet," Mr. Shiftlet continued, "as a boy's mother. She taught him his first prayers at her knee, she give him love when no other would, she told him what was right and what wasn't, and she seen that he done the right thing. Son," he said, "I never rued a day in my life like the one I rued when I left that old mother of mine."

The boy shifted in his seat but he didn't look at Mr. Shiftlet. He unfolded his arms and put one hand on the door handle.

"My mother was a angel of Gawd," Mr. Shiftlet said in a very strained voice. "He took her from heaven and giver to me and I left her." His eyes were instantly clouded over with a mist of tears.

The boy turned angrily in the seat. "You go to the devil!" he cried. "My old woman is a flea bag and your's is a stinking pole cat!" and with that he flung the door open and jumped out with his suitcase into the ditch.

Mr. Shiftlet was so shocked that for about a hundred feet he drove along slowly with the door still open like his mouth. Then he reached over and shut both. A cloud, the exact color of the boy's hat and shaped like a turnip, had descended over the sun, and another, worse looking, crouched behind the car. Mr. Shiftlet felt that the rottenness of the world was about to engulf him. He raised his arm and let it fall again to his breast. "Oh Lord!" he prayed, "break forth and wash the slime from this earth!"

The turnip continued slowly to descend. After a few minutes there was a guffawing peal of thunder from behind and fantastic raindrops, like tin can tops, crashed over the rear of Mr. Shiftlet's car. Very quickly he pushed in his clutch and stepped on the gas and, with his stump sticking out the window, he raced the galloping shower into Mobile.

[OLD SERIES VOL. XV, NO. 2 / SPRING 1953]

Konstantinos Kavaphes

Translated from Greek by Richmond Lattimore

Waiting for the Barbarians

Why are we all assembled and waiting in the market place?

It is the barbarians; they will be here today.

Why is there nothing being done in the senate house?
Why are the senators in session but are not passing laws?

Because the barbarians are coming today.
Why should the senators make laws any more?
The barbarians will make the laws when they get here.

Why has our emperor got up so early
and sits there at the biggest gate of the city
high on his throne, in state, and with his crown on?

Because the barbarians are coming today
and the emperor is waiting to receive them
and their general. And he has even made ready
a parchment to present them, and thereon
he has written many names and many titles.

Why have our two consuls and our praetors
come out today in their red embroidered togas?
Why have they put on their bracelets with all those amethysts
and rings shining with the glitter of emeralds?
Why will they carry their precious staves today
which are decorated with figures of gold and silver?

Because the barbarians are coming today
and things like that impress the barbarians.

Why do our good orators not put in any appearance
and make public speeches, and do what they generally do?

Because the barbarians are coming today
and they get bored with eloquent public speeches.

Why is everybody beginning to be so uneasy?
Why so disordered? (See how grave all the faces have
become!) Why do the streets and the squares empty so quickly,
and they are all anxiously going home to their houses?

Because it is night, and the barbarians have not got here,
and some people have come in from the frontier
and say that there aren't any more barbarians.

What are we going to do now without the barbarians?
In a way, those people were a solution.

[OLD SERIES VOL. XVII, NO. 2 / SPRING 1955]

W. S. MERWIN

The Nine Days of Creation

The first day of Creation
All things, love, alone were,
Darkness the lonely creature;
Clove us then Love with good light
For two can be together,
And partly we were bright,
Each other so to look on.

The second day of Creation
But water was our body
In one place that lay;
Sundered us then Love
And part raised firm, that we
The hard sky too might have
And be both up and down.

The third day of Creation
Framed Love from our same sea
The good land to broach drily;
Sometime was I seed,
But, love, you first were a tree;
In your fruit I was glad,
You from my joy green.

The fourth day of Creation,
That sing might we,
As the sun Love shaped me
And you the moon there shining;
Stars also and planets we
Then together singing
And the song one.

The fifth day of Creation
Love, to multiply,
Formed us fish in sea,
Beasts for the wood,
Fowls to fly;
We went as we would,
And sense to joy in.

The sixth day of Creation
Love was a wind high
In the dust that was dry,
Male and female that made us
With a word suddenly,
So our warmth told was
Bare in a garden.

The seventh day of Creation
All that good day
Love and we in Sabbath lay,
Our praise and sole conceiving
Was ease and idly,
In all our parts Love resting
As before we began.

The eighth day of Creation
You, love, from your still tree
Such fruit did offer Time and me

As did taste immortal,
And we knew mutability
Even as a turning wheel
Recalling season and season.

At that time in our whirling station
Love set us Memory,
And our love more to purify,
That other angel, Forgetfulness
Of all our bodies but these only
Where dearest we love, and all other faces,
And blessed joy with pain.

The ninth day of Creation
Love with most perfect care
Wrought us fear there
For casting out, and last
Was even death about our nature
To bind our natures fast
Till all things but this Love be gone.

[OLD SERIES VOL. XVIII, NO. 3 / SUMMER 1956]

All the Beautiful Are Blameless

Out of a dark into the dark she leaped
Lightly this day.
Heavy with prey, the evening skiffs are gone,
And drowsy divers lift their helmets off,
Dry on the shore.

Two stupid harly-charlies got her drunk
And took her swimming naked on the lake.
The waters rippled lute-like round the boat,
And far beyond them dipping up and down,
Unmythological sylphs, their names unknown,
Beckoned to sandbars where the evenings fall.

Only another drunk would say she heard
A natural voice
Luring the flesh across the water.
I think of those unmythological
Sylphs of the trees.

Slight but orplidean shoulders weave in dusk
Before my eyes when I walk lonely forward
To kick beer-cans from tracked declivities.
If I, being lightly sane, may carve a mouth
Out of the air to kiss, the drowned girl surely

Listened to lute-song where the sylphs are gone.
The living and the dead glide hand in hand
Under cool waters where the days are gone.
Out of the dark into a dark I stand.
The ugly curse the world and pin my arms
Down by their grinning teeth, sneering a blame.

Closing my eyes, I look for hungry swans
To plunder the lake and bear the girl away,
Back to the larger waters where the sea
Sifts, judges, gathers the body, and subsides.
But here the starved, touristic crowd divides
And offers the dead
Hell for the living body's evil:
The girl flopped in the water like a pig
And drowned dead drunk.

So do the pure defend themselves. But she,
Risen to kiss the sky, her limbs still whole,
Rides on the dark tarpaulin toward the shore;
And the hired saviours turn their painted shell
Along the wharf, to list her human name.
But the dead have no names, they lie so still,
And all the beautiful are blameless now.

[OLD SERIES VOL. XX, NO. 4 / AUTUMN 1958]

Awaiting the Swimmer

Light fails, in crossing a river.
The current shines deeply without it.
I hold a white cloth in my hands.
The air turns over one leaf.
One force is left in my arms
To handle the cloth, spread it gently,
And show where I stand above water.

I see her loosed hair straining.
She is trying to come to me, here.
I cannot swim, and she knows it.
Her gaze makes the cloth burn my hands.
I can stand only where I am standing.
Shall she fail, and go down to the sea?
Shall she call, as she changes to water?

She swims to overcome fear.
One force is left in her arms.
How can she come, but in glory?
The current burns; I love
That moving-to-me love, now passing
The midst of the road where she's buried.
Her best motions come from the river;

Her fear flows away to the sea.
The way to walk upon water

Is to work lying down, as in love.
The way to wait in a field
Is to hold a white cloth in your hands
And sing with the sound of the river.
Called here by the luminous towel,

My rib-humming breath, and my love,
She steps from the twilit water.
At the level of my throat, she closes
Her eyes, and ends my singing.
I wrap her thin form in the towel,
And we walk through the motionless grasses
To the house, where the chairs we sit in

Have only one force in their arms.
The bed like the river is shining.
Yet what shall I do, when I reach her
Through the moon opened wide on the floor-boards?
What can I perform, to come near her?
How hope to bear up, when she gives me
The fear-killing moves of her body?

[OLD SERIES VOL. XXI, NO. 4 / AUTUMN 1959]

THOMAS PYNCHON

Entropy

> Boris has just given me a summary of his views. He is
> a weather prophet. The weather will continue bad, he
> says. There will be more calamities, more death, more
> despair. Not the slightest indication of a change any-
> where. . . . We must get into step, a lockstep toward the
> prison of death. There is no escape. The weather will
> not change.
> —Tropic of Cancer

Downstairs, Meatball Mulligan's lease-breaking party was moving into its 40th hour. On the kitchen floor, amid a litter of empty
champagne fifths, were Sandor Rojas and three friends, playing
spit in the ocean and staying awake on Heidseck and benzedrine
pills. In the living room Duke, Vincent, Krinkles and Paco sat
crouched over a 15-inch speaker which had been bolted into the
top of a wastepaper basket, listening to 27 watts' worth of *The
Heroes' Gate at Kiev.* They all wore horn rimmed sunglasses and
rapt expressions, and smoked funny-looking cigarettes which
contained not, as you might expect, tobacco, but an adulterat-
ed form of *cannabis sativa.* This group was the Duke di Angelis
quartet. They recorded for a local label called Tambú and had to
their credit one 10" LP entitled *Songs of Outer Space.* From time
to time one of them would flick the ashes from his cigarette into
the speaker cone to watch them dance around. Meatball himself
was sleeping over by the window, holding an empty magnum to
his chest as if it were a teddy bear. Several government girls, who
worked for people like the State Department and NSA, had passed
out on couches, chairs and in one case the bathroom sink.

This was in early February of '57 and back then there were a lot of American expatriates around Washington, D.C., who would talk, every time they met you, about how someday they were going to go over to Europe for real but right now it seemed they were working for the government. Everyone saw a fine irony in this. They would stage, for instance, polyglot parties where the newcomer was sort of ignored if he couldn't carry on simultaneous conversations in three or four languages. They would haunt Armenian delicatessens for weeks at a stretch and invite you over for bulghour and lamb in tiny kitchens whose walls were covered with bullfight posters. They would have affairs with sultry girls from Andalucía or the Midi who studied economics at Georgetown. Their Dôme was a collegiate Rathskeller out on Wisconsin Avenue called the Old Heidelberg and they had to settle for cherry blossoms instead of lime trees when spring came, but in its lethargic way their life provided, as they said, kicks.

At the moment, Meatball's party seemed to be gathering its second wind. Outside there was rain. Rain splatted against the tar paper on the roof and was fractured into a fine spray off the noses, eyebrows and lips of wooden gargoyles under the eaves, and ran like drool down the windowpanes. The day before, it had snowed and the day before that there had been winds of gale force and before that the sun had made the city glitter bright as April, though the calendar read early February. It is a curious season in Washington, this false spring. Somewhere in it are Lincoln's Birthday and the Chinese New Year, and a forlornness in the streets because cherry blossoms are weeks away still and, as Sarah Vaughan has put it, spring will be a little late this year. Generally crowds like the one which would gather in the Old Heidelberg on weekday afternoons to drink Würtzburger and to sing Lili Marlene (not to mention The Sweetheart of Sigma Chi) are inevitably and incorrigibly Romantic. And as every good Romantic knows, the soul (*spiritus, ruach, pneuma*) is nothing, substantially, but air; it is only natural that warpings in the atmosphere should be recapitulated in those who breathe it. So that

over and above the public components—holidays, tourist at-
tractions—there are private meanderings, linked to the climate
as if this spell were a *stretto* passage in the year's fugue: haphazard
weather, aimless loves, unpredicted commitments: months one
can easily spend *in* fugue, because oddly enough, later on, winds,
rains, passions of February and March are never remembered in
that city, it is as if they had never been.

The last bass notes of *The Heroes' Gate* boomed up through
the floor and woke Callisto from an uneasy sleep. The first thing
he became aware of was a small bird he had been holding gently
between his hands, against his body. He turned his head side-
wise on the pillow to smile down at it, at its blue hunched-down
head and sick, lidded eyes, wondering how many more nights
he would have to give it warmth before it was well again. He had
been holding the bird like that for three days: it was the only
way he knew to restore its health. Next to him the girl stirred
and whimpered, her arm thrown across her face. Mingled with
the sounds of the rain came the first tentative, querulous morning voices of the other birds, hidden in philodendrons and small
fan palms: patches of scarlet, yellow and blue laced through this
Rousseau-like fantasy, this hothouse jungle it had taken him
seven years to weave together. Hermetically sealed, it was a tiny
enclave of regularity in the city's chaos, alien to the vagaries of
the weather, of national politics, of any civil disorder. Through
trial-and-error Callisto had perfected its ecological balance, with
the help of the girl its artistic harmony, so that the swayings of its
plant life, the stirrings of its birds and human inhabitants were all
as integral as the rhythms of a perfectly-executed mobile. He and
the girl could no longer, of course, be omitted from that sanctuary; they had become necessary to its unity. What they needed
from outside was delivered. They did not go out.

"Is he all right," she whispered. She lay like a tawny question
mark facing him, her eyes suddenly huge and dark and blinking
slowly. Callisto ran a finger beneath the feathers at the base of the
bird's neck; caressed it gently. "He's going to be well, I think. See:

he hears his friends beginning to wake up." The girl had heard the rain and the birds even before she was fully awake. Her name was Aubade: she was part French and part Annamese, and she lived on her own curious and lonely planet, where the clouds and the odor of poincianas, the bitterness of wine and the accidental fingers at the small of her back or feathery against her breasts came to her reduced inevitably to the terms of sound: of music which emerged at intervals from a howling darkness of discordancy. "Aubade," he said, "go see." Obedient, she arose; padded to the window, pulled aside the drapes and after a moment said: "It is 37. Still 37." Callisto frowned. "Since Tuesday, then," he said. "No change." Henry Adams, three generations before his own, had stared aghast at Power; Callisto found himself now in much the same state over Thermodynamics, the inner life of that power, realizing like his predecessor that the Virgin and the dynamo stand as much for love as for power; that the two are indeed identical; and that love therefore not only makes the world go 'round but also makes the boccie ball spin, the nebula precess. It was this latter or sidereal element which disturbed him. The cosmologists had predicted an eventual heat-death for the universe (something like Limbo: form and motion abolished, heat-energy identical at every point in it); the meteorologists, day-to-day, staved it off by contradicting with a reassuring array of varied temperatures.

But for three days now, despite the changeful weather, the mercury had stayed at 37 degrees Fahrenheit. Leery at omens of apocalypse, Callisto shifted beneath the covers. His fingers pressed the bird more firmly, as if needing some pulsing or suffering assurance of an early break in the temperature.

It was that last cymbal crash that did it. Meatball was hurled wincing into consciousness as the synchronized wagging of heads over the wastebasket stopped. The final hiss remained for an instant in the room, then melted into the whisper of rain outside. "Aarrgghh," announced Meatball in the silence, looking at the empty magnum. Krinkles, in slow motion, turned, smiled and held out a cigarette. "Tea time, man," he said. "No, no,'" said Meatball. "How many times I got to tell you guys. Not at my place. You ought to know, Washington is lousy with Feds." Krinkles looked wistful. "Jeez, Meatball," he said, "you don't want to do nothing no more." "Hair of dog," said Meatball. "Only hope. Any juice left?" He began to crawl toward the kitchen. "No champagne, I don't think," Duke said. "Case of tequila behind the icebox." They put on an Earl Bostic side. Meatball paused at the kitchen door, glowering at Sandor Rojas. "Lemons," he said after some thought. He crawled to the refrigerator and got out three lemons and some cubes, found the tequila and set about restoring order to his nervous system. He drew blood once cutting the lemons and had to use two hands squeezing them and his foot to crack the ice tray but after about ten minutes he found himself, through some miracle, beaming down into a monster tequila sour. "That looks yummy," Sandor Rojas said. "How about you make me one." Meatball blinked at him. "*Kitchi lofass a shegitbe*," he replied automatically, and wandered away into the bathroom. "I say," he called out a moment later to no one in particular. "I say, there seems to be a girl or something sleeping in the sink." He took her by the shoulders and shook. "Wha," she said. "You don't look too comfortable," Meatball said. "Well," she agreed. She stumbled to the shower, turned on the cold water and sat down crosslegged in the spray. "That's better," she smiled.

"Meatball," Sandor Rojas yelled from the kitchen. "Somebody is trying to come in the window. A burglar, I think. A second-story man." "What are you worrying about," Meatball said. "We're on the third floor." He loped back into the kitchen. A shaggy woebegone figure stood out on the fire escape, raking his fingernails down the windowpane. Meatball opened the window. "Saul," he said.

"Sort of wet out," Saul said. He climbed in, dripping. "You heard, I guess."

"Miriam left you," Meatball said, "or something, is all I heard."

There was a sudden flurry of knocking at the front door. "Do come in," Sandor Rojas called. The door opened and there were three coeds from George Washington, all of whom were majoring in philosophy. They were each holding a gallon of Chianti. Sandor leaped up and dashed into the living room. "We heard there was a party," one blonde said. "Young blood," Sandor shouted. He was an ex-Hungarian freedom fighter who had easily the worst chronic case of what certain critics of the middle class have called Don Giovannism in the District of Columbia. *Purche porti la gonnella, voi sapete quel che fa.* Like Pavlov's dog: a contralto voice or a whiff of Arpege and Sandor would begin to salivate. Meatball regarded the trio blearily as they filed into the kitchen; he shrugged. "Put the wine in the icebox," he said "and good morning."

Aubade's neck made a golden bow as she bent over the sheets of foolscap, scribbling away in the green murk of the room. "As a young man at Princeton," Callisto was dictating, nestling the bird against the gray hairs of his chest, "Callisto had learned a mnemonic device for remembering the Laws of Thermodynamics: you can't win, things are going to get worse before they get better, who says they're going to get better. At the age of 54, confronted with Gibbs' notion of the universe, he suddenly realized that undergraduate cant had been oracle, after all. That spindly maze of equations became, for him, a vision of ultimate, cosmic heat-death. He had known all along, of course, that nothing but a theoretical engine or system ever runs at 100% efficiency; and about the theorem of Clausius, which states that the entropy of an isolated system always continually increases. It was not, however, until Gibbs and Boltzmann brought to this principle the methods of statistical mechanics that the horrible significance of it all dawned on him: only then did he realize that the isolated system—galaxy, engine, human being, culture, whatever—must evolve spontaneously toward the Condition of the More Probable. He was forced, therefore, in the sad dying fall of middle age, to a radical reëvaluation of everything he had learned up to then;

all the cities and seasons and casual passions of his days had now to be looked at in a new and elusive light. He did not know if he was equal to the task. He was aware of the dangers of the reductive fallacy and, he hoped, strong enough not to drift into the graceful decadence of an enervated fatalism. His had always been a vigorous, Italian sort of pessimism: like Machiavelli, he allowed the forces of *virtú* and *fortuna* to be about 50/50; but the equations now introduced a random factor which pushed the odds to some unutterable and indeterminate ratio which he found himself afraid to calculate." Around him loomed vague hothouse shapes; the pitifully small heart fluttered against his own. Counterpointed against his words the girl heard the chatter of birds and fitful car honkings scattered along the wet morning and Earl Bostic's alto rising in occasional wild peaks through the floor. The architectonic purity of her world was constantly threatened by such hints of anarchy: gaps and excrescences and skew lines, and a shifting or tilting of planes to which she had continually to readjust lest the whole structure shiver into a disarray of discrete and meaningless signals. Callisto had described the process once as a kind of "feedback": she crawled into dreams each night with a sense of exhaustion, and a desperate resolve never to relax that vigilance. Even in the brief periods when Callisto made love to her, soaring above the bowing of taut nerves in haphazard double-stops would be the one singing string of her determination.

"Nevertheless," continued Callisto, "he found in entropy or the measure of disorganization for a closed system an adequate metaphor to apply to certain phenomena in his own world. He saw, for example, the younger generation responding to Madison Avenue with the same spleen his own had once reserved for Wall Street: and in American 'consumerism' discovered a similar tendency from the least to the most probable, from differentiation to sameness, from ordered individuality to a kind of chaos. He found himself in short, restating Gibbs' prediction in social terms, and envisioned a heat-death for his culture in which ideas, like heat-energy, would no longer be transferred, since each point in it would ultimately have the same quantity of energy; and intellectual motion would, accordingly, cease." He glanced up suddenly. "Check it now," he said. Again she rose and peered out at the thermometer. "37," she said. "The rain has stopped." He bent his head quickly and held his lips against a quivering wing. "Then it will change soon," he said, trying to keep his voice firm.

Sitting on the stove Saul was like any big rag doll that a kid has been taking out some incomprehensible rage on. "What happened," Meatball said. "If you feel like talking, I mean."

"Of course I feel like talking," Saul said. "One thing I did, I slugged her."

"Discipline must be maintained."

"Ha, ha. I wish you'd been there. Oh Meatball, it was a lovely fight. She ended up throwing a *Handbook of Chemistry and Physics* at me, only it missed and went through the window, and when the glass broke I reckon something in her broke too. She stormed out of the house crying, out in the rain. No raincoat or anything."

"She'll be back."

"No."

"Well." Soon Meatball said: "It was something earth-shattering, no doubt. Like who is better, Sal Mineo or Ricky Nelson."

"What it was about," Saul said, "was communication theory. Which of course makes it very hilarious."

"I don't know anything about communication theory."

"Neither does my wife. Come right down to it, who does? That's the joke."

When Meatball saw the kind of smile Saul had on his face he said: "Maybe you would like tequila or something."

"No. I mean, I'm sorry. It's a field you can go off the deep end in, is all. You get where you're watching all the time for security cops: behind bushes, around corners. MUFFET is top secret."

"Wha."

"Multi-unit factorial field electronic tabulator."

"You were fighting about that."

"Miriam has been reading science-fiction again. That and *Scientific American*. It seems she is, as we say, bugged at this idea of computers acting like people. I made the mistake of saying you can just as well turn that around, and talk about human behavior like a program fed into an IBM machine."

"Why not," Meatball said.

"Indeed, why not. In fact it is sort of crucial to communication, not to mention information theory. Only when I said that she hit the roof. Up went the balloon. And I can't figure out *why*. If anybody should know why, I should. I refuse to believe the government is wasting taxpayers' money on me, when it has so many bigger and better things to waste it on."

Meatball made a moue. "Maybe she thought you were acting like a cold, dehumanized amoral scientist type."

"My god," Saul flung up an arm. "Dehumanized. How much more human can I get? I worry, Meatball, I do. There are Europeans wandering around North Africa these days with their tongues torn out of their heads because those tongues have spoken the wrong words. Only the Europeans thought they were the right words."

"Language barrier," Meatball suggested.

Saul jumped down off the stove. "That," he said, angry, "is a good candidate for sick joke of the year. No, ace, it is *not* a barrier. If it is anything it's a kind of leakage. Tell a girl: 'I love you.' No trouble with two-thirds of that, it's a closed circuit. Just you and she. But that nasty four-letter word in the middle, *that's* the one you have to look out for. Ambiguity. Redundance. Irrelevance, even. Leakage. All this is noise. Noise screws up your signal, makes for disorganization in the circuit."

Meatball shuffled around. "Well, now, Saul," he muttered, "you're sort of, I don't know, expecting a lot from people. I mean, you know. What it is is, most of the things we say, I guess, are mostly noise."

"Ha! Half of what you just said, for example."

"Well, you do it too."

"I know." Saul smiled grimly. "It's a bitch, ain't it."

"I bet that's what keeps divorce lawyers in business. Whoops."

"Oh I'm not sensitive. Besides," frowning, "you're right. You find I think that most 'successful' marriages—Miriam and me, up to last night—are sort of founded on compromises. You never run at top efficiency, usually all you have is a minimum basis for a workable thing. I believe the phrase is Togetherness."

"Aarrgghh."

"Exactly. You find that one a bit noisy, don't you. But the noise content is different for each of us because you're a bachelor and I'm not. Or wasn't. The hell with it."

"Well sure," Meatball said, trying to be helpful, "you were using different words. By 'human being' you meant something that you can look at like it was a computer. It helps you think better on the job or something. But Miriam meant something entirely—"

"The hell with it."

Meatball fell silent. "I'll take that drink," Saul said after a while.

The card game had been abandoned and Sandor's friends were slowly getting wasted on tequila. On the living room couch, one of the coeds and Krinkles were engaged in amorous conversation. "No," Krinkles was saying, "no, I can't put Dave *down*. In fact I give Dave a lot of credit, man. Especially considering his accident and all." The girl's smile faded. "How terrible," she said. "What accident?" "Hadn't you heard?" Krinkles said. "When Dave was in the army, just a private E-2, they sent him down to Oak Ridge on special duty. Something to do with the Manhattan Project. He was handling hot stuff one day and got an overdose of radiation. So now he's got to wear lead gloves all the time." She shook her head sympathetically. "What an awful break for a piano-player."

Meatball had abandoned Saul to a bottle of tequila and was

about to go to sleep in a closet when the front door flew open and the place was invaded by five enlisted personnel of the U.S. Navy, all in varying stages of abomination. "This is the place," shouted a fat, pimply seaman apprentice who had lost his white hat. "This here is the hoorhouse that chief was telling us about." A stringy-looking 3rd class boatswain's mate pushed him aside and cased the living room. "You're right, Slab," he said. "But it don't look like much, even for Stateside. I seen better tail in Naples, Italy." "How much, hey," boomed a large seaman with adenoids, who was holding a Mason jar full of white lightning. "Oh, my god," said Meatball.

Outside the temperature remained constant at 37 degrees Fahrenheit. In the hothouse Aubade stood absently caressing the branches of a young mimosa, hearing a motif of sap-rising, the rough and unresolved anticipatory theme of those fragile pink blossoms which, it is said, insure fertility. That music rose in a tangled tracery: arabesques of order competing fugally with the improvised discords of the party downstairs, which peaked sometimes in cusps and ogees of noise. That precious signal-to-noise ratio, whose delicate balance required every calorie of her strength, seesawed inside the small tenuous skull as she watched Callisto, sheltering the bird. Callisto was trying to confront any idea of the heat-death now, as he nuzzled the feathery lump in his hands. He sought correspondences. Sade, of course. And Temple Drake, gaunt and hopeless in her little park in Paris, at the end of *Sanctuary*. Final equilibrium. *Nightwood*. And the tango. Any tango, but more than any perhaps the sad sick dance in Stravinsky's *L'Histoire du Soldat*. He thought back: what had tango music been for them after the war, what meanings had he missed in all the stately coupled automatons in the *cafés-dansants*, or in the metronomes which had ticked behind the eyes of his own partners? Not even the clean constant winds of Switzerland could cure the *grippe espagnole*: Stravinsky had had it, they all had had it. And now many musicians were left after Passchendaele, after the Marne? It came down in this case to seven: violin, double-bass. Clarinet, bassoon. Cornet, trombone. Tympani. Almost as if any tiny troupe of saltimbanques had set about conveying the same information as a full pit-orchestra. There was hardly a full complement left in Europe. Yet with violin and tympani Stravinsky had managed to communicate in that tango the same exhaustion, the same airlessness one saw in the slicked-down youths who were trying to imitate Vernon Castle, and in their mistresses, who simply did not care. *Ma maitresse.* Celeste. Returning to Nice after the second war he had found that cafe replaced by a perfume shop which catered to American tourists. And no secret vestige of her in the cobblestones or in the old pension next door; no perfume to match her breath heavy with the sweet Spanish wine she always drank. And so instead he had purchased a Henry Miller novel and left for Paris, and read the book on the train so that when he arrived he had been given at least a little forewarning. And saw that Celeste and the others and even Temple Drake were not all that had changed. "Aubade," he said, "my head aches." The sound of his voice generated in the girl an answering scrap of melody. Her movement toward the kitchen, the towel, the cold water, and his eyes following her formed a weird and intricate canon; as she placed the compress on his forehead his sigh of gratitude seemed to signal a new subject, another series of modulations.

"No," Meatball was still saying, "no, I'm afraid not. This is not a house of ill repute. I'm sorry, really I am." Slab was adamant. "But the chief said," he kept repeating. The seaman offered to swap the moonshine for a good piece. Meatball looked around frantically, as if seeking assistance. In the middle of the room, the Duke di Angelis quartet were engaged in a historic moment. Vincent was seated and the others standing: they were going through the motions of a group having a session, only without instruments. "I say," Meatball said. Duke moved his head a few times, smiled faintly, lit a cigarette, and eventually caught sight of Meatball. "Quiet, man," he whispered. Vincent began to fling his arms around, his fists clenched; then, abruptly, was still, then repeated the performance. This went on for a few minutes while Meatball sipped his drink moodily. The navy had withdrawn to the kitchen. Finally at some invisible signal the group stopped tapping their feet and Duke grinned and said, "At least we ended together."

Meatball glared at him. "I say," he said. "I have this new conception, man," Duke said. "You remember your namesake. You remember Gerry."

"No," said Meatball. "I'll remember April, if that's any help."

"As a matter of fact," Duke said, "it was Love for Sale. Which shows how much you know. The point is, it was Mulligan, Chet Baker and that crew, way back then, out yonder. You dig?"

"Baritone sax," Meatball said. "Something about a baritone sax."

"But no piano, man. No guitar. Or accordion. You know what that means."

"Not exactly," Meatball said.

"Well first let me just say, that I am no Mingus, no John Lewis. Theory was never my strong point. I mean things like reading were always difficult for me and all—"

"I know," Meatball said drily. "You got your card taken away because you changed key on Happy Birthday at a Kiwanis Club picnic."

"Rotarian. But it occurred to me, in one of these flashes of insight, that if that first quartet of Mulligan's had no piano, it could only mean one thing."

"No chords," said Paco, the baby-faced bass.

"What is he trying to say," Duke said, "is no root chords. Nothing to listen to while you blow a horizontal line. What one does in such a case is, one *thinks* the roots."

A horrified awareness was dawning on Meatball. "And the next logical extension," he said.

"Is to think everything," Duke announced with simple dignity. "Roots, line, everything."

Meatball looked at Duke, awed. "But," he said.

"Well," Duke said modestly, "there are a few bugs to work out."

"But," Meatball said.

"Just listen," Duke said. "You'll catch on." And off they went again into orbit, presumably somewhere around the asteroid belt. After a while Krinkles made an embouchure and started moving his fingers and Duke clapped his hand to his forehead. "Oaf!" he roared. "The new head we're using, you remember, I wrote last night?" "Sure," Krinkles said, "the new head. I come in on the bridge. All your heads I come in then." "Right," Duke said. "So why—" "Wha," said Krinkles, "16 bars, I wait, I come in—" "16?" Duke said. "No. No, Krinkles. Eight you waited. You want me to sing it? A cigarette that bears a lipstick's traces, an airline ticket to romantic places." Krinkles scratched his head. "These Foolish Things, you mean." "Yes," Duke said, "yes, Krinkles. Bravo." "Not I'll Remember April," Krinkles said. "*Minghe morte*," said Duke. "I *figured* we were playing it a little slow," Krinkles said. Meatball chuckled. "Back to the old drawing board," he said. "No, man," Duke said, "back to the airless void." And they took off again, only it seemed Paco was playing in G sharp while the rest were in E flat, so they had to start all over.

In the kitchen two of the girls from George Washington and the sailors were singing Let's All Go Down and Piss on the Forrestal. There was a two-handed, bilingual *mura* game on over by the icebox. Saul had filled several paper bags with water and was sitting on the fire escape, dropping them on passersby in the street. A fat government girl in a Bennington sweatshirt, recently engaged to an ensign attached to the Forrestal, came charging into the kitchen, head lowered, and butted Slab in the stomach. Figuring this was as good an excuse for a fight as any, Slab's buddies piled in. The *mura* players were nose-to-nose, screaming *trois, sette* at the tops of their lungs. From the shower the girl Meatball had taken out of the sink announced that she was drowning. She had apparently sat on the drain and the water was now up to her neck. The noise in Meatball's apartment had reached a sustained, ungodly crescendo.

Meatball stood and watched, scratching his stomach lazily. The way he figured, there were only about two ways he could cope: (a) lock himself in the closet and maybe eventually they would all go away, or (b) try to calm everybody down, one by one. (a) was certainly the more attractive alternative. But then he started thinking about that closet. It was dark and stuffy and he would be alone. He did not feature being alone. And then this crew off the good ship Lollipop or whatever it was might take it upon themselves to kick down the closet door, for a lark. And if that happened he would be, at the very least, embarrassed. The other way was more a pain in the neck, but probably better in the long run.

So he decided to try and keep his lease-breaking party from deteriorating into total chaos: he gave wine to the sailors and separated the *mura* players; he introduced the fat government girl to Sandor Rojas, who would keep her out of trouble; he helped the girl in the shower to dry off and get into bed; he had another talk with Saul; he called a repairman for the refrigerator, which someone had discovered was on the blink. This is what he did until nightfall, when most of the revellers had passed out and the party trembled on the threshold of its third day.

Upstairs Callisto, helpless in the past, did not feel the faint rhythm inside the bird begin to slacken and fail. Aubade was by the window, wandering the ashes of her own lovely world; the temperature held steady, the sky had become a uniform darkening gray. Then something from downstairs—a girl's scream, an overturned chair, a glass dropped on the floor, he would never know what exactly—pierced that private time-warp and he became aware of the faltering, the constriction of muscles, the tiny tossings of the bird's head; and his own pulse began to pound more fiercely, as if trying to compensate. "Aubade," he called weakly, "he's dying." The girl, flowing and rapt, crossed the hothouse to gaze down at Callisto's hands. The two remained like that, poised, for one minute, and two, while the heartbeat ticked a graceful diminuendo down at last into stillness. Callisto raised his head slowly. "I held him," he protested, impotent with the wonder of it, "to give him the warmth of my body. Almost as if I were communicating life to him, or a sense of life. What has happened? Has the transfer of heat ceased to work? Is there no more . . ." He did not finish.

"I was just at the window," she said. He sank back, terrified. She stood a moment more, irresolute; she had sensed his obsession long ago, realized somehow that that constant 37 was now decisive. Suddenly then, as if seeing the single and unavoidable conclusion to all this she moved swiftly to the window before Callisto could speak; tore away the drapes and smashed out the glass with two exquisite hands which came away bleeding and glistening with splinters; and turned to face the man on the bed and wait with him until the moment of equilibrium was reached, when 37 degrees Fahrenheit should prevail both outside and inside, and forever, and the hovering, curious dominant of their separate lives should resolve into a tonic of darkness and the final absence of all motion.

[OLD SERIES VOL. XXII, NO. 2 / SPRING 1960]

The Beekeeper's Daughter

A garden of mouthings. Purple, scarlet-speckled, black
The great corollas dilate, peeling back their silks.
Their musk encroaches, circle after circle,
A well of scents almost too dense to breathe in.
Hieratical in your frock coat, maestro of the bees,
You move among the many-breasted hives,

My heart under your foot, sister of a stone.

Trumpet-throats open to the beaks of birds.
The Golden Rain Tree drips its powders down.
In these little boudoirs streaked with orange and red
The anthers nod their heads, potent as kings
To father dynasties. The air is rich.
Here is a queenship no mother can contest—

A fruit that's death to taste: dark flesh, dark parings.

In burrows narrow as a finger, solitary bees
Keep house among the grasses. Kneeling down
I set my eye to a hole-mouth and meet an eye
Round, green, disconsolate as a tear.
Father, bridegroom, in this Easter egg
Under the coronal of sugar roses

The queen bee marries the winter of your year.

[OLD SERIES VOL. XXII, NO. 4 / AUTUMN 1960]

WILLIAM STAFFORD

Adults Only

Animals own a fur world;
people own worlds that are variously, pleasingly, bare.
And the way these worlds are once arrived for us kids
  with a jolt,
that night when the wild woman danced
in the giant cage we found we were all in
at the state fair.

Better women exist, no doubt, than that one,
and occasions more edifying, too, I suppose.
But we have to witness for ourselves what comes
  for us,
nor be distracted by barkers of irrelevant ware;
and a pretty good world, I say, arrived that night
when that woman came farming right out of her clothes,
  by God,

At the state fair.

[OLD SERIES VOL. XXII, NO. 4 / AUTUMN 1960]

ROBERT LOWELL

Saturday Night in the Village

The day
is ready to close;
the girl takes the downward
path homeward from the vineyard,
and jumps from crevice to crevice
like a goat, as she holds a swath
of violets and roses
to decorate her hair and bodice
tomorrow as usual for the Sabbath.

Her grandmothier sits,
facing the sun going out,
and spins and starts to reason
with the neighbors, and renew the day,
when she used to dress herself for the holiday
and dance away
the night—still quick and healthy,
with the boys, companions of her fairer season.

Once again the landscape is brown,
the sky drains to a pale blue,
shadows drop from mountain and thatch,
the young moon whitens.
As I catch

the clatter of small bells,
sounding in the holiday,
I can almost say
my heart takes comfort in the sound.
Children place their pickets
and sentinels,
and splash round and round
the village fountain.
They jump like crickets,
and make a happy sound.
The field hand,
who lives on nothing,
marches home whistling,
and gorges on the day of idleness at hand.

Then all's at peace;
the lights are out;
I hear the rasp of shavings,
and the rapping hammer
of the carpenter, working all night
by lanternlight —
hurryinig and straining himself
to increase his savings
before the whitening day.

This is the most kind
of the seven days; tomorrow, you will wait
and pray for Sunday's boredom and anguish
to be extinguished
in the workdays' grind
you anticipate.
Lively boy,
the only age you are alive
is like this day of joy,
a clear and breathless Saturday

that heralds life's holiday.
Rejoice, my child,
this is the untroubled instant.
Why should I undeceive you?
Let it not grieve you,
if the following days are slow to arrive.

The Infinite

That hill pushed off by itself was always dear
to me and the hedges near
it that cut away so much of the final horizon.
When I would sit there lost in deliberation,
I reasoned most on the interminable spaces
beyond all hills, on their antediluvian resignation
and silence that passes
beyond man's possibility.
Here for a little while my heart is quiet inside me;
and when the wind lifts roughing through the trees,
I set about comparing my silence to those voices,
and I think about the eternal, the dead seasons,
things here at hand and alive,
and all their reasons and choices.
It's sweet to destroy my mind
and go down
and wreck in this sea where I drown.

[OLD SERIES VOL. XXIII, NO. 4 / AUTUMN 1961]

Message in a Bottle

There are days when the world pauses, gets stuck, senselessly, like one of those machines that ought to give cigarettes or make balls bump round but simply becomes an object that takes kicks, shakes, unyieldingly. You drop out of step with the daily work or habit that carries you along and stare about. Halt, halt! It's fatal. This is not Sunday, with cows beside winter willows and dried-up streams, and white egrets catching up with their own forward-jerking necks. I notice a face in the strip of mirror attached with crystal knobs to the pillar in the coffee shop. An uneven face, looks as if it's been up all night for years: my own. Once I had no face to speak of, only a smile, bright eyes and powdered cheeks, nicely arranged. I order two coffees, one for myself, one for the child — "Would you like a cup of coffee?": it is a piece of clumsy flattery, a status I confer upon her because she has just been to a doctor and suffered a painful treatment. She accepts it, her token smile knowing its worth.

She shivers a little, from shock, in her dusty school clothes; at this time of the morning, she ought to be doing mental arithmetic. I am in my work clothes too, interrupted by necessity. I do not know what to talk to the child about because she has plumbed cheerful, jollying reassurances over months of pain, and efforts at distraction she takes as a kind of insult. She resents my sympathy because I have not her pain; my solicitously gentle voice is easy enough for me, it does not help her, she has discovered. So we don't talk, and I eat a piece of cheesecake, not so much because I want it, but to show her that life must go on.

By such moves and signals do we conduct the battle that is waged between the sick and the well.

I eat the cheesecake and look again at the only other two customers in the place at this time on a Wednesday morning. I half-saw them when we came in, but my awareness was merely of a presence that brought to light my old trousers and cardigan. An oldish man and a blonde girl out of a fashion magazine. She is tall as they always are and she sits not with her knees under the table but with the length of her body from seat to head turned diagonally toward him and supported by her elbow on the table. From the door, without detail, they fell into an image of a girl making up to a man. But she is weeping. Tears fill and refract marvellously the one eye I can see and then run slowly down the pale beige cheek. She stretches the muscles of her face to hold them and puts up the forefinger of a clenched hand to catch them. One distinctly runs over the finger and drops to the tablecloth. There will be a little splotch there, where it fell.

I look away, but when I look back again the tears are still coming, in slow twos and threes down the matte and perfect cheek. She is talking all the time to the man, not looking at him but talking without a sound that I can hear, directly to his ear with the dark shadow in it that must be a tuft of hair. That tense tendon in her neck may become permanent when she is older; but there is no reason why she will be so unhappy often. It looks like the kind of misery one grows out of.

She is a beautiful girl dressed from head to foot in pale beige that matches her face and hair. He would be ugly if he were a poor man, sucked dry, at his age, and leathery; but his crowded features, thin ridged nose and eyes and line of mouth, are filled out, smoothly built up, deal by deal, as a sculptor adds clay daub by daub, by ease and money-making. He has never been a good-looking young man, never. While she talks he looks out across the room, listening. He does not look at her but at the waiters passing, the door opening, the woman at the cash register ringing up the sale of a packet of cigarettes. It is a face that has put love into making money. Yes, he is ugly, but I do not know whether I imagine that she already has the look of one of those lovely creatures whose beauty—that makes them feel they may have any man—brings them nothing but one of these owners of textile factories; while we others, who are ignored by the many, carry off the particular prizes, the distinguished, the gentle, the passionately attractive, the adventurous. Is she pleading with him not to break off an affair? The one remark I do hear belies this: "... what about that boy friend of yours, doesn't he ... " The very tone of his voice, raised plainly above the confidential, is that of the confidant importuned, stonily turning nasty and wanting to give up his privilege to anyone who seems under a more valid obligation to deal with the situation. Yet I don't know. She is still pleading, clearly going over and over what she has said a dozen times before. How beautifully she weeps, without a bloated nose; why should one feel not moved by her just because she is beautiful, why, in spite of everything, is there the obstinate cold resentment that her face is more than she deserves?

The man's eyes (he is obviously keenly long-sighted) follow the passing of someone on the other side of the glass barrier, in the street. As he changes focus we meet, my piece of cheesecake halfway to my mouth. We know each other, this morning, above the heads of the child and the weeping one. I should never have thought it; but you don't always choose the ones you know. The girl has not paused in her desperate monologue and the child, beside me, has her one uncovered eye screwed up, nuzzling toward brightness without seeing, like a mole.

I pay and the child and I walk out just behind the other two. There is a big black car outside the door and a black chauffeur, fat henchman, opens the door for them. One feels the girl likes this, it turns up the fragment of a fairy tale. She steps inside elegantly, with a certain melancholy pleasure, balanced like a brimming glass.

I drive out of the city to an address where the child is to have a culture made from the infected tissues in her eyelids. The doctor has drawn a little map for me; through suburbs, past country clubs and chicken farms, everywhere the sun shines evenly through a bloom of blue smoke that marks the position of the city, from far off, like the spout of a whale. The research institute is spread out pleasantly on a rise; there are gardens, and horses standing in a field. We get out of the car and it's as if a felt-lined door has been shut—the sound of life in the city comes only as a slight vibration under one's feet. I take her by the arm and we cross some grass, city people in the sunlight, and wander from building to building. They are white inside and, although we hear voices through frosted doors, all desks are empty. We see an African in a white coat blocking the light at the end of corridor. He directs us to another building. He has a kind of trolley full of small cages with dark shapes in them that don't move. Out of the clean buildings, round the goldfish ponds (she is too old to want to linger beside them any more), we come into a courtyard full of gray monkeys in cages. She forgets about her eye and breaks away from me, finding her way: "Oh aren't they sweet!" They swing from gray tails, they have black masks through which amber eyes shine with questions. They have patches where the fur has been shaved and the skin has been punctured again and again and painted with medicaments; oh why, but why? She pulls back from my arm when I tell her. There are rats, crouched guinea pigs, piles of empty cages in yards. The horses, that were standing so peacefully in the field, have glazed eyes and the hopelessness of working animals who have come out of the shafts for good. On their rumps and necks are the shaved and painted patches. Their stalls are being swilled out and scrubbed by men in rubber boots; it is so clean, all this death and disease.

"Now we're going to try and grow these nasty goggas from your eye, dear, we're going to grow them in an egg and see whether we can make you well." The woman in the white coat talks soothingly as she works on the eye. While she is out of the laboratory for a moment we listen to a kettle that is singing up to the boil, and I say, "Don't rub it." The child says after a silence,

"I wish I could be the one who sits and watches." Pain is taking her innocence, she is getting to know me. But if she indicts, she begins at the same time to take on some of the guilt: "They will grow mine in an egg? Only in an egg?" The sun is high; we do not know what time it is, driving back. She tells time by the school bell, I by the cardboard file growing thinner.

My husband has a story to tell when he comes home in the evening. An acquaintance, who took him out shooting, last weekend, has committed suicide. He does not tell it baldly like this but begins slowly at what led up to the beginning, although we can tell, almost from the beginning, what is coming. "He was in wonderful form. I stood next to him and watched him bring down four birds with five cartridges. Alba worked so well and he asked me whether I couldn't ask Jack Strahan to sell him one from the next litter. He couldn't get over the way Alba worked; he said he'd never seen a dog like it, for range. And he asked when I was going to bring you on a shoot again, when're you going to bring your wife out here with you, he said; he remembered that time last year when we had such a good time in the camp."

The man kissed his wife, dropped his children at their school, telephoned his office to say he would be a little late, and then drove out into the veld. "Shut himself in the boot of the car and shot himself through the head." I scarcely knew the man, met him only that once at the camp, but, at this detail of the manner of his death, I suddenly think of something: "But don't you remember, hie used to shut his hunting dogs in the boot? He did it that day, and when I picked him out about it he said it wasn't cruel and they didn't mind being shut up in there!" Nobody knows why he killed himself, he has gone without a word to anyone—except this. The stranger who cannot remember clearly what he looked like is the one into whose hands his last message has fallen. What can I do with it? It's like a message picked up on the beach, that may be a joke, a hoax, or a genuine call of distress—one can't tell, and ends by throwing the bottle back into the sea. If it's genuine, the sender is beyond help already. Or someone else may pick it up and know what it's all about.

If I keep it perhaps I might crack the code one day? If only it were the sort of code that children or spies use, made out of numbers or lines from the Bible. But it is made of what couldn't be equated or spelled out to anyone in the world, that could leave communication only in the awkward movement of his body through the air as he scrambled into the smell of dust and petrol, where the dogs had crouched, and closed the lid over his head.

For no reason at all, my mind begins to construct a dialogue with the girl—that girl. I see her somewhere, years later. She is laughing, she is conscious of her beauty. I say to her quite abruptly, "What happened that morning, anyway? —You know, he has developed hardened arteries and his teeth are giving him trouble. He's on a strict diet—no wine, no red meat—and his old wife cooks for him again. He never goes out."

The child comes in and stands squarely before me. She has put her dark glasses on and I can't see her eyes. "And if the egg should hatch," she says, "if the egg hatches?"

[OLD SERIES VOL. XXIV, NO. 2 / SPRING 1962]

Three Dream Songs

I

In a state of chortal sin — once he reflected,
swilling tomato juice — live I, and did
more than my thirsty years.
To Hell then will it haul me? for good talk
& gripe of retail loss? I dare say not.
I don't think there's that place

save somewhat here! where from she flies tonight
retrieving her whole body, which I need.
I recall a coon treed,
flashlights, & barks, and I was in that tree,
and something can (has) been said for sobriety
but very little.

The guns. Ah, darling, it was late for me,
midnight, at seven. (How in famished youth
could I foresee Henry's sweet seed
unspent across so flying barren ground,
where would my loves dislimn whose dogs abound?)
I fell out of the tree.

II

Some remember ("Pretty well") the Korean war.
The unrecruited memory seems to embrace

82

the Bay of Pigs, Franklin Roosevelt. Who has in mind
with a shudder Cold Harbor,—
Henry is schlaft in his historical moode,—
with pity & horror the Bloody Angle?
Good Friday, and the end?

Three like terrifying political murders
have cast, as Adams sighed, no shadow on the Whites' House.
—Adhere, Sir Bones, to Heaven; tho' the shrine is still,
what here or there but by the will
of hidden God git done? Ah ask.
—I have an answer lost here on my desk:

Pakistan may Pakistan, well, find;
or not.
Henry couldn't care less.
—Mr. Bones, cares for all men!
—Overloaded. It is my country   in my country only
cast is our lot.

III

For John Crowe Ransom

His mother goes. The mother comes & goes.
Chen Lung's too came, came and crampt & then
that master's mother was gone.
It seem we don't have no good bed to lie on,
forever. While he drawing his first breath,
while skinning his knees,

while he was so beastly with love for Charlotte Coquet
he skated up & down in front of her house
wishing he could, sir, die,
while being bullied & he dreamt he could fly—
during the irregular verbs—them world-sought bodies
safe in the Arctic lay:

Strindberg rocked in his niche, the great Andrée
by muscled Fraenkel under what's of the tent,
torn like then limbs, by bears
over fierce decades, harmless. Up in pairs
go we not, but we have a good bed.
I have said what I had to say.

[OLD SERIES VOL. XXVI, NO. 1 / WINTER 1964]

V. S. Naipaul

The Baker's Story

Look at me. Black as the ace of spades, and ugly to match. Nobody looking at me would believe they looking at one of the richest men in this city of Port of Spain. Sometimes I find it hard to believe it myself, you know, especially when I go out on some of the holidays that I start taking the wife and children to these days, and I catch sight of the obzocky black face in one of those fancy mirrors that these expensive hotels have all over the place, as if to spite people like me.

Now everybody—particularly black people—forever asking me how this thing start, and I does always tell them I make my dough from dough. Ha! You like that one? But how it start? Well, you hearing me talk, and I don't have to tell you I didn't have no education. In Grenada, where I come from—and that is one thing these Trinidad black people don't forgive a man for being: a black Grenadian—in Grenada I was one of ten children, I believe—everything kind of mix up out there—and I don't even know who was the feller who hit my mother. I believe he hit a lot of women in all the other parishes of that island, too, because whenever I go back to Grenada for one of those holidays I tell you about, people always telling me that I remind them of this one and that one, and they always mistaking me for a shop assistant whenever I in a shop. (If this thing go on, one day I going to sell somebody something, just for spite.) And even in Trinidad, whenever I run into another Grenadian, the same thing does happen.

Well, I don't know what happen in Grenada, but mammy

85

bring me alone over to Trinidad when she was still young. I don't know what she do with the others, but perhaps they wasn't even she own. Anyway, she get a work with some white people in St. Ann's. They give she a uniform; they give she three meals a day; and they give she a few dollars a month besides. Somehow she get another man, a real Trinidad 'rangoutang, and somehow, I don't know how, she get somebody else to look after me while she was living with this man, for the money and the food she was getting was scarcely enough to support this low-minded Trinidad rango she take up with.

It uses to have a Chinee shop not far from this new aunty I was living with, and one day, when the old girl couldn't find the cash no how to buy a bread — is a hell of a thing, come to think of it now, that it have people in this island who can't lay their hands on enough of the ready to buy a bread — well, when she couldn't buy this bread she send me over to this Chinee shop to ask for trust. The Chinee woman — eh, but how these Chinee people does make children! — was big like anything, and I believe I catch she at a good moment, because she say nothing doing, no trust, but if I want a little work that was different, because she want somebody to take some bread she bake for some Indian people. But how she could trust me with the bread? This was a question. And then I pull out my crucifix from under my dirty merino that was more holes than cloth and I tell she to keep it until I come back with the money for the bake bread. I don't know what sort of religion these Chinee people have, but that woman look impressed like anything. But she was smart, though. She keep the crucifix and she send me off with the bread, which was wrap up in a big old *châle-au-pain*, just two or three floursack sew together. I collect the money, bring it back, and she give me back the crucifix with a few cents and a bread.

And that was how this thing really begin. I always tell black people that was God give me my start in life, and don't mind these Trinidadians who does always tell you that Grenadians always praying. Is a true thing, though, because whenever I in any little business difficulty even these days I get down bam! straight on my two knees and I start praying like hell, boy.

Well, so this thing went on, until it was a regular afternoon work for me to deliver people bread. The bakery uses to bake ordinary bread — hops and pan and machine — which they uses to sell to the poorer classes. And how those Chinee people uses to work! This woman, with she big-big belly, clothes all dirty, sweating in front of the oven, making all this bread and making all this money, and I don't know what they doing with it, because all the time they living poor-poor in the back room, with only a bed, some hammocks for the young ones, and a few boxes. I couldn't talk to the husband at all. He didn't know a word of English and all the writing he uses to write uses to be in Chinee. He was a thin nashy feller, with those funny flapping khaki short pants and white merino that Chinee people always wear. He uses to work like a bitch, too. We Grenadians understand hard work, so that is why I suppose I uses to get on so well with these Chinee people, and that is why these lazy black Trinidadians so jealous of we. But was a funny thing. They uses to live so dirty. But the children, man, uses to leave that ramshackle old back room as clean as new bread, and they always had this neatness, always with their little pencil-case and their little rubbers and rulers and blotters, and they never losing anything. They leaving in the morning in one nice little line and in the afternoon they coming back in this same little line, still cool and clean, as though nothing at all touch them all day. Is something they could teach black people children.

But as I was saying this bakery uses to bake ordinary bread for the poorer classes. For the richer classes they uses to bake, too. But what they would do would be to collect the dough from those people house, bake it, and send it back as bread, hot and sweet. I uses to fetch and deliver for this class of customer. They never let me serve in the shop; it was as though they couldn't trust me selling across the counter and collecting money in that rush. Always it had this rush. You know black people: even if it only have one man in the shop he always getting on as if it have one hell of a crowd.

Well, one day when I deliver some bread in this *châle-au-pain* to a family, there was a woman, a neighbor, who start saying how nice it is to get bread which you knead with your own hands and not mix up with all sort of people sweat. And this give me the idea. A oven is a oven. It have to go on, whether it baking one bread or two. So I tell this woman, was a Potogee woman, that I would take she dough and bring it back bake for she, and that it would cost she next to nothing. I say this in a sort of way that she wouldn't know whether I was going to give the money to the Chinee people, or whether it was going to cost she next to nothing because it would be I who was going to take the money. But she give me a look which tell me right away that she wanted me to take the money. So matter fix. So. Back in the *châle-au-pain* the next few days I take some dough, hanging it in the carrier of the bakery bicycle. I take it inside, as though I just didn't bother to wrap up the *châle-au-pain*, and the next thing is that this dough mix up with the other dough, and see me kneading and baking, as though all is one. The thing is, when you go in for a thing like that, to go in brave-brave. It have some people who make so much fuss when they doing one little thing that they bound to get catch. So, and I was surprise like hell, mind you, I get this stuff push in the oven, and is this said Chinee man, always with this sad and sorrowful Chinee face, who pulling it out of the oven with the long-handled shovel, looking at it, and pushing it back in.

And when I take the bread back, with some other bread, I collect the money cool-cool. The thing with a thing like this is that once you start is damn' hard to stop. You start calculating this way and that way. And I have a calculating mind. I forever sitting down and working out how much say .50 a day every day for seven days, and every week for a year, coming to. And so this thing get to be a big thing with me. I wouldn't recommend this to any- and everybody who want to go into business. But is what

I mean when I tell people that I make my dough by dough.

The Chinee woman wasn't too well now. And the old man was getting on a little funny in a Chinee way. You know how those Chinee fellers does gamble. You drive past Marine Square in the early hours of the Sabbath and is two to one if you don't see some of those Chinee fellers sitting down outside the Treasury, as though they want to be near money, and gambling like hell. Well, the old man was gambling and the old girl was sick, and I was pretty well the only person looking after the bakery. I work damn' hard for them, I could tell you. I even pick up two or three words of Chinee, and some of those rude black people start calling me Black Chinee, because at this time I was beginning to dress in short khaki pants and merino like a Chinee and I was drinking that tea Chinee people drinking all day long and I was walking and not saying much like a Chinee. And, now, don't believe what these black people say about Chinee and prejudice, eh. They have nothing at all against black people, provided they is hard-working and grateful.

But life is a funny thing. Now when it look that I all set, that everything going fine and dandy, a whole set of things happen that start me bawling. First, the Chinee lady catch a pleurisy and dead. Was a hell of a thing, but what else you expect when she was always bending down in front of that fire and then getting wet and going out in the dew and everything, and then always making these children too besides. I was sorry like hell, and a little frighten. Because I wasn't too sure how I was going to manage alone with the old man. All the time I work with him he never speak one word straight to me, but he always talking to me through his wife.

And now, look at my crosses. As soon as the woman dead, the Chinee man like he get mad. He didn't cry or anything like that, but he start gambling like a bitch, and the upshot was that one day, perhaps about a month after the old lady dead, the man tell his children to pack up and start leaving, because he gamble and lose the shop to another Chinee feller. I didn't know where

I was standing, and nobody telling me nothing. They only packing. I don't know, I suppose they begin to feel that I was just part of the shop, and the old man not even saying that he sorry he lose me. And, you know, as soon as I drop to my knees and start praying, I see it was really God who right from the start put that idea of the dough in my head, because without that I would have been nowhere at all. Because the new feller who take over the shop say he don't want me. He was going to close the bakery and set up a regular grocery, and he didn't want me serving there because the grocery customers wouldn't like black people serving them. So look at me. Twenty-three years old and no work. No nothing. Only I have this Chinee-ness and I know how to bake bread and I had this extra bit of cash I save up over the years.

I slip out of the old khaki short pants and mero and I cruise around the town a little, looking for a work. But nobody want bakers. I had about $700.00, and I see that this cruising around would do but it wouldn't pay, because the money was going fast. Now look at this. You know, it never cross my mind in those days that I could open a shop of my own. Is how it is with black people. They get so use to working for other people that they get to believe that because they black they can't do nothing else but work for other people. And I must tell you that when I start praying and God tell me to go out and open a shop for myself I feel that perhaps God did mistake or that I didn't hear Him good. Because God only saying to me, "Youngman, take your money and open a bakery. You could bake good bread." He didn't say to open a parlor, which a few black fellers do, selling rock cakes and mauby and other soft drinks. No, He say open a bakery. Look at my crosses.

I had a lot of trouble borrowing the extra few hundred dollars, but I eventually get a Indian feller to lend me. And this is what I always tell young fellers. That getting credit ain't no trouble at all if you know exactly what you want to do. I didn't go round telling people to lend me money because I want to build house or buy lorry. I just did want to bake bread. Well, to cut a long story short, I buy a breakdown old place near Arouca, and I spend most of what I had trying to fix the place up. Nothing extravagant, you understand, because Arouca is Arouca and you don't want to frighten off the country-bookies wth anything too sharp. Too besides, I didn't have the cash. I just put in a few second-hand glass case and things like that, I write up my name on a board, and, look, I in business.

Now the funny thing happen. In Laventille the people couldn't have enough of the bread I was baking — and in the last few months was me was doing the baking. But now trouble. I baking better bread than the people of Arouca ever see, and I can't get one single feller to come in like man through my rickety old front door and buy a penny hops bread. You hear all this talk about quality being its own advertisement? Don't believe it, boy. Is quality plus something else. And I didn't have this something else. I begin to wonder what the hell it could be. I say is because I new in Arouca that this thing happening. But no. I new, I get stale, and the people not flocking in their hundreds to the old shop. Day after day I baking two or three quarts good and all this just remaining and going dry and stale, and the only bread I selling is to the man from the government farm, buying stale cakes and bread for the cows or pigs or whatever they have up there. And was good bread. So I get down on the old knees and I pray as though I want to wear them out. And still I getting the same answer: "Youngman" — was always the way I uses to get call in these prayers — "Youngman, you just bake bread."

Pappa! This was a thing. Interest on the loan piling up every month. Some months I borrow from aunty and anybody else who kind enough to listen just to pay off the interest. And things get so low that I uses to have to go out and pretend to people that I was working for another man bakery and that I was going to bake their dough cheap-cheap. And in Arouca cheap mean cheap. And the little cash I picking up in this disgraceful way was just about enough to keep the wolf from the door, I tell you.

Jeezan. Look at confusion. The old place in Arouca so damn'

out of the way—was why I did buy it, too, thinking that they didn't have no bakery there and that they would be glad of the good Grenadian-baked—the place so out of the way nobody would want to buy it. It ain't even insure or anything, so it can't get in a little fire accident or anything—not that I went in for that sort of thing. And every time I go down on my knees, the answer coming straight back at me: "Youngman, you just bake bread."

Well, for the sake of the Lord I baking one or two quarts regular every day, though I begin to feel that the Lord want to break me, and I begin to feel too that this was His punishment for what I uses to do to the Chinee people in their bakery. I was beginning to feel bad and real ignorant. I uses to stay away from the bakery after baking those quarts for the Lord—nothing to lock up, nothing to thief—and, when any of the Laventille boys drop in on the way to Manzanilla and Balandra and those other beaches on the Sabbath, I uses to tell them, making a joke out of it, that I was "loafing." They uses to laugh like hell, too. It have nothing in the whole world so funny as to see a man you know flat out on his arse and catching good hell.

The Indian feller was getting anxious about his cash, and you couldn't blame him, either, because some months now he not even seeing his interest. And this begin to get me down, too. I remember how all the man did ask me when I went to him for money was: "You sure you want to bake bread? You feel you have a hand for baking bread?" And yes-yes, I tell him, and just like that he shell out the cash. And now he was getting anxious. So one day, after baking those loaves for the Lord, I take a Arima Bus Service bus to Port of Spain to see this feller. I was feeling brave enough on the way. But as soon as I see the old sea and get a whiff of South Quay and the bus touch the Railway Station terminus my belly start going pweh-pweh. I decide to roam about the city for a little.

Was a hot morning, *petit-carême* weather, and in those days a coconut uses still to cost .04. Well, it had this coconut cart in the old square and I stop by it. It was a damn' funny thing to see. The seller was a black feller. And you wouldn't know how funny this was, unless you know that every coconut seller in the island is Indian. They have this way of handling a cutlass that black people don't have. Coconut in left hand; with right hand bam, bam, bam with cutlass, and coconut cut open, ready to drink. I ain't never see a coconut seller chop his hand. And here was this black feller doing this bam-bam-bam business on a coconut with a cutlass. It was as funny as seeing a black man wearing dhoti and turban. The sweetest part of the whole business was that this black feller was, forgetting looks, just like a Indian. He was talking Hindustani to a lot of Indian fellers, who was giving him jokes like hell, but he wasn't minding. It does happen like that sometimes with black fellers who live a lot with Indians in the country. They putting away curry, talking Indian, and behaving just like Indians. Well, I take a coconut from this black man and then went on to see the feller about the money.

He was more sad than vex when I tell him, and if I was in his shoes I woulda be sad, too. Is a hell of a thing when you see your money gone and you ain't getting the sweet little kisses from the interest every month. Anyway, he say he would give me three more months' grace, but that if I didn't start shelling out at the agreed rate he would have to foreclose. "You put me in a hell of a position," he say. "Look at me. You think I want a shop in Arouca?"

I was feeling a little better when I leave the feller, and who I should see when I leave but Percy. Percy was a old rango who uses to go to the Laventille elementary school with me. I never know a boy get so much cut-arse as Percy. But he grow up real hard and ignorant with it, and now he wearing fancy clothes like a saga boy, and talking about various business offers. I believe he was selling insurance—is a thing that nearly every idler doing in Trinidad, and, mark my words, the day coming when you going to see those fellers trying to sell insurance to one another. Anyway, Percy getting on real flash, and he say he want to stand

me a lunch for old times' sake. He make a few of the usual ignorant Trinidadian jokes about Grenadians, and we went up to the
Angostura Bar. I did never go there before, and wasn't the sort of
place you would expect a rango like Percy to be welcome. But we
went up there and Percy start throwing his weight around with
the waiters, and, mind you, they wasn't even a quarter as black as
Percy. Is a wonder they didn't abuse him, especially with all those
fair people around.

After the drinks Percy say, "Where you want to have this
lunch?"

Me, I don't know a thing about the city restaurants, and when
Percy talk about food all I was expecting was rice and peas or a
roti off a Indian stall or a mauby and rock cake in some parlor.
And is a damn' hard thing to have people, even people as ignorant as Percy, showing off on you, especially when you carrying
two nails in your pocket to make the jingling noise. So I tell Percy
we could go to a parlor or a bar. But he say, "No, no. When I treat
my friends, I don't like black people meddling with my food."

And was only then that the thing hit me. I suppose that what
Trinidadians say about the stupidness of Grenadians have a little
truth, though you have to live in a place for a long time before
you get to know it really well. Then the thing hit me, man.

When black people in Trinidad go to a restaurant they don't
like to see black people meddling with their food. And then I see
that though Trinidad have every race and every color, every race
have to do special things. But look, man. If you want to buy a
snowball, who you buying it from? You wouldn't buy it from a
Indian or a Chinee or a Potogee. You would buy it from a black
man. And I myself, when I was getting my place in Arouca fix
up, I didn't employ Indian carpenters or masons. If a Indian in
Trinidad decide to go into the carpentering business the man
would starve. Who ever see a Indian carpenter? I suppose the
only place in the world where they have Indian carpenters and
Indian masons is India. Is a damn' funny thing. One of these days
I must make a trip to that country, to just see this thing. And as

we walking I seeing the names of bakers: Coelho, Pantin, Stauble. Potogee or Swiss or something, and then all those other Chinee places. And, look at the laundries. If a black man open a laundry, you would take your clothes to it? *I* wouldn't take my clothes there. Well, I walking to this restaurant, but I jumping for joy. And then all sorts of things fit into place. You remember that the Chinee people didn't let me serve bread across the counter? I uses to think it was because they didn't trust me with the rush. But it wasn't that. It was that, if they did let me serve, they wouldn't have had no rush at all. You ever see anybody buying their bread off a black man?

I ask Percy why he didn't like black people meddling with his food in public places. The question throw him a little. He stop and think and say, "It don't *look* nice."

Well, you could guess the rest of the story. Before I went back to Arouca that day I make contact with a yellow boy call Macnab. This boy was half black and half Chinee, and, though he had a little brown color and the hair a little curly, he could pass for one of those Cantonese. They a little darker than the other Chinee people, I believe. Macnab I find beating a steel pan in somebody yard—they was practicing for Carnival—and I suppose the only reason that Macnab was willing to come all the way to Arouca was because he was short of the cash to buy his costume for the Carnival band.

But he went up with me. I put him in front of the shop, give him a merino and a pair of khaki short pants, and tell him to talk as Chinee as he could, if he wanted to get that Carnival bonus. I stay in the back room, and I start baking bread. I even give Macnab a old Chinee paper, not to read, because Macnab could scarcely read English, but just to leave lying around, to make it look good. And I get hold of one of those big Chinee calendars with Chinee women and flowers and waterfalls and hang it up on the wall. And when this was all ready, I went down on my knees and thank God. And still the old message coming, but friendly and happy now: "Youngman, you just bake bread."

And, you know, that solve another problem. I was worrying to hell about the name I should give the place. New Shanghai, Canton, Hongkong, Nanking, Yang-tse-Kiang. But when the old message come over I know right away what the name should be. I scrub off the old name — no need to tell you what that was — and I get a proper sign painter to copy a few letters from the Chinee newspaper. Below that, in big letters, I make him write:

YUNG MAN

BAKER

I never show my face in the front of the shop again. And I tell you, without boasting, that I bake damn' good bread. And the people of Arouca ain't that foolish. They know a good thing. And soon I was making so much money that I was able to open a branch in Arima and then another in Port of Spain self. Was hard in the beginning to get real Chinee people to work for a black man. But money have it own way of talking, and when today you pass any of the Yung Man establishments all you seeing behind the counter is Chinee. Some of them ain't even know they working for a black man. My wife handling that side of the business, and the wife is Chinee. She come from down Cedros way. So look at me now, in Port of Spain, giving Stauble and Partin and Coelho a run for their money. As I say, I only going in the shops from the back. But every Monday morning I walking brave brave to Marine Square and going in the bank, from the front.

[OLD SERIES VOL. XXVI, NO. 3 / SUMMER 1964]

Don DeLillo

Coming Sun. Mon. Tues.

The bitterness and urgency of today's rebellious youth
. . . tender and lyrical . . . A social document of aimless
teenagers seeking their identity . . . evocative and bitter-
sweet . . . the tragic boomerang of adolescent passions
. . . A visual treat . . . somewhat controversial.
—The Times

It is Fifth Avenue in late afternoon in autumn and the shadows
darken the street. The boy wears a heavy sweater and desert
boots. He has long hair. The girl is pretty. She is wearing a heavy
sweater. It is Fifth Avenue or Grosvenor Square. She has lovely
eyes. They look in the shop windows. Mannequins in fur and
diamonds. Ladies' shoes atop red velvet. An eight million dollar
necklace. She whirls and pirouettes, dreaming of inaugural balls
or being presented to the Queen. A few middle-aged people stare
at her and shake their heads. What is the world coming to. She
giggles and takes the boy's hand and they skip away to the park.
They walk in the park. Leaves are falling. It is that golden time of
day. There are boats on the lake. The sun is going down behind
the Dakota Apartments or the London Hilton and she chases a
squirrel across the grass in the soft darkening afternoon. Then
they are drinking wine. They are in his small room drinking wine.
Her eyes are lovely. The boy is talking. He is being bitter about
something. Eventually it becomes clear. It's the world. He is being bitter about the world. He chain-smokes and drinks a lot of
wine. It is Greenwich Village or the West Side. It is either of those
or it is Soho or it is Montmartre. After a while she does a little
pirouette and he gets up and stands in front of the bathroom

mirror and makes funny faces in the mirror. Then they make funny faces together. He kisses her. She becomes pregnant. She is pregnant and they talk to an abortionist. The abortionist's office is cold and sterile. Everything in the office is white. The boy and girl are nervous but the abortionist's nurse is not nervous. The nurse has hooded eyes. She smokes a cigarette. The abortionist is smooth and very much to the point. He's been through this scene thousands of times. He has a moustache and long, elegant fingers. He tells them to come back next Tuesday. They leave the office. The boy puts his arm around the girl. They are not on Fifth Avenue. They are near the waterfront. A drunk is sleeping in a doorway. They are trying to decide what to do. The girl writes a letter to her mother in the suburbs and then tears it up. The boy runs from one end of Chicago to the other. Then he looks for a job to get the money for the abortion. He is interviewed by a series of tall men with elegant fingers and they all tell him that they'll let him know if anything turns up. He insults one of the men, an old school chum of his father's who is the president of a management consultant firm and cannot understand why the boy did not finish college. The boy insults him beautifully. The man is so out of it that he is not even sure he has been insulted. Then the boy and girl go to a store in San Francisco or Toronto or Liverpool. They steal some groceries. They leave the store laughing with the groceries under their heavy sweaters. Then the boy stops at a flower stand and steals a flower for the girl. Then they go home and she cries. Then they go to a party. Everybody at the party is a phony except for one guy who's a West Indian or an American Negro or a French Canadian. This guy tells them that they don't know the first thing about being bitter. They have no right to be bitter. He tells them a thing or two about life and death. Everybody else is doing the freddy and this guy is telling them about real suffering, real pain. Telling it like it is. Then he rolls up his sleeve and shows them how he was wounded in Vietnam or Mississippi. Meanwhile everybody is doing the freddy and talking about Andy Warhol or the Animals. The boy and girl go home again. The Vietnam or Mississippi thing has put their troubles in a truer perspective. They play hide-and-seek under the covers of his tiny bed. Then they take turns feeling the girl's belly. They go to the Louvre and the girl sticks out her tongue at the Mona Lisa. Some middle-aged people shake their heads. The next day the girl gets up early and goes to school and the boy sits around smoking and looking in the mirror. Then he steals a car. He drives past all the ancient monuments of Rome or Athens. He sees his father come out of a hotel with a woman who is not his mother. He slumps down low in the driver's seat and watches. His father talks to the woman for a few seconds and then kisses her and they walk off in different directions. The boy just sits there. He sits there. Cars are piling up behind him and horns are blowing. Then he is standing on a bridge above the Thames. Leaves and garbage float by. He goes home and sees that the flower he had stolen for the girl is dead. He throws the flower away so she won't see it when she gets home from school. Then she gets home and tells him to return the stolen car. He gives her a hard time, saying basically that nothing means anything so why bother. She says if that's your concept of life I don't want to see you anymore. So she goes home to the suburbs. She has roast beef and mashed potatoes with her mother and father and older sister. Dessert is chocolate cake. Her mother wants to know why she's failing Civics and Arithmetic and where she's been the last three days and nights. The girl tries to be nice. Things are different now, mom. It's not like when you were growing up. The father makes an attempt at paternal understanding. Takes the positive approach. Compliments her on the fine job she's been doing in English Lit. Says he *likes* the Beatles. Then the older sister's date shows up. He has a crew-cut and wears a button-down shirt. He makes a lot of comments about the junior chamber of commerce and the local country club. He's in the executive training program of a huge management consultant firm. He's also a lieutenant in the Air Force Reserve. Brags about the fact that his country club just admitted its first Jew. The girl wants to know why they didn't do

it twenty years ago. Older sister gets mad and tells her to go to
her room. In her room she looks in the mirror. Then she feels
her belly for a few minutes and repacks her suitcase. The boy
stands in front of a movie theater looking at a poster of Jean
Paul Belmondo. He goes to a bar. The place is full of hookers
and pimps. Derelicts slip from their bar stools and lie in the sawdust. The juke is playing mean, lowdown jazz. The bartender is
fat and ugly. A very clean-cut man comes up to the boy and ar-
rests him. The boy's father visits him in jail and they have an
argument. The boy doesn't want to mention the strange woman
he had seen with his father but in the heat of the argument it
slips out. The father is ashamed. He offers to foot all the bills if
the boy would only go to the Sorbonne or Michigan State. The
boy calls this gesture a moral bribe and he laughs sardonically.
Then he is released in the custody of his father and he goes back
to his small flat in Chelsea and looks in the mirror. His parole officer tries to talk some sense into him. The parole officer is a nice
guy. He has kids of his own, same age as the boy. The boy goes
to his room and plays the guitar. He runs through the mad Los
Angeles night. Then the girl comes in with her suitcase and they
live together. Both of them wear heavy sweaters and blue jeans
and desert boots. The girl whirls and pirouettes. She is not too
good-looking but she has lovely eyes. They go to Coney Island
or Brighton. They ride on the roller coaster and the carousel and
they look at themselves in the distorted mirrors. He is nine feet
tall and very skinny. She is short and squat and it reminds her
that she is pregnant. They think of the abortionist. She feels her
belly and smiles. They are going to have the baby. Then he chases
her along the beach. Seagulls slant across the dying afternoon.
They go behind a sand-dune and kiss. They go home. He kills a
roach. They see what their life together is going to be like.

The end.

[OLD SERIES VOL. XXVIII, NO. 3 / SUMMER 1966]

JOHN CROWE RANSOM

Winter Remembered

Two evils, monstrous either one apart,
Possessed me, and were long and loath at going:
A cry of Absence, Absence, in the heart,
And in the wood the furious winter blowing.

Think not, when fire was bright upon my bricks,
And past the tight boards hardly a wind could enter,
I glowed like them, the simple burning sticks,
Far from my cause, my proper heat and center.

Better to walk forth in the frozen air
And wash my wound in the snows; that would be healing;
Because my heart would throb less painful there,
Being caked with cold, and past the smart of feeling.

And where I walked, the murderous winter blast
Would have this body bowed, these eyeballs streaming,
And though I think this heart's blood froze not fast
It ran too small to spare one drop for dreaming.

Dear love, these fingers that had known your touch,
And tied our separate forces first together,
Were ten poor idiot fingers not worth much,
Ten frozen parsnips hanging in the weather.

Janet Waking

Beautifully Janet slept
Till it was deeply morning. She woke then
And thought about her dainty-feathered hen,
To see how it had kept.

One kiss she gave her mother,
Only a small one gave she to her daddy
Who would have kissed each curl of his shining baby;
No kiss at all for her brother.

"Old Chucky, Old Chucky!" she cried,
Running on little pink feet upon the grass
To Chucky's house, and listening. But alas,
Her Chucky had died.

It was a transmogrifying bee
Came droning down on Chucky's old bald head
And sat and put the poison. It scarcely bled,
But how exceedingly

And purply did the knot
Swell with the venom and communicate
Its rigour! Now the poor comb stood up straight
But Chucky did not.

So there was Janet
Kneeling on the wet grass, crying her brown hen
(Translated far beyond the daughters of men)
To rise and walk upon it.

And weeping fast as she had breath
Janet implored us, "Wake her from her sleep!"
And would not be instructed in how deep
Was the forgetful kingdom of death.

[FROM SELECTED POEMS, THIRD EDITION 1969]

Robert Hass

Picking Blackberries with a Friend Who Has Been Reading Jacques Lacan

August is dust here. Drought
stuns the road,
but juice gathers in the berries.

We pick them in the hot
slow-motion of midmorning.
Charlie is exclaiming:

for him it is twenty years ago
and raspberries and Vermont.
We have stopped talking

about *L'Histoire de la vérité*,
about subject and object
and the mediation of desire.

Our ears are stoppered
in the bee-hum. And Charlie,
laughing wonderfully,

beard stained purple
by the word *juice*,
goes to get a bigger pot.

[VOL. I, NO. 1 / WINTER 1979]

ANNIE DILLARD

Observations and Experiments in Natural History

from the book of that title by Alan Dale

Observations

Observations are usually not too difficult to make.

To make sure of seeing the phosphorescent light,
obtain a fresh herring and place it on an open plate.
Leave it for one or two days and then
examine it in the dark. If it is not glowing
leave it a little longer.

> It is a fact that small trout
> are caught very easily. They are returned
> to the water, and have presumably learned
> some sort of lesson. They may be caught again
> and again as little ones, but
> as they grow larger
> they seem to learn that danger

is associated with artificial flies;
perhaps it is the hook in them.

It is best to use cold water
to thaw a spider.

Personal Notes

Once I was walking across fields in Shropshire
to a river which, because of a rise in the ground,
I could not see.

When I was living in Tamworth,
one year, towards the end of September,
many of the leaves of my cherry tree
became rather odd in appearance.

Experiments

Catch butterflies and clip their wings
with scissors.
　　　　　Do your observations
outside, where the butterflies are numerous.

　　　　　If you can obtain several caterpillars
　　　　　of a species that spins a cocoon,
　　　　　experiments can be performed . . .

　　　　　As the cocoon nears completion
　　　　　cut a "window" in it
　　　　　with sharp scissors. Great care
　　　　　must be taken not to injure the caterpillar

which should be left undisturbed
to give it an opportunity
to repair the damaged cocoon
if it is so disposed.

If it does —
it may take 6-12 hours —
cut away another piece.

Liberate a grasshopper from its container and . . .
cause it to jump by touching it.

Make it jump again — and again —
and again.
        Do its leaps
get more feeble? In addition,
does the insect become more reluctant
to jump again after each leap?

Can you so exhaust the insect
that it can make only the feeblest attempt . . . ?

Pinch through ten worms
about one quarter of the way along the body.
Put all the heads and tails in one tin.
Repeat this for a second group of worms, but
this time break each worm about halfway along . . .
Break another ten worms
about three-quarters of the way along the body . . .

Put ten whole worms in the fourth tin.
These are control worms, and if
they soon die, the experiment is no good.
If these control worms live, however,

it will show that the other worms
could have lived,
                    and if these others die
it will be due to their being broken.

Further Experiments

Which end of an aphid is born first?

Are insects that pass the winter as adults always female?

Are haws eaten?

How do duckweeds pass the winter?

Can the tail of a worm burrow?

What do you think?

Further Personal Notes

There is a poem by John Drinkwater
called *Pike Pool* which has always
appealed strongly to me.

> I once saw a frog
> attacked and turned over by my dog
> and it lay quite still on its back.

> I am positive that it made
> quite a separate movement
> to put its front feet over its ears.
> Why did it?

I have preferred to know
"less and less about more and more."

[VOL. XII, NO. 2 / SPRING 1990]

ANNIE SPRINKLE

Section 4 of Andrea Dwarkin's Anti-pornography Civil Rights Law Cut Up with a Paragraph from *Screw* Magazine

Outer golden moaning discrimination
to coerce, intimidate, or moist crevices.
Soon blouses, bras, skirts sued for damages,
including to eliminate the product(s) of the
pearly teeth as her mouth enclosed hereafter.
Public view. Unlawful practices on the bed.
Heather howled her way through any person,
including transsexual, into performing porno-
graphy. "oooh, ooh, ahhh." she sued for
damages. Exhibitor(s), seller(s), and dis-
tributor(s) of said thing up the injury.
"Coerce," deep into her statement of policy.

[VOL. XII, NO. 2 / SPRING 1990]

ABBY FRUCHT

Steps Out

The stairway leading from the front hall to the second floor of
Ben and Lea's house consists of six steps, then a broad, bare landing where a window looks out, then five more steps climbing to a
corridor always littered with stray bits of laundry. At the landing
the stairs jackknife, and the window frames a view of a lawn sloping down to the creek, where some saplings are planted. On the
ground floor just behind the front hall, beneath the six ascending
steps, is a cubby lined with coat hooks and high, narrow shelves
where Ben and Lea store an assortment of items: boots, gloves,
hats, binoculars, even a set of barbells. Hanging among the coats
are several net bags and leather-handled baskets, one — Lea's favorite — with a purple stripe woven into the straw. On the floor
is a mess of shoes and toys, also the telephone. The oddest thing
is a medicine cabinet hung on the wall, mirrored door and all.
Inside, on the flimsy glass shelves, is where they stack the bills.

Tonight Ben pulls handfuls of bills off the shelves, then sits
on the floor to sort through them for clues. Simon is quiet in
his father's lap, one torn envelope balanced on his knee. He is
picking his nose. First, Ben scans the long-distance calls on the
telephone bills — her mother, his mother, her sister, her glaze
supplier in New Jersey-but finding only the usual, begins shuffling aimlessly hoping for letters from travel agents, from airlines,
even sweepstakes announcements. There's nothing, though, and
that's just it, because whatever it was, she would have taken it
with her. Daniel has a plan; we listen, we nod, and pretty soon
we're all busy looking for what's gone. At once, I find a missing

pair of canvas platform sandals; that is, they are not on the shelf where they are ordinarily, and Daniel finds a raincoat missing from the second coat hook. The purple-striped basket is gone, as well, along with a twenty-pound barbell and a wide-brimmed hat. Lea's sunglasses are not on the dining room table, but then again, they often need to be hunted. So, we hunt, and give the hunt seven minutes which is how long it usually takes Lea to find them.

Afterwards we gather at the wobbly table, empty-handedly bearing our hodgepodge of clues. Lea, it seems, was not taken entirely by surprise. ("Taken by surprise" has become, in this town, a horrifying pun, as if "surprise"—winged, taloned—might swoop down at any moment and take any one of us.) Clearly Lea had a plan, as the things she brought with her add up to a kind of forecast—sunshowers, we agree, and we identify a few possibilities: Vancouver, Mississippi, Seattle, Maine, really anywhere damp as long as it's far enough away, because she took the whole stack of Sunday *Times* magazines as if for reading on a train. She chose a cookbook, too, although it takes us a while to figure out which one's missing from the shelf. It was a present from Ben, a book of international sweets. For a minute we imagine her preparing those foods—the pastries, the syrups, the delicate custards—for a tableful of guests whose faces and names we don't recognize. Once, because she found it amusing, she read to us a passage from a recipe for Indian Jamuns. "Display the sweetmeats on a serving platter of unusual beauty," Lea read, and recalling this I quickly open the cabinet where she keeps her serving platters, but all of them are there: the Raku, the stippled pastel, the handpainted floral.

"She must be headed someplace where she can work on pots," I say, and Daniel stares at me as if I've said something really stupid, which of course I have.

"She can work on pots here any damn time she wants," says Ben, bewildered, wounded. Simon pulls a platter from the open cabinet, distracting us, until we notice all at once that little Stevie is not in the room; we haven't seen him in a couple of minutes, he's gone, he's missing, and we stand unnaturally until hearing the noise of his footsteps.

Ben considers the presence of Lea's winter jacket still hanging on a coat hook an encouraging sign, suggesting that she plans to return before winter if only to pick it up, but I don't tell him Lea mentioned to me recently that she was due for a new one; the armpits on that one have always been tight. We were strolling to the reservoir a bit behind the men, talking about *possessions.* About how much *things* mattered. I commented on the men's cutoffs, so threadbare and torn we could peek at their bottoms.

We did, for a moment.

"Men's bodies never change," I remarked. "Any clothing a woman had that was that old wouldn't fit her anymore." It was a fact to which I alone am an exception among the women I know.

"Really," Lea said. "Anything pre-Simon, forget it, it doesn't fit me under the armpits these days. Across the back."

Then, the thing about the winter coat. Which seems portentous, now, as if she'd known we three would be sitting here. She didn't, though. Not in advance, and I believe that with all my heart. She must have realized all at once that she was leaving, too late to stop it from happening. The straw basket over her elbow, the rain hat crammed into the sleeve of the coat, the sunglasses askew on the top of her head amid haphazard strands of hair. Then a second later she was gone.

"I have this feeling she couldn't possibly have known what she was doing," says Ben after a while. He looks at us questioningly over the mute top of Simon's head, and Daniel and I nod, both of us thinking. At least she didn't take Simon; she left him for Ben to hang on to. And later the three of us agree: Naturally she must have been in some kind of a trance, because otherwise why would she have taken the barbell? Just to keep her arms in shape for throwing pots? Well, maybe.

And that's how it goes; we sit there three hours, four, talking, not talking, never ever alert to the possibility of Lea's step on the front porch because we know we won't hear it. What's possible is that maybe she'll write Ben a letter, either soon or not, and tell him she misses him, because that's what they, do, usually. Certain people do. I know because I've seen quite a few such letters, always on real (apologetic) stationery—illustrated note cards, gilt-edged papers, matching envelopes. I've managed to read some, each routinely simple and unyielding. They say: "Missing you. Come see me soon," but then say neither where, nor when, nor how. So I'm thinking, if Lea writes such a letter, do I deliver it to Ben, or should I spare him the grief?

Spare him, I think.

"Deliver it," says Daniel, later on in bed. How innocent he is. He is truly astounded. "You don't have a choice. You're a *mailman*."

"I'm a TLC," I argue. Temporary Letter Carrier.

Daniel sighs, rolls over on his stomach, reconsiders, migrates, lays his head on my belly. Case closed. I don't know. But maybe she won't write the letter. And how terrible *that* would be. It's not impossible, considering the sunglasses and raincoat. An odd combination, more suitable for subterfuge, I've begun to realize, than for Oregon or Maine. The rain hat, too.

Ben was sitting on the couch when he got his last glimpse of her. She was climbing the steps. Going up. She was crossing the landing, It was half past eight. Ben was reading Simon a favorite bedtime book—cartoons about slugs—and Lea went upstairs to get Simon's pajamas. Simple enough. Through the living room archway he could watch her climb the stairs as usual. She was barefoot. Lea's ankles are strong, erect, broad-boned. She wore a dress to midcalf (I know this although Ben didn't say), and the wood creaked under her step. Then the creaking ceased. Ben thought, She's in the bathroom. Then he thought, She's looking out the window in Simon's room at some kids playing under the bridge in the creek. Then he thought, She's reading something at the desk, some newspaper or something. She's on the phone, he thought. She's steaming her face. She can't find any matching pajamas.

But Lea had never cared about matching pajamas, before.

He thought, She hit her head.

And he went up to take a look.

There's a closet in their bedroom, under the eaves. The door is childsized. The interior, slant-ceilinged space extends straight across the width of the house with room enough for boxes, crates, camp trunks—the floor roughhewn, the rafters showing in the sides, no insulation, the air close and smelling of bats. After looking upstairs and finding no sign of Lea, and after looking downstairs, in the kitchen, in the basement, in the backyard whose barbecue still smoldered from dinner, and in the playroom, and then checking on Simon, and then checking the front porch and up and down the street and even over in the creek where the boys were still tossing stones, and after checking upstairs in the bathroom again and in Simon's room behind the crib where she kept some of his clothing, Ben opened the door to the eaves and looked in there, first without a flashlight, then with. He showed the flashlight beam around and called, "Hey, Lea," in what he described to us as a perfectly natural voice, because at the time it seemed entirely likely to him that she was in there. Then, Simon started crying downstairs, and the telephone rang. It was me. I was calling to see if they wanted to go for a walk.

"I think Lea already went for a walk, or something," Ben said.

"Oh. Is she headed this way?"

"She is?"

"What?"

"Is she headed your way?"

"I don't know, Ben. How should I know? Let me see . . ." I took a look out the front door.

"Call me if she gets there," Ben said. He sounded pissed off. I figured they'd been having an argument. Daniel and Stevie and

I went out for our own walk, around the reservoir. The evening was humid, and there was still enough light that the turtles were basking, their small heads blindly lifted toward the sloping rays. Nobody was sitting on the bench, but there was popcorn scattered round it and pigeons eating. The pigeons roosted high up on the stone water tower, and we had seen them flock down on our way over.

We kept walking until it was dark, then started home along Plum Creek past Ben and Lea's. Their porch light was off, but we could see Ben standing near the railing among the hanging spider plants, holding Simon in his arms. That in itself was a frightening sight, because Simon doesn't like to be held in such heat. He's a rambunctious baby. But he was not so much as tugging at the fronds of the plants, so the pots hung motionless. We were climbing the slope, slowly, pushing Stevie in the stroller, when Ben turned around and went inside. When we got there Simon was under the table with a cookie and Ben was washing dinner dishes. He had put on rubber gloves, but I could see that the water was cold. I brought Simon upstairs, dressed him in his pajamas, ran a washcloth round his face and the palms of his hands, and put him in bed. I found a night-light on a shelf and plugged it into its socket, but the fan on the dresser had already been switched on.

What hurts us most, I suppose, is that she left with the mystery still intact. Somehow we must all have believed that if the secret were revealed to one of us, it would be shared, or at the very least, suggested. A bus ticket stub might suffice, a canceled check, even a door left ajar might point us in the direction of understanding. As it is, we can't be certain that she even *used* a door.

Which leaves me contemplating the very scariest possibility of all: that not even Lea can pinpoint the method of departure. Of transition. She might simply have ended up somewhere. In the Southwest, maybe, throwing pots in an adobe studio. She might be longing for us—for Simon, for Ben, but unable to draw herself away. A prisoner of desire. Of her heart's content. Out the window a view of the dry bed of a river, then the walls of a canyon dotted with scrub pines and Indian ruins, that sort of thing, in the distance a little town. The pots are plain red clay, vessel-shaped as if for the storage of actual food and water.

Later on she is wearing that trench coat, its collar turned up, her head erect inside it, her long legs scissoring under the hem. The day is sunstruck; the sidewalk leads her to a bank, a utilities office, and then, further north, along a roadside mall whose pay telephone she passes without slowing, without thinking, even.

She's not thinking about us. We can't fault her for that; there's no malice involved, no neglect, even. We don't occur to her. That's all. She feels, as she passes the telephones, a little buzz of indecipherable concern.

And, if it happened to Lea, what's to stop it from happening to me?

I mention this to Daniel.

He doesn't want to talk about it.

But he says, "That's ridiculous. It's not something that *happened* to her. It's something she *did*."

"Well," I say, "what's to stop *me* from doing it, too?"

"In spite of yourself?" says Daniel.

"In spite of myself," I say.

I am holding Daniel's hand. I give it a squeeze. After that we don't move a muscle.

[VOL. XII, NO. 3 / SUMMER 1990]

RON SMITH

Learner's Permit
on Skyline Drive

We sit in back
where we can't be caught
in the nervous eyecorner.
Four hands in her lap,
one knotty ball. My fingers
have been numb for miles.

This is where we first learned to let go.

And our son is taking us again
along the spine of the Blue Ridge.
The Olds drifts to the solid line
white as a cloud, grinds in the gravel
next to a low stone wall
we will have to leap or penetrate
to fly into the valley.

On the road is all I will let myself say.

October, the leaves all golden,
the 5 p.m. light golden and clear
in the windshield. A net
of purple finches

starts from the roadway
as we swing from a curve.

He slows to 30 on an uphill, hurtles to 50

down and into a turn I know
will be our last. *Stay on the road!*
she whispers as tires float to the grab
of shoulder. Across the valley the mountains
soften to gray folds.

His frightened eyes in the mirror see only the blacktop
snaking, falling, rising beyond
the hood. *Just relax*, I say,
my heart unclenching, settling in
for the mistake
that changes everything.
It was October then, too, but cold
and dark in the big Chevy. *No*, she said, *no*,
and what did I say but *yes* and *yes*,

as if either of us knew the difference.

[VOL. XII, NO. 3 / SUMMER 1990]

JUDITH BERKE

Old Eight-by-Ten Glossy

Her eyebrows are raised
and seem to hold the rest of her features taut,
like the bars that hold the strings of a marionette.
"Listen," I say, and her face opens a little.
"Speak up," I say, and she does: *I don't like
this pose*, she says to the photographer,
and musses her hair, and smells the smell
of that place which is stuffy and stale
as he is. Last night, the two guys
went down to the alley and fought
about her. She didn't go. Too nice
for that, too good, always, but now I let
her go down, and bite her knuckles,
and root for one of them, for both
of them. She even begins to laugh at herself
(*too wide, too big*, the photographer says,
but she laughs anyway—even with her nostrils
that flare like a horse's, even with her canine
teeth they say are too big and pointy).
I tell her to follow the two guys to the bar
afterwards, and she does, agreeing
with them when they say she's a bitch, agreeing
that she's vain and flighty and wild,
yes, and dopey and shy and whatever,
like the rest of us. I tell her that now

and she smiles, she laughs, and snap,
the photographer gets it, though it's hard
when there's so much life, almost a moving
picture.

[VOL. XII, NO. 4 / FALL 1990]

Lewis Hyde

The Freedom to Talk Dirt*

The current debate over obscenity, government funding, and the arts has set me to thinking about dirt, what it is and why we have such trouble with it.

"Dirt is matter out of place," goes an old saying. Egg on my plate is breakfast, but egg on my face is dirt. Shoes in the closet are tidy, but shoes on the table are not. Certain movies shown in Covington, Kentucky, are commerce; across the Ohio River in Cincinnati they are filth.

Dirt is also the anomalous, not just what is out of place but what has no place at all, or at least no place in the center of things. Cleaning house, we take those items that belong nowhere, call them "trash," and haul them to the dump at the edge of town. "Dirt" that belongs no place may be hard to get rid of, but at least we can keep it out of sight.

"Out of place" or "out of sight," either way, dirt is a sort of by-product of creating order. Where there is dirt there is always a system of some kind, and an argument about dirt is always an argument about the system. An argument about obscenity is a *serious* argument about the system (the Latin roots of "obscene" mean "really dirty").

Debates over dirt will always be with us, I think, partly because we recurrently discover we have been mistaken in our system building. Sometimes, when life goes a little dead on us or

* This editorial was originally written for the American Institute of Graphic Arts *Journal*.

unexpected trouble arises, we come to see that we need the very thing we once called dirty.

Examples are common in erotic life: sexual attraction is disruptive enough that it often seems useful to treat it as dirt, but Eros has a way of escaping from the trash. Nor are the only examples of dirt's return sexual. I may believe some secret childhood wound has dirtied me, only to find, as I mature, that strength and purpose come when I let the secret out. Or a nation, as it matures, may find it cannot realize its ideals without enfranchising an entire group it had earlier marginalized and treated, as they say, "like dirt."

Reimagining the order of things in this fashion is a kind of "dirt work," and different societies have different ways to go about it. Many traditional cultures, for example, have annual rituals with a kind of intentionally scandalous air. Carnivals of the medieval Church included all sorts of shameless acting out—the men dressed as women, people wore grotesque masks, sang indecent songs in the choir loft, told smutty jokes, played at dice, and so on. At a set time each year, native American tribes allowed themselves to tell the off-color stories of trickster figures such as sneaky old Coyote. The citizens of ancient Athens, during an annual festival, paraded phallic images of Dionysus through the streets.

Such rituals provide a kind of controlled contact with dirt and, risqué as they seem, actually have a conservative function. They keep dirt in its place. Rather than upsetting the order of things, they solidify that order by allowing a short-term exception. In a hierarchical society, hierarchy is reaffirmed by its brief inversion.

Democracies have quite different institutions to ensure that the order of things can periodically be reimagined or remade. I am thinking in particular of freedom of speech (which prohibits the cry of "obscenity" in serious debate) and the separation of church and state (which prohibits one group's moral system from becoming state doctrine). Democratic institutions allow contact with what the system excludes and—if we add free elections to the list—they even allow the system itself to change. People and topics that have been out of sight can become visible; those that do not like their place can work to change it.

If, with these ideas in mind, we turn to the current, end-of-the-millenium debate over obscenity, one thing to note immediately is that, although there is a lot of dirt around, the laundry list we have been offered is short and particular. To judge from the grants recently proposed by peer panels but denied by the NEA staff, we're asked to consider two candidates for dirt status: homosexuals and feminists. Four performance artists whose grant requests were refused were Karen Finley, Holly Hughes, John Fleck, and Tim Miller. In each case the work has clear feminist content or the performer is gay. Hughes was quoted in the *New York Times* (June 30, 1990): "I think the reason my work was overturned is because it is chock-full of good old feminist satire and, secondly, I am openly lesbian."

Before commenting on the candidates for dirt status, allow me to offer two candidates of my own by way of contrast. In the Philippines there is a town, Olongapo City, whose economy is almost entirely based on prostitution: twenty thousand bar girls and streetwalkers depend for their livelihood on the seven thousand American servicemen stationed with the Seventh Fleet. I like to imagine a politician who finds that obscene and seeks ways to redirect the Navy's wealth so that Olongapo City might diversify its economy.

Or, knowing how addictive nicotine is, I like to imagine a politician who would not only urge us to stop subsidizing tobacco farming but go on to propose that members of Congress pledge to refuse all nicotine dollars offered their campaigns.

Two cases—sex and drugs—but neither, I realize, is a serious candidate for dirt status at the moment. Neither the traffic in nicotine nor the traffic in women is sufficiently "out of place" to make Jesse Helms's list. Why, then, homosexuals and feminists?

I assume it is because in these areas we are having what I called at the outset a *serious* argument about our system. Serious changes are upon us. In 1970, fewer than half of all American women worked for wages; now more than half do, but they still earn less than seventy cents for every dollar a man earns. Small wonder, then, that there are artists whose performances ask us to reflect on how we imagine women.

As for how we imagine homosexuals, the question has a particular urgency now because of the AIDS crisis. Perhaps some earlier era could afford to keep homosexuals out of sight, but such invisibility now seems perilous. If we are to respond to AIDS, we must be free to speak of and understand images of homosexual love, exactly the images that those who cry "obscene" hope to remove from sight.

Here let us come back to how democracy deals with dirt. There have always been societies with little tolerance for reconsidering the order of things; they tend to be both more stable and more repressive than our own. If they are homogeneous or small (the medieval Church, a Hopi village in the seventeenth century, say) they may not even be repressive in any modern sense. But America is not homogeneous or small; it is pluralistic and huge.

No such mass society can long endure whose citizens cannot talk freely about dirt. The Soviet experience makes this clear. For decades the Soviets repressed not just artists but humanists, religious leaders, psychologists, dissident politicians—everyone, that is, whose work might lead them to reconsider what the system excludes. The result was a nation repressive and, in the end, *un*stable, unstable because unable to respond to change, unable to reimagine itself.

Now it is suggested that we ask American artists and humanists to pledge to exclude all dirt from their work. If we do so, we also ask them to stop offering alternative images of our future. It seems an odd way to close the Cold War, as if we'd rather bring repression home than end it. It also seems dangerous because democracy's longevity, I suspect, is linked to its tolerance for discussing what at first blush seems to be "really dirty."

[VOL. XII, NO. 4 / FALL 1990]

Susan Hahn

In the ambulance between the quick
decisions made on the two-way
radio and the moans of the man inches
from the muddied floor, whose clothes
the paramedics tore off,
they kept asking me who I was,
could I spell my name and
over and over I'd tell them
susan hahn s-u-s-a-n-h-a-h-n.
It sounded wrong—
too bland, too short
with all those double s's, a's, h's, n's.
A drab white kept coming
to mind like a rag,
a too easily grabbed
burial cloth. I wanted more

letters as if that would hold me
to the solid world I'd just left
before the smack and spin from the other
car—that driver's desperate rush
to take his doubled-up passenger
to the hospital and how now
I was going too. I'm not ready

to know what happened to the man
they harnessed to the steel board —
his sleepy eyes slowly rolling off
course as the men who worked on him
shouted *What's Your Name.*
Only once did he say it as we sped
to Emergency. When they carried him away
I whispered in a scratched voice
something I can't quite remember
and which he probably didn't
hear, like *take care, be fine
please*, his name, then mine.

[VOL. XIII, NO. 1 / WINTER 1991]

James Harms

'When You Wish upon a Star that Turns into a Plane'

The Replacements

My clothes are standing up without me,
though it's just the bus is here,
the noise of people pulling things
into line. And I don't want a ride
but the driver leans out the door
as if to pull me into heaven.

So I light a french fries wrapper
and think: Go away, and he does.
The doors fold shut and, woosh,
there goes the bus.

A bum sits down next to me and cups
a cigarette that isn't there —
he shakes his hand and takes a drag.
The air is brown around us, like an old
snapshot; I spend three minutes
trying not to breathe, just sipping a little,
then walk up to Sunset Boulevard
where on good days with God willing

I can hitchhike all the way to the beach.
I am sure that the sea will rise one day
and drive its way inland, but not today.
Today will end with a colorful dusk,
a stain the length of California
fading as the sun goes down.

When I was small there was always a meal
that everyone agreed on, and the stars
falling over the city.
I'd watch the ocean from my parents' roof
and Catalina on some days, like a cupped
hand above the smog. It's fourteen miles and three
transfers from here to Pasadena,
and my mother has said on the phone
that she loves me regardless of what
I'm taking. What am I taking?
I remember who I am and where I'm from
and I don't remember why.
But this is nothing to cry about,
so I don't. I sit down
and wave past another bus.
I watch myself flicker in its windows.

[VOL. XIII, NO. 1 / WINTER 1991]

Dead Doe: I

for Huck

The doe lay dead on her back in a field of asters: no.

The doe lay dead on her back beside the school bus stop: yes.

Where we waited.
Her belly white as a cut pear. Where we waited: no: off

from where we waited: yes:

at a distance: making a distance
we kept,
as we kept her dead run in sight, that we might see if she chose
to go skyward;
that we might run, too, turn tail
if she came near
and troubled our fear with presence: with ghostly blossoming:
    with the fountain's

                                 unstoppable blossoming
                  and the black stain the algae makes when the water
                                        stays near.
We can take the gilt-edged strolling of the clouds: yes.
But the risen from the dead: no!

The haloey trouble shooting of the goldfinches in the bush:
                    yes: but *in season*:

kept within bounds,
not in the pirated rows of corn,
not above winter's pittance of river.

The doe lay dead: she lent
    her deadness to the morning, that the morning might have
           weight, that our waiting might matter: be up-
           held by significance: by light on the rhododen-
           dron, by the ribbons the sucked mint loosed
                          on the air,
by the treasonous gold-leaved passage of season, and you

from me/child/from me/

from . . . not mother: no:
but the weather that would hold you: yes:

hothouse you to fattest blooms: keep you in mild unceasing rain,
    and the fixed stations of heat: like a pedalled note: or the held
                breath: sucked in, and stay: yes:
stay

but: no: not done: can't be:

the doe lay dead: she could
do nothing:

the dead can mother nothing . . . nothing
but our sight: they mother that, whether they will or no:

they mother our looking, the gap the tongue prods when the
    tooth is missing, when
                    fancy seeks the space.

The doe lay dead: yes: and at a distance, with her legs up and
    frozen, she tricked
                              our vision: at a distance she was
                                   for a moment no deer
at all

but two swans: we saw two swans
        and they were fighting
    or they were coupling
      or they were stabbing the ground for some prize
            worth nothing, but fought over, so worth *that*, worth
the fought-over glossiness: the morning's fragile-tubed glory.

And this is the soul: like it or not. Yes: the soul comes down: yes:
comes into the deer: yes: who dies: yes: and in her death twins
herself into swans: fools us with mist and accident into believing
her newfound finery

and we are not afraid
though we should be

and we are not afraid as we watch her soul fly on: paired

as the soul always is: with itself:
    with others.

                Two swans ...

Child. We are done for
in the most remarkable ways.

[VOL. XIII, NO. 3 / SUMMER 1991]

COLLEEN J. MCELROY

A Little Traveling Music

This is not a planet I would want to inherit—
With its inventory of mountainous sorrows
There is hardly a place to lay a good night's
Sleep before tomorrow's bad news arrives,

And hardly a road I want to travel.
I know these woods are no longer gentle
And love no longer runs through dry grass
Clean as the country we once dreamed of—

Out here hard times grind into thin skin
With needle tracks and pock marks
That make the going rough even for those
Of us who have gone straight.

Listen to the reports: arteries and alternates
Twist and back up all the way out, cyclists
Spin out in heavy water and trashy sunlight.
Long distance hauls jackknife in lanes too narrow

To carry weight limits for any major move, and Western
High rises are clogged to the exits—I can't get home,
Can't get back to ghettos where uncles drove jitneys
Because white cabbies couldn't read the English
Of broken street signs, even in broad daylight.

I want something more than a two-lane either-or
World still mapped by tribal law, or reflections
Of my grandmother stuck black in a window, watching
The traffic of each year move faster, sighing,
"We all got to go when the wagon comes."
And when it comes — its door open — I want more
Than the temptation to go in and see if I have arrived
At century's end without stalling out on bad memory.

[VOL. XIII, NO. 4 / FALL 1991]

TERESE SVOBODA

I Dreamt He Fell
Three Floors and Lived

The rest of the world pretends it is normal. A few birds cough up
from the black-budded trees, two cars miss each other. Looking
out the window, away from the bed, I begin to swell, filling the
whole room. The nurse has a hard time getting to my son, and
my mother is almost squeezed out of the room entirely. It's that
I'm allergic to his death; I think it's a reaction. Then, pop, I need
a Hershey's and a bathroom, but that's it. Dad says I have to live
with it.

OK.

I look around at all these people stuffed in the tiny, green
room. Hospitals are for the modern, small family or for getting
them smaller, not like the bumper crop we have. They sit in chairs
stolen from Detox and look at me. Who's taking care of the dog?
I think to say.

Angie, says my second sister. Tacos twice a day.

With hot sauce. Honest. That is the dog-feeder herself, my
third sister, her lap holding a *Post* that has slipped. It shows me,
my blond hair framing a Munch moment, my hands clamped to
the side of my face.

Laughter pitches from me, a whole lot of green leaves falling
for no reason, what must have happened outside. I sit up in my
chair. What is this, day three?

My next-to-last brother, leaning up against the wall, stretches, but has the sense not to say. The yes comes from Mom, the yes

she uses after someone exclaims So many children! As the eldest, I am the one who counts them. I learned to count first. I am not good at counting backwards. Blast off, I want to say now. Instead I ask: Is it OK to take off my clothes and rub my face in the dirt and howl?

It's winter, says my brother.

That's how much they take me seriously.

OK.

The machine overhead practices its single red line. The nurse tells me I have another ten minutes to decide, then takes all my son's thin chart with her.

Didn't you go to Prague last summer? I ask the third sister.

Year before.

He made a turret out of blocks the other day, I say. He hurt his finger when they all came down. No keystone. I touch his cool, perfect finger, then pretend to have a headache.

Where is that doctor?

That is my mother again.

Thick ropes of green, the wall paint, straighten out in front of me. I say What I'd like is another Hershey's.

Someone looks relieved and volunteers to find one. There is that much more air in the room when he leaves. With more air, I can turn my head; I can see my husband in a schlump in the chair beside me. He makes a tiny smile the size of an apostrophe, but he isn't the father. The father won't come to the hospital. He is too upset. Instead, he gives the papers the school photo, which hardly resembles what lies before us now.

My own dad is standing behind my husband's chair, using it as a sort of barricade, to keep what is happening on the bed at bay. He doesn't cry, however, unlike everybody else here, even the nurses. Instead, getting out of the taxi this morning, he falls on a tree guard and loses two teeth. He can't even smile.

Let's sing, I say.

We know only two kinds of songs—carols and "I've Been Working on the Railroad." The carols all have to do with baby boys.

We're in full force, even Dad, moving his face around the stumps of his teeth, when the nurse comes back. I keep on singing while she hands me forms that read Corneas, Kidneys—all the spares. These aren't my favorites anyway, I say, then get the hiccups.

The next day we wake, which is how I like to make a basically wordless party sound active. A little girl, not one of my son's friends, arrives last, clutching her father. She's so skittery I must be a lesson for her, a cautionary tale. The father smiles at her with a pride I'm not supposed to miss, which says: I have mine.

Look, I am the mother who did not take care of her child. I whisper to her, Boo! She runs away. To celebrate, I eat a whole plateful of kisses.

Someone says they ran the story in both papers. I saw them, I lie, looking away when he offers copies. Then I hear my mother tell that someone I'd recover. She says it the way you would if I had a cold with complications. I start to exude a toxic, green chemical so everyone will stay away. It works. Only the sculptor hugs me. And he's the one who tells the story of a kid who falls another hundred feet and survives.

Nobody my age has children. This is before the baby boom boomed. They just mill around, eating pâté the way they do at openings. One of them blurts out that their dog died, is it like that? I start to swell again.

My husband likes parties. He is trying not to talk about anything, but I catch him discussing a movie. It had a good ending, he says, and can't go on.

The father is fighting with his girlfriend. I can tell because she is eating with her back to him, eating a lot the way I used to, to annoy him. He doesn't look to be too grief stricken, I notice. But, then, he didn't have to sign for body parts. I'm the one with custody.

Without.

I myself have eaten only air and chocolate for the last few

days. Not eating helps with the swelling. I get lighter easily and hit the ceiling fast, go as far away as I can without going. My family is going at six. Instead, they play Scrabble but keep the vocabulary limited, no past tense.

On some anniversary, I'm at the lawyer's and he says: What's wrong?

After I tell him, he reveals his wife was murdered ten years ago and he has their three kids.

So do I get mouse ears with the membership? I ask.

He looks at me as if I am a case on consignment. I won't charge you for telephone time, he says, and takes a call.

At night before I fall asleep — fall, I tell you, it's even a season — I see the distance between us and how I didn't catch him and I start to swell again, now into an ambulance, and all the sirens on the street join in riotous medley, with him whole inside me.

[VOL. XVII, NO. 2 / SPRING 1995]

REBECCA McCLANAHAN

To the Absent Wife of the Beautiful Poet at the Writers' Conference

I want you to know that nothing happened,
and everything that might have is now sewn
into the hoop of Arizona sky
that stretched above our heads that shy
evening of talk when we left our books
and went out to read the papery news
of bougainvillea. Here was vegetation
more animal than plant, the dangerous spine
of cactus, its fleshy stem and thistle,
and those rubbery tongues lolling speechless
in the desert air where even domestic
herbs turn wild, parsley and dill spilling
over their planned containers. When your husband
broke off a piece of rosemary and held it
out to me, I smelled the sharp clean scent
of marriage, the scent that fills my loved world
three time zones away. My garden, the spotted
cat and aged brandy, the bed pillow minted
with the imprint of my husband's head.
Yet I confess that part of me wanted
to take, in that moment, the man you more
than half-made, knowing that what I love

most in married men is what is given
by wives. The elbow he leans upon
is your elbow, his listening quiet,
your quiet, practiced in twenty years
of bedtime conversation. If he loved,
in that instant, anything in me, it was
the shape and smell of one whole woman
made from the better halves of two —
your hard-earned past and my present, briefly
flaming. Not long ago I watched a girl
I might have been twenty years ago, sit
literally at my husband's feet and adore him.
There are gifts we can give our husbands,
but adoration is not one. If I could,
I would be one woman diverging, walk
one road toward those things that matter
always, the difficult trail long love requires.
The other, for what burned in the eyes
of your husband as he asked, *What is the secret
to a long marriage?* I gave my grandfather's
bald reply: *You don't leave and you don't die.*
There are no secrets. Together, the four of us —
your beautiful husband, mine, you, and I,
have lasted. I started to say forty
married years, but no, it is eighty,
each of us living those years sometimes,
by necessity, singly, the whole of love
greater than the sum of its combined hearts.
That's what I mean about the sky. Its blueness
and the way it goes on forever. An old
teacher told me if you break a line in half
again and again, you will never reach an end.
Infinity is measured by the broken spaces
within as well as by the line spooling out
as far as we can see. I love my husband.

Still, there were spaces in that evening
that will go on dividing our lives. And if
the sky had not begun in that moment
to blink messages of light from stars I thought
had died out long ago, I might have answered
your husband's eyes another way.
And there would have been heaven to pay.

[VOL. XVIII, NO. 1 / WINTER 1996]

ALLISON JOSEPH

Barbie's Little Sister

How terrible it would be
to be Barbie's little sister,
suspended in perpetual pre-adolescence
while Barbie, hair flying behind her
in a tousled blond mane, dashed
from adventure to adventure,
ready for space travel or calf roping
or roller disco in campy, flashy clothes
that defied good taste and reason.
Stuck with the awful nickname Skipper,
Barbie's little sis never got out much,
a mere boarder in Barbie's three-story
hot-pink Dream House, too young
to wear the thousands of outfits
stashed in the bedroom closets:
purple-beaded Armani evening gowns,
knit sweater dresses by Donna Karan,
specially commissioned tennis togs
sewn personally by Oleg Cassini.
Skipper had to buy off the rack
at Kmart, condemned to wear
floral sunsuits with Peter Pan collars.
Unlike her bosomy sister,
Skipper had no chest
for the boys to ogle,
until some bright toymaker

gave us "Growing Up Skipper":
with a twist of her right arm,
she grew taller, breasts sprouting
where there once were none,
a thick rubber band inside her
pushing her chest up and out
until the band snapped
and Skipper was stuck at age 15,
never the same again.
For consolation, she turned to
Barbie's black friend Christie —
who was just figuring out
all the fuss about equal rights —
and Barbie's best pal Midge,
who was tired of hearing
about spats with Ken, knowing
he was cheating on America's sweetheart
with every new celebrity doll on the market —
Brooke Shields, Cher, Dorothy Hamill.
Together, those three decided
they'd had enough of Toyland —
so they pooled their cash,
swiped Barbie's camper,
and tore out of California
for Las Vegas, where they bought
a little establishment not too far
from the gaming houses,
a restaurant for all of us
without thick manes of hair
or upturned noses, without
impossibly slender ankles
and tiny feet, without
perfectly molded breasts.

[VOL. XVIII, NO. 2 / SPRING 1996]

BARON WORMSER

My Wife Asks Me Why I Keep Photographs in a Drawer

Beneath T-shirts and underwear,
A few almost-sepia photographs
Of my mother and father — before they knew me.

My mother stands in front of the school
Where she first taught fourth grade.
She's young and lovely and smiling
In a summer dress. Her shoulders are bare,
Her eyes alight with candid feeling.
The year before, she'd worked in
A department store where she'd read Tolstoy
During her breaks. One day she came back
To her counter red-eyed; her supervisor inquired
About her. "Anna died," my mother blurted.

My father sits at a table. He holds some cards
And smiles. All the other guys at the table
Are soldiers too and they smile. They're going
To live through the war. It's aces and swell
Broads and highballs and homeruns for them.

I should set up some sort of shrine for these
Bouquets of time, something more visible. They
Lie there in my drawer as I stutter through
My slice of time—from semi-hippiedom
To that middle-age wariness
That signals a flagging of mortal belief.

I never take them out. I know them too well.
It's dark in the drawer and common and hidden.
Photos tell you that people can smile at
The dark eye of oblivion. Albums and walls are
Too insistent. What's part of every fumbling
Morning is closer to the fleeting mark.

[VOL. XIX, NO. 1 / WINTER 1997]

BILLY COLLINS

The Night House

Every day the body works in the fields of the world
mending a stone wall
or swinging a sickle through the tall grass—
the grass of civics, the grass of money—
and every night the body curls around itself
and listens for the soft bells of sleep.

But the heart is restless and rises
from the body in the middle of the night,
leaves the trapezoidal bedroom
with its thick, pictureless walls
to sit by herself at the kitchen table
and heat some milk in a pan.

And the mind gets up too, puts on a robe
and goes downstairs, lights a cigarette
and opens a book on engineering.
Even the conscience awakens
and roams from room to room in the dark,
darting away from every mirror like a strange fish.

And the soul is up on the roof
in her nightdress, straddling the ridge,
singing a song about the wildness of the sea
until the first rip of pink appears in the sky.

Then, they all will return to the sleeping body
the way a flock of birds settles in a tree,

resuming their daily colloquy,
talking to each other or themselves
even through the heat of the long afternoons.
Which is why the body — that house of voices —
sometimes puts down its metal tongs, its needle, or its pen
to stare into the distance,

to listen to all its names being called
before bending again to its labor.

[VOL. XX, NO. 2 / SPRING 1998]

JEFFREY HARRISON

Horseshoe Contest

East Woodstock, Connecticut
Fourth of July

After the parade
of tractors and fire trucks,
old cars and makeshift floats,
after speeches by
the minister and selectman,
after the cakewalk and hayrides
and children's games
are over and the cornet band
has packed up its instruments
and left the gazebo,
the crowd on the town
green begins to gather
around the horseshoe pit
where a tournament
has been going on all day
and is now down
to the four or five
best players—the same ones
every year, these old guys
who, beneath their feigned
insouciance, care about this
more than anything.
The stakes are high:
their names on a plaque,

their pride, their whole idea
of who they are,
held onto since high school
when they played football
or ran track — something
unchanging at their core,
small but of a certain heft.
Limber as gunslingers
preparing for a showdown,
they step up in pairs
to take their turns
pitching the iron shoes,
lofting these emblems
of luck with a skill
both deliberate and
offhand, landing ringer
after ringer, metal
clashing against metal,
while the others, those
who entered the contest
just for the hell of it
and who dropped out
hours ago, their throws
going wild or just
not good enough, stand
quietly at the sidelines,
watching with something close
to awe as their elders
stride with the casual
self-consciousness of heroes,
becoming young again
in the crowd's hush
and the flush of suspense,
elevated for these moments
like a horseshoe hanging

in the sunlit air
above them, above their lives
as dairymen and farmers,
their bodies moving
with a kind of knowledge
unknown to most of us
and too late for most of us
to learn—though I'd give
almost anything
to be able to do anything
that well.

[VOL. XXI, NO. 1 / WINTER 1999]

Virgil Suárez

Arroz

comes to El Volcan, the corner *bodega*
run by El Chino Chan,
along with the food rations
the people of Arroyo Naranjo, Cuba,
line up and wait for, in the meantime
they listen as Chan
calls out "*alo, alo,*" Spanish-Chinese
for *arroz*. Rice. I, six or seven, stand
in line, my mother next to me in the shade
of the *guayaba* trees, we watch as people
move in and out of the sun and heat.
Women fan their faces. Talk and gossip
buzz like the horseflies that fly up
from the ravine and brook. Chan tells
stories of when the great poet jumped
into the river and the villagers, to keep
the fish from gobbling up the poet, tossed in
rice dumplings wrapped in bamboo leaves.
Arroz. The blessing at weddings. Constant
staple with its richness of spirit. Sustenance.
Slowly the rations are filled and the line
moves and my mother and I reach the counter.
Behind it hang *papalotes,* kites made
of colorful rice paper, next to them
the countless oriental prints of carp,
egrets, tigers, and dragons. Chan talks

about the grain of rice kept in a glass
case at El Capitolio in the city, a love poem
etched on it in print so small one needs
more than a magnifying glass to read
what it says. Chan, rice, magic — the gift
of something different to pass the time.
Now, so many miles and years from this life,
in the new place called home, rice,
like potatoes, goes unnoticed when served.
Often, my daughters ignore it
and I won't permit it. Rice, I say, to them,
needs respect, needs worship,
their full attention, for blessed is that
which carries so many so far.

[VOL. XXI, NO. 1 / WINTER 1999]

Nancy Zafris

Stealing the Llama Farm

There came a day when I stole the llama farm from Amy Boyd. I was in love with Amy Boyd and once long ago I had saved her father's life and felt the sun charge through my body. I think almost everyone would say I was not the kind of person who would steal someone's llama farm right out from under them, but whatever made me do it must have been waiting there inside me.

Amy Boyd was the first smart woman I'd ever met, at least to my knowledge, which didn't kick in until twenty years had passed. When it finally did it was like all the desire from the lower half of my body moved upwards to my head. I wanted to express to her what this felt like but the words could not be found in the tangle of my brain, the jungle in there having been tended all these years by the many dumb women, starting with my mother, who had set about watering it. Not that I lay my troubles on these women, but they didn't help.

Besides running the llama farm Amy Boyd wrote stories, and all her stories had llamas in them: llamas giving birth to other llamas, llamas passing on the wisdom of llamas, llamas wondering what to do with themselves, biorhythmic llamas, llamas practicing euthanasia on other llamas. I said "Amy, put some people in these stories" and Amy Boyd didn't like hearing that. But, for example, you don't see movies with venetian blinds as the main characters, two venetian blinds trying to adopt a tiny solid-white blind for their little baby window in the bathroom. You don't see that in the movies — maybe there's a reason.

As usual Amy didn't answer me. I was starting to see what my two ex-wives had found so annoying about me. "You should be glad I don't argue," I'd told them. "I'm just a mellow guy." But now there was nothing more I would have liked than a heated discussion leading to a heated argument. "Well, let's just talk about it," I suggested to Amy. "Maybe you have seen a movie about venetian blinds. Have you? Amy?"

But she had pulled on her rubber knee-highs and was already out the door. I followed her to the llama barns and we passed the hallowed circle where I had saved her father's life, her father now long dead so what had been the point of saving him, really, a waste of a perfectly good foot that had not yet seen its prime. Amy was careful to avoid this permanent dead image in the grass where it had happened. It softened her some, I could see by the slump of her shoulders, to remember her father and how he would have died a little bit earlier if not for me, just a little bit earlier, that little bit of extra time hardly worth mentioning now, but how were we to divine such a thing on that day, how were we to know he might not have a life dull and interminable ahead of him. God knows he had been dull and interminable up to that point. There was no reason to think it might not continue.

The dead spot in the grass, still recognizably shaped to the imaginative eye as a lower torso, set my foot to clawing inside its boot, and when my foot hurt like that it felt like something punching its way out of a box and only a sturdy box could contain it, which is why I always cage my feet in cowboy or steel-toed work boots. I couldn't help but look up as we passed the spot where it happened; I can't help looking up everywhere I go, and everywhere I notice the same thing: how low the high-tension wires are, how low they hover, how low certain death is strung out above us.

Amy's father had been struggling with his new extension ladder, showing off how to carry something forty feet long, and was heading straight toward these wires. And when I ran to push him away both his clenched hands knocked back from the ladder, flicking one of mine against it, and what was in that wire shot through my arm and fired out my foot. The whole town drove by to check out the scorch burns on the grass and for more than a month I got a happy buzz out of my charred foot and was proud of the two toes I was going to lose, and my twenty-one-year-old self had plenty of time to perfect the many jokes about what to do with those toes. Then the skin grafts and rehab started. By then the miracle of simply being alive had receded into the forgotten background where daily living day after day always managed to put it and I was in a terrible misery compounded by morphine addiction and I vowed then and it's a vow I've kept that I had done my good deed for the afternoon and anybody else bearing a ladder toward a high tension wire was on their own. I'd yell out, sure, try to get their attention, but that's as far as it would go—unless of course it was Amy Boyd and then I would sacrifice all.

I trailed Amy to the llama barns where she began scooping food pellets from a bin. A false spring had passed and we were back to winter again. Amy said another big snowstorm was sweeping over the Great Lakes. I thought less about the snowstorm and more about the fact that Amy had freely offered a line of conversation. "Pedro!" she then hollered, sounding mean. The llamas began shuffling toward the food, her beloved Pedro, Jesus, and Maria, the three llamas she talked about most; then Felipe, Carmita, and Sean. A half dozen more after that. Their number had dwindled since her father's day when almost a hundred roamed the place—it was hard, however, to call that time a heyday. So many disgusting llamas and something extra and human, a low-hanging unhappiness, had brought a scrounging kind of gloom to the place. The Boyd farm was without topsoil or beauty and eventually it had caused Amy's mother to go AWOL with Amy's little brothers, and Amy was left alone with her father until she went off to college at Miami University. I thought Oxford, Ohio, would claim her for good, but two years after graduation her dad was dead and the English major was back to save the farm.

I backed away from the barn. I positioned myself at a safe distance from the llamas shoving in to eat. Don't even get me started on llamas and how much I hate them. Llamas bite, they hiss and spit, they lie down and get a mood on and won't get up, they're ugly, they kick, from a distance they look like ostriches, up close they look like llamas, they have no social graces, they bite, they have not a jot of affability, they bite, they refuse to look you in the eye, they bite, if you attempt friendly eye contact they spit at you, if you do worse and flash a smile at them they turn around and release their dung at your feet. I've seen this happen too many times not to know it's deliberate.

And it wasn't as if the llamas liked Amy but hated the rest of us. They appeared to hate her, too. They saved some of their best spitting and kicking and biting just for her, just for their Amy. It was a sick marriage between Amy and her llamas, and despite a compelling case of domestic abuse up and down her arms, bite marks on her thighs and quail egg hematomas on her calves, she stuck it out, she spent her days caring for them and her nights writing about them, hunched over in the dark with pencils that kept breaking she pressed so hard, writing stories about my arch rivals—Pedro, Felipe, and Jesus—why did smart women get sucked into these kinds of relationships? With me it was easy, I married dumb, we were two shallow wells and when our wells ran dry, there were no permanent hard feelings, just a need to fill up elsewhere—it didn't seem so bad so I tried it all over again, and life moved on.

It was past five o'clock and I had to be going. For the five hundredth time I asked Amy if she wanted to meet up at Chi-Chi's—meet up was how I always said it, not a date, just two cars happening upon each other in the same lot, a meeting up. For the five hundredth time Amy didn't bother to answer me and I headed for my truck, rehearsing a final positive remark about Pedro (*good appetite tonight!*) so I would be welcomed back into her good graces the next day without having to limp for it, when I turned and saw Amy's eyes glaring right at me, sunken and black. It had been so long since I had seen them focused my way, I welcomed their fierce glare, my heart rose at the sight. I loved everything about her, even her eye sockets tunneling to a hateful squint, because everything about her was nothing I'd ever known. I can't say it was good, I can't say it was bad. It was something I ignored for twenty years.

"Yes or no?" she was demanding. "Are you going to do it or not?"

"Well yeah," I said. "Absolutely. What time do you wanna meet up?"

At Chi-Chi's that night I sat alone. Ours was a town of 8,700 though it felt like fifty, all of that fifty usually hanging out at Chi-Chi's every night. To my knowledge Amy had never been inside and she had just increased her streak by another cipher. She had not wanted to eat with me. She had wanted me to take care of her llamas while she drove to Pittsburgh to pick up her brother at the airport; she was sure she'd get caught in a snowstorm and have to stay the night. She asked me to feed Pedro and the others but she never said *please* to me, she never said *thank you.* She was losing all her manners. She hardly ever made eye contact. I had to dance in a ring to keep up with her averted stares.

Chi-Chi's was the only restaurant to speak of in the town. It was three years old and had quickly driven out of business the only other major restaurant—a smorgasbord with a coal mining motif that surprisingly was not named The Black Lung Buffet. We had turned away from all-you-can-eat and strip-mining; we had embraced Mexico and Mexico had embraced us.

"Ready to order?" the waitress asked. Still in high school, she wore somebody's varsity jacket over her uniform—somebody from Steubenville. "Do you want to hear the specials?"

"No, just give me the Hearty Olé!" I said.

It embarrassed me even to say it. I dreamed of a time when no one bothered to order off the Chi-Chi menu anymore and the sweet broad faces of the waitresses had to press back a smile at the mention of chimichangas. We ate simple and pure, *arroz y pollo* or, if we got lucky, *arroz y llama*, and one of us, afterwards, always drove to the house where the person he loved lived alone with her creatures and he stretched out on her grass picking the charmed scorched spot for his bed. And for the rest of the night whatever he dreamed belonged to him.

The next morning I drove to Amy's farm. She was already gone. Her note told me Pedro and pals had been fed. The crabbed handwriting seemed to scowl as fiercely as she did, no mention of a thank you, no mention of a please, no mention of a help yourself to tap water for doing this, but at the end of this sour note she had drawn a big smiley face with a single spitcurl on top and one above each ear. That big smiley face with three hairs propelled me to the pantry where I sorted through the keys hanging on the key jockey and found the one to the ancient stake body truck. I had to excavate the equipment barn to clear a path for it; then I drove it to the llama field and loaded as many of those animals as I could on it. They kept trying to bite me. Their matted fleeces gave me a coughing fit. I took off my belt and flailed and coughed and yanked them to the truck. I had to hope that special llama mood wouldn't strike because if they decided to belly down on me I'd never be able to budge them off the ground. But I got six of them loaded up in that ancient truck without any hissing or spitting. Their necks rested over the boards I had, one long-ago summer, staked into the flat bed for Amy's father, and for the moment at least they seemed content enough.

I looked across the Boyd farm. A line of dark junipers rose from the damaged land. Strip-mining had drawn our horizon ragged and had forever shifted the landscape; now neither its beauty nor its ugliness was natural. I felt I was living a lie in a landscape that itself was carved into a lie. And you might well say to this, you might say, Why didn't you simply extricate yourself from the lie, why didn't you leave? But that's just it, that's the thing. Why didn't I leave, why don't I now? That's the point, isn't it?

I got in the truck and drove off. I knew of a gravel pit in front of Wilma Lipinski's deserted place and I turned into the dirt road heading there. The house stood on a moraine. Gravel pit operations had been threatening to swallow it for years, but the house still stood. I drove down into Wilma's gravel pit with a ton and a quarter's worth of llamas and there I had to unload them one by one. Then I went back for another vesselful and it was afternoon before I was done. The sun was clouded over. Snow flurries flickered the grayness; the light was already preparing to leave. The door to the empty Lipinski house was gone, I saw. The windows were broken into glass daggers. I could see some stuff still inside. I wondered if Amy knew about the love affair her father was having with Wilma before his not-so-old heart, for once fighting out of its bag of dullness, stopped just like that. The wind was blowing in a stronger snow. Amy had been right about the weather. I walked back to the truck and retrieved her rifle and a box of 30-06 calibre cartridges.

I would have started with Pedro if he hadn't been bunched in the pack. I took aim at his protective circle. One shot, one llama down, one echo rolling back, and with each crack of the rifle my love for Amy Boyd grew. The Ruger 77 was burning up my hands with only five llamas dropped, but I'd known a burning much worse, much worse, and I kept going. Maria's front hooves had made it over the lip of the pit when I got her—that doomed, frantically stubborn gal was more like Amy than any of them. The rest just stood there like the dumb llamas they were. Jesus waited calmly, true to his namesake, and hiding behind him but not for long was Pedro—for once his raggedy hide shone. Inside my shaking boot a three-toed foot that hardly belonged to me was spewing a geyser of pain and fire and clawing to get out. The gray sun was reduced to a scrap of driftwood but once the whole of that bright star had traveled through me.

One shot, one llama down, one echo rolling back. I had never killed so many things in a row and been able to take my time about it, my own good time that was my own secret song I was now discovering, and if I had a soul it was awakening. The rhythm was powerful as the morphine and just as quick in its addiction, and when I was finished with the llamas I turned my sights on Wilma Lipinski's house and saw people from the town inside, people I liked, and I shot every one of them with the rest of Amy's cartridges.

Then I went to Chi-Chi's. I knew the limp had started. I sat at a table hoping to be alone but already some of the guys I had killed were patting me on the back and saying hey how's it going. One of them said, with only mild interest, "Didn't I see you shooting some llamas over at the Lipinski place?" I said, "Coulda been." I held onto my cup of coffee. I looked down at my burning hands. I said to myself, Now what are you going to do? Are you going to do something with your life or are you going to sit here and drink coffee for the rest of its unfolding?

Right on cue the high school waitress, in somebody's Steubenville varsity jacket, came to my table holding up her glass pot. The young chubbiness of her face hid all the bones, and she could have been Mexican, or Mayan, or even Asian. She asked, "Warm it up?" and I said yes, honey, just keep it coming for the rest of my life, coffee coffee coffee, coffee till my brain explodes and drips back south where it belongs.

If I couldn't have her, no one would, that's what the world would be saying in two days when Amy started packing and called in her brothers to help her move. The snowstorm would be bringing with it a wretched gift of pain for my foot and when everybody was at the height of talking about me I would be limping my worst and trying not to show it, which would show it even more. Once I had saved a man, it was a hundred years ago, and now I would save his daughter. There was no reason for this, it was just something I wanted to do. If I couldn't have her, then someone would. I'd sent her on her way.

Daniel Mark Epstein

Magic for Houdini

After the feast in his honor, the magician
Checked his watch, blinked, palmed a yawn,
As amateurs turned water into wine, or wine
Into water, and beamed at his applause. Next?
One held a cigarette paper rolled betwixt
Thumb and forefinger, and beguiled
The crowd with faultless patter promising
To turn this sheer paper into a live moth.

Gracefully he rolled the paper. Smiling,
He made a fist. But then the Truth
Upstaged the actor, as it sometimes does.
When he opened up his hand again,
The smile that had been poised above success,
Died on his lips. Where life should have been,
A flutter of fresh wings as the moth flew free,
Death left its ashes, the poor bug's remains.

Knowing the greatest illusion ends in folly
As even the best magicians fail sometimes
To make the incredible act a certainty,
Houdini raised his hands to start a round
Of clapping to mask the man's embarrassment,
A simple trick of professional courtesy
For the thing boldly attempted, bravely lost —
And maybe a little sympathy for the moth.

Then the audience drew in its breath.
A living moth came flying from nowhere
And circled the mortified magician's hair,
Once, twice, three times. Crackling applause
That might have come from pity came from fear.
And no one's dread ran deeper than the master's,
Who was all too familiar with these powers
Of darkness. He would be dead within a year.

[VOL. XXIII, NO. 1 / WINTER 2001]

LINDA GREGERSON

Cranes on the Seashore

For Thomas Lynch

1.

Today, Tom, I followed the tractor ruts north
        along
           the edge of Damien's pasture. I missed all the

dung slicks but one. The calves did not judge me
        or, comely
           darlings, judged me benign. The ditches

and the token bits of barbed wire weren't, I like
        to think,
           intended to halt my trespass much more than they

did. The hedge-crowned chassis might have been one
        of my father's
           own. And then at the rise, Tom, the promised

North Atlantic, and I'm fixed. Salt cure for
        rheum. Rock
           cure for bureaucracy and blood-borne grudge.

The farmers on Orkney favored this time of year
            for pillage. Took
        to the sea just after the crops were in. Cleared

the mind.

2.

           Megan
     is not happy with her drawing of the

rock face. She has fastened on only this one pure
            thing:
       the light-shot swells of the tide do not move her,

the shattered interlacements and the rolling
            greens,
       she'd trade them all for the one right likeness

of ice-thrust slate. Megan is not by nature
           ascetic — her
       paper has smudged and the pencil lead snapped —

she's after proof the earth leaps too

3.

           At eight
     o'clock on a Wednesday evening, eighteen

hundred seventy-four, one Jeremiah Dowling
           (this
       was June quite near the solstice, therefore

light) took aim "as he thought" at a pair of cranes.
           The girls
       in question, both of them in service at the

Leadmore farm, were washing skeins of new-spun
             wool
      in the surf. And must have bloodied

the wool when they fell, but did not die,
             or had not
      when the county paper went to press.

Of Mr. Dowling's youth and upright family
             the writer
      cannot say enough (his obvious

promise, their moneyed remorse); we may thank
             our different
      pieties we're less inclined to think these

help. We'd like to think our present dis-
             positions
      bear more scrutiny, that girls

may be lovely as cranes and safe.

4.

             Behind
      the row of holiday villas, the hay

has started to rot in the fields. On the weather,
             the hay
      and the holiday makers agree. But Damien's

calves have all been sound, and three to
             come,
      and Damien's father is glad for the extra (villas

need carpenters) work. It's like this at home now, the parts
                    you sell in order
        to pay for the parts you keep, till my uncle

is told by the barman one day would he please
                    not come in
        in his farm clothes, it puts off trade. A little

longer, barman, bid the locals then, A little
                    while
        is all we'll take. I lied

about the calves, though; you can see the smallest
                    Holstein's
        lame. Emma had thought he was simply less

greedy, so late did he turn toward the bucket of mash,
                    and now
        she can hardly bear to look. God

keep us from the gun sight. Here is
                    one
        for the landlord and one (we're almost

gone) for the road.

[VOL. XXIII, NO. 1 / WINTER 2001]

CZESLAW MILOSZ

Translated from Polish by the author and Robert Hass

To Robert Lowell

I had no right to talk of you that way,
Robert. An émigré's envy
Must have prompted me to mock
Your long depressions, weeks of terror,
Presumed vacations in the safety of the wards.
It was not from pride in my normalcy.
Insanity, I knew, was insinuating itself
In a thin thread into my very being
And only waited for my permission
To carry me into its murky regions.
And I was watchful. Like a lame man,
I used to walk upright to hide my affliction.
You didn't have to. For you it was permitted.
Not for me, a refugee on this continent
Where so many newcomers vanished without a trace.
Forgive me my mistake. Your will was of no use
Against an illness that held you like a stigma.
Beneath my anger was the vanity,
Unjustifiable, of the humiliated. Belatedly
I write to you across what separates us:
Gestures, conventions, idioms, illusions.

[VOL. XXIII, NO. 2 / SPRING 2001]

PABLO NERUDA

Translated from Spanish by Lewis Hyde

The Widower's Tango

Oh Maligna, now you've found the letter,
now you've cried with rage,
and you've insulted the memory of my mother,
calling her a rotten bitch and the mother of dogs,
now you've drunk the afternoon tea alone, lonely,
staring at my old shoes, empty forever,
and now you can't recall my illnesses, my night dreams, my meals,
without cursing me out loud as if I were still there
complaining about the tropics, about the *corringhis* coolies,
about the poison fevers that hurt me so much
and about the dreadful Englishmen, whom I still hate.

Maligna, the truth, what an immense night,
what a lonely earth!
Once again I've come to lonely sleeping rooms,
to eating my cold breakfast in restaurants, and once again
I throw my pants and shirts on the floor,
my room has no coat racks, no portraits of anyone on the walls.
How much of the shadow that's in my soul I would give to have
    you back,
and how threatening the names of the months seem to me
and how the word winter sounds like a sorrowful drum.

Later you'll find, buried by the coconut palm,
the knife I hid there for fear you'd kill me,

and now, suddenly, I'd like to smell its kitchen steel
accustomed to the weight of your hand and the shine of your foot:
under the dampness of the earth, among the deaf roots,
of the human languages only that of the poor could know
    your name,
and the heavy earth doesn't understand your name
made out of impenetrable, divine substances.

This is how it hurts me to think of the clear day of your legs
resting like suspended and firm water from the sun,
and the swallow that lives in your eyes, sleeping and flying,
and the dog of rage that you shelter in your heart,
and this is also how I see the dead who are between us from now on,
and I breathe the air made of ashes and ruins,
the long, lonely space that surrounds me forever.

I'd give this wind from the gigantic sea for your rough breathing
heard in the long nights without a trace of forgetfulness,
uniting itself with the atmosphere like the whip on the horse's hide.
And just to hear you pissing in the dark at the back of the house,
as if you were spilling a thin, trembling, silvery, insistent honey,
how many times I would deliver up this chorus of shadows
    I possess,
and the sound of useless swords that can be heard in my soul,
and the pigeon of blood that's all alone on my forehead
calling for things that are missing, missing people,
substances strangely inseparable and lost.

[VOL. XXIII, NO. 2 / SPRING 2001]

WISLAWA SZYMBORSKA

Translated from Polish by Vuyelwa Carlin and Sylwester Cygan

Cat in an Empty Apartment

Die—you can't do that to a cat.
What is it to do, the cat,
in an empty apartment,
but climb the walls,
and rub against the furniture?
It's as if nothing is changed
—yet everything is out of true:
as if nothing has been moved,
and yet, there's a void.
And of an evening, the lamp's not lit.

Footsteps on the stairs—
but not the right ones:
and an unfamiliar hand
puts fish on the plate.

Things here aren't beginning
in their usual seasons.
Nothing takes place as it should.
Someone who was, and was,
suddenly is no more—
and remains, stubbornly, no more.

All the wardrobes have been investigated;
every shelf nosed over;
the crawlspace between carpet and floor, checked:
even the forbidden papers
have been riffled through and scattered.
What more is there to do
but sleep, and wait?

Well, just let him come back —
just let him show his face!
He'll find out, all right,
what a cat does, and does not, permit.
It will edge to his side,
as if most loth — little by little,
padding in high dudgeon.
And — for the time being — no jumping up;
a buttoned lip.

[VOL. XXIII, NO. 2 / SPRING 2001]

Sixty-first Birthday

By the toe of my boot,
a pebble of quartz,
one drop of the earth's milk,
dirty and cold.
I held it to the light
and could almost see through it
into the grand explanation.
Put it back, something told me,
put it back and keep walking.

Walking on Tiptoe

Long ago we quit lifting our heels
like the others—horse, dog, and tiger—
though we thrill to their speed
as they flee. Even the mouse
bearing the great weight of a nugget
of dog food is enviably graceful.
There is little spring to our walk,
we are so burdened with responsibility,
all of the disciplinary actions
that have fallen to us, the punishments,
the killings, and all with our feet
bound stiff in the skins of the conquered.

But sometimes, in the early hours,
we can feel what it must have been like
to be one of them, up on our toes,
stealing past doors where others are sleeping,
and suddenly able to see in the dark.

Praying Hands

There is at least one pair
in every thrift shop in America,
molded in plastic or plaster of paris
and glued to a plaque,
or printed in church-pamphlet colors
and framed under glass.
Today I saw a pair made out of
lightweight wire stretched over a pattern
of finishing nails.
This is the way faith goes
from door to door,
cast out of one and welcomed at another.
A butterfly presses its wings like that
as it rests between flowers.

[VOL. XXIV, NO. 1 / WINTER 2002]

W. S. MERWIN

Under the Day

To come back like autumn
to the moss on the stones
after many seasons
to recur as a face
backlit on the surface
of a dark pool one day
after the year has turned
from the summer it saw
while the first yellow leaves
stare from their forgetting
and the branches grow spare

is to waken backward
down through the still water
knowing without touching
all that was ever there
and has been forgotten
and recognize without
name or understanding
without believing or
holding or direction
in the way that we see
at each moment the air.

[VOL. XXIV, NO. 1 / WINTER 2002]

CHARLES WYATT

From *The Spirit Autobiography of S. M. Jones*

I was born in 1836 with a veil over my face, a fact to which some might attribute the story I am about to tell. I write not to gain eccentric notoriety, but do so out of a good and honest heart, through the influence of some mysterious power. The candid reader may accredit all that is herein written, for they are veritable facts.

Invisible Kittens

Evenings we often sat and read, our conversation desultory as the sounds of the log falling to pieces in the fireplace. I liked those quiet times, especially when Mother would tell us her stories. On the occasion I have in mind, I was seven or eight, not long recovered from my illness—Tommy was playing with his lead soldiers, arranging them in rows like the corn standing in the back of the garden. I suppose I was tormenting him by secretly causing them to fall when Mother put down her sewing.

Mother began to tell us one of Tommy's favorite stories about the little people—the little people lived in the garden and were small enough to hide in milkweed pods. Like mankind, they made mischief and did good in more or less equal measure, but were most amazing in their ability to avoid detection. They could simply tell when we were going to look their way. "Can't you feel when someone is watching you?" Mother asked us. "The little people can feel when you are about to see them, and they hide."

"Why can't I hide like the little people?" Tommy complained. "Sylvester always finds me when I hide."

"Then you must persuade them to teach you their art."

"But no one can see the little people. How could I catch one?"

"The little people would never help you if you try to catch them, but they listen from their hiding places. Sometimes they teach children how to hide the way they do. But you would need a better reason than Sylvester always finding you."

"I know a good reason," Tommy said, "but I'm not going to tell."

"You don't have to tell me," I said. "You have to tell them and you don't know where to find them."

Mother said we might hear them singing among the crickets (whom they tended) and katydids (which they did not tend, as anyone could tell by listening). And later, Tommy and I began to play a game of turning suddenly in the hope of catching one unaware. Sometimes I felt I had seen a small figure, especially in the tall weeds near the fence row, but Tommy's sightings, and this was usual in our games, were both more frequent and fervent than mine. This night, Mother's story was of the little people sailing over the meadows, using silken threads they had stolen from spiders. They were bringing secrets of the world to the hiding children, the children they had taught the secrets of their invisibility.

I had chosen a small rocking chair with flat comfortable arms, and I had grown quite drowsy as the story developed, as Mother's stories often did, into a listing of all the plants of the meadow and the properties of healing and harm they contained. Suddenly I felt something fall into my lap. Had I been touched by a moth, or had some projectile winged its way past me, perhaps in retribution for my recent mischief? I looked at Tommy, but he seemed to be innocent. Sensing my gaze, he looked up from his squadrons.

"What is it?" he asked.

"I don't know," I said. "Something fell into my lap, but it's not here now."

Then something brushed against my hand on the arm of the chair away from Tommy. It was fairly dark in the room because the fire had died down, but I could see that there was nothing there.

"Who threw that?" I asked. And to the ensuing silence, I demanded, "Who . . . who threw that?"

At this point, Mother, who had taken up her mending again at the end of her story, suggested that we go to bed. I was a nervous child. I would always be a nervous child, inclined to disrupt her quieter moments. After she had tucked us in, and we had said our prayers, and only the candle in the hallway was left burning, I felt again that soft impression of something falling on my bedclothes.

"Did you throw that, Tommy?" I asked. Already half asleep, he only mumbled.

"Wake up, wake up. There is something strange going on." As I spoke I groped about the bedspread, searching for the object that had fallen on it. Then I grasped it, something small, furry, and wiggling—unquestionably a kitten. I could feel its tiny claws, but it made no sound at all. I was filled with the kind of loathing that the sight of maggots brings, part from the suddenness of the vision, part from sympathy for the once living thing they have so awfully transformed. The eye refuses to take it in. The mind cannot deal in swarming things. I felt there was some like thing in my hand. I threw it out of the bed. When it should have struck the floor, it did not. At least, there was no sound at all. Tommy began to snore softly. I felt another small thump on the bed, and then another. Groping around me, I gathered them up. It was dark, but not so dark that I could not see what I was grasping: nothing. But I could feel the fur and the tiny squirming limbs, ending in needle-sharp claws. One by one, I threw them out of the bed. Again, there was no sound.

"Tommy, wake up," I hissed repeatedly, as they came like a slow rain or hail against the bedclothes.

"What is it?" He sounded awake by now. I continued to perform my charade of gathering, grasping, and throwing. "Get down on the floor and feel around," I whispered. "There should be something there. I am throwing them."

"Throwing what?"

"Kittens. You should be able to feel them."

"Are you awake?"

"Yes, yes, I am awake. What can you feel there? Reach under the bed."

He struggled out from under the covers and groped about on the floor. It was a cold night, and I could hear him shivering.

"Well, what do you feel?"

"Nothing. There isn't anything here. What in the world have you been doing?"

"Come here then. I have gathered them all around me."

Then when Tommy came over to my bedside, I realized that they were gone.

"They were kittens. And they were invisible. I could feel their tiny claws and teeth. And when I threw them, they disappeared. Well, they finished disappearing. I threw them and there was no sound at all. But they kept falling on my bed."

"You were dreaming," he said. "I have had dreams like that before. In fact," he said thoughtfully, "I have had a dream very like this. Invisible kittens. But I had forgotten it."

"No, it was no dream. Come here and bring the candle." And by its light, I showed him the scratches on my hands and wrists.

The Magic Box

When Tommy was five and I was six, we were playing in the attic one day and found the little box. It was a large attic and the cat had favored it to hide her kittens. All week we looked for them, getting ourselves dirty enough to be scrubbed raw by Peach, who still did not seem to mind our playing there. We found them finally, but their eyes were closed — they were too tiny for us to play with. The box we found near the cat's nest was sturdy but old, about eighteen inches square. I suppose the wood was oak or maple. It had a lid and hinges, but these were broken, so the lid merely lay across the top. The box seemed ordinary, but useful, and we included it in our games, using it to store marbles and the like. Then, when we were playing at soldiers and had taken them all out of the box, Tommy gave a queer look, and laying his hands on the lid, which he placed back on the box, said, "Who's there?" And with this utterance, the lid slipped off the box under his hands. I thought it was a good game and asked if I could try it, too. "Who's there?" I called dramatically, and the lid bucked under my hands as if the box contained something alive. I was as shocked as I had been the year before when the heavy door of the feed store in town had closed on my hand and I could not cry out because of the pain or the surprise. Finally I was able to speak. "Tommy, what was in the box?"

"There's nothing in the box," he said simply, holding it for me to see.

The inside of the box was bare and a little dusty. I felt carefully around it to detect some secret feature, but the boards were plain.

Satisfied that there was no snake or creature in the box, I was content to ignore its tendency to toss off its lid. We kept the lead soldiers, special stones, and arrowheads in it and occasionally brought it out for play.

One Sabbath there was a neighbor visiting at the house, named Fitzpatrick. He was, I think, an especially strong young man. I remember particularly his bulging arms. Tommy and I were playing on the floor, and when the box was emptied of our playthings, the "who's there" game commenced. We would hold our little hands on the lid, call out "who's there," and off the lid would tip. Farmer Fitzpatrick came over to us and asked us what we were playing. We explained the game and he asked if he could try, also. Laying his hand on the box lid, he called out, "Who's there?" Instantly the lid tipped off the box. With a look of astonishment on his face, he picked up the box and examined it minutely. Then he asked if he might repeat the experiment. This second time, he laid both his large rough hands on the box lid, and called out the words with rather more an inflection of genuine curiosity than before. Again, the box lid tipped off, this time causing Farmer Fitzpatrick to fall back with a heavy thump.

I remember that Mother had come into the room, causing Farmer Fitz to swallow some of the epithets he had been applying freely to the box and its unknown inhabitants. "May I try one more time?" he asked politely. We offered no objections. He took the box to the doorway, placed it on the jamb rock, and bracing himself above it, held down the lid with both his hands, his muscles straining in anticipation. "Who's there?" he called through clenched teeth. At these words, the lid came off the box again, violently pitching Farmer Fitz out the door and onto his backside in the dusty lane. He lay there for a moment as if the wind had been knocked out of him, but when my mother inquired if he were hurt, he slowly got to his feet, dusted himself off and said, "I am satisfied." With those words, he turned on his heel and did not visit our house again.

At dinner, Father smiled at our story, but then became thoughtful and said the box would have to go. Tommy and I protested tearfully, and Mother suggested that it was a useful box, that she could keep it in the kitchen. Father assented to this arrangement.

Now Mother and Peach often sang as they bustled about preparing meals. The little box was placed in a corner; and when the women sang, it would make a tapping noise, its lid jigging along in perfect time. Mother stopped her work, and, after wiping her hands on her apron, picked up the box and held it before her.

"Is anyone in there?" she asked. "Can you speak?"

From inside the box came a loud sound of hissing, just like the hissing of a goose. Mother put the box back in its corner and did not look inside, as the others had done. Soon she and Peach were singing again and the box resumed its rhythmic tapping.

One day I noticed that the box was no longer in its corner in the kitchen and I asked Mother what had become of it.

"I have put it away," she replied, bustling about and not looking at me. "Your father has decided it is unseemly for us to have a singing spirit box, or whatever it might be."

"But where have you put it?" I cried, for it was like an old pet to me.

Mother would not answer me, but from that day on, the door to the attic was locked, and Peach would not let us play there.

Hellmoffring

What is your name what is my name whats in a name there under a rock you see them spelling it spelling what spelling isnt telling who was that hellmoffring yes my name is hogmoffring who was I indeed I was an indian chief a large dog large red dog with bristles in a quiver like to shake a snake who is with me oh we are several here where here its not cold its like the barn falling from the hayloft all the time whats it like all the time falling you get used to it yes hellmoff what does it mean it means this bush not that why should I tell you yes hogmiff well what is yours the bear the bear the bear came over oh we can talk we like to sing who who who my frings my wings my dings my my awfuls oh play for us sylvester slay for us pylvester

The writing began, as did all things really, in those days when Tommy and I were together. Tommy could do it and I learned that I could as well. It was simply a matter of sitting quietly, pen in hand. "Put yourself away," Tommy said, and then the pen would move. At the time, Tommy could only write his name, but he discovered the trick, nonetheless. He would hold the pen loosely and it would dart about the page. He insisted that it was doing those things of its own accord. So, at his behest, I held the pen and made a blank of my mind, something I was surprised to discover I could do easily. Then the pen would move and often wrote gibberish and vile, bad words. Still, it was amusing, and we played at it often enough until Mother caught us at it. She said it was wrong and sacrilege, and it seemed suddenly to us that it was so. We were not punished that I can recall, and that was the end of it.

That was the end of it until about the time of my discourses with Dudley upon the spirit world. I found myself drifting off over Latin exercises or even the notes I sometimes wrote at end of day on my practicing. Hellmoffring is the name I use, but it called itself by many names, asking and answering its own questions (although its answers were seldom satisfactory). It became a nuisance for me because I sometimes became thoughtful when I was writing in my journal, and then I was likely to come to myself over a page of such scribbling—and odd it was, all swirls and swoops as if the pen itself had taken on the character of a water beetle. I could get it to go away, it seemed, or to please it for a while, by playing my violin. It seemed to wish for me to play, and this I was willing enough to do. Was it a dog or an Indian chief or a crooked tree as it once insisted? I can only say it had a voice. Perhaps it was that only, a voice.

[VOL. XXV, NO. 1 / WINTER 2003]

Thomas Glave

Interview
with the Not-Poem

Interviewer: "But how can you call yourself
                 a 'not-poem'?

                 You look, from all appearances,
                 like a poem.

                 You crouch,
                 shuffle,
                 swing and sway
                 and arrange your lines,
                 syllables,
                 metaphors and similes
                 like a poem.

                 Your flesh
                 resembles that of a poem,
                 of all poems,
                 as do all your other parts.

                 So how,
                 pray tell,
                 can you not be a poem?
                 Explain if you will
                 this 'not-poem'-ness,
                 this state of un."

Not-Poem: "But then do not call me a poem,
for no, I am not one.

I came recently from that country
(about which by now you surely will have heard)
in which it was most unwise,
ungood,

simply *un*,
to be a poem.

Entire poems were murdered
in silent fields.

Stanzas,
though begging for their lives,
their limbs,
were strung up
and destroyed.

Delicate lines
and vulgar ones,
those both insensitive to light and fond of it,
and even mere epithets,
cries in ignorance and mediocrity,
simple daily failure
but also joy,
were torched,
leaving only ashes,

bare ashes,
in their wake.

Erased unto oblivion.

Scratched out of paper villages,
books unimaginable.

Books that, though outlawed,
were somewhere dreamt.

The smell of burning poem flesh,
rancid, sooty
and profane,

shrouded entire cities,
coastal plains.

Poem conversations were spied on
by poem-despising agents,
and entire towns of poems
emptied,
laid waste.

Rounded up and deported.
Torched, as I said.
Stoned.

So no, do not call me a poem.
I will never be a poem again."

Interviewer: "But still, you do look much like a poem,
                and sound like one.
                You smell—"

Not-Poem: "But then you know nothing, I see,
                of the flags that, in that time, so swiftly, were raised.
                Raised within days.

Yes, raised over twenty million roofs,
hoisted high over one hundred million TV antennas.

Flags, proud flags.
Flaggery everywhere.

Flags raised against poems
and those who resembled them.

Flags sprouted in airports.
Especially in airports.

At all security points,
and all customs checks.
Proof of citizenship so critical,
fealty more so.

But flags too in previously bland shopping malls,
and across yawning suburban lawns.

Poems dared not walk unaccompanied to the market,
nor — no, not ever — to worship
in poem holy places.

Poems were wrenched off planes
by those too edgy to fly with them.

'Who knows, they could be one of them!' some
            shouted,
teeth bared but shoulders cowering —
rocks in their dreams,
if not yet in their hands.

For — yes, did you not know?
Poem — children began ducking stones at school,

and more than one poem
(or anyone who looked like one)
was felled by bullets.

Bullets—
the good old-fashioned kind that still served.

Better than the national pastime, and more to
      the point.

Bullets still good enough to bring down a dirty
      poem,
to blow the heads off poem motherfuckers
who should anyway have had the sense,
long ago,
to go back where they came from.

Dirty poems,
cocksucking poems,
poems that didn't speak the language,
that chattered only in an outlandish gibberish.

Poems that stole jobs
and their dreams,
those elusive dreams.
The dream.

Poems that flooded the nation, bred like rabbits.
Poems that fucked with life as they knew it.

Poems that prayed too much or too little,
always with those awful accents,
that savage garb.

Poems without flags,
the flag.

Bullets urged on by flags
that stated, loudly,
This is who I am, and what I believe.
And you, they asked, *who are you?*"

Interviewer: "Do you actually expect us to believe —"

Not-Poem: "Only that I am a not-poem.
Not a poem."

Interviewer: "But you have said that flags were used to —"

Not-Poem: "O, but let me tell you.
They, they believed in their flag —
its supposed nobility, its invincibility.

Is not a flag
(though it may blare, loudly enough, its share of red)
easier to gaze upon, caress,

than one million and counting scorched hands
       in a field?

Than sixty million legs and limbs suspended
between leaves?

Than two hundred thousand eyes peering outward
from crouching hoods?

Than deserts baked with dead poems
and with fingers, knees?

A flag doesn't answer back, after all.
It makes no pretensions to having a right to its
        own life.
It couldn't care less about hunger, or thirst.
It loves bombs, which inform the songs
droned out, routinely, in its name.

It drapes coffins at will, and with grace.
And most of all—yes, most important—
it adores histories that never were,
that were never taught,
known,
and will never be.
Not-history."

Interviewer: "And so the poems—"

Not-Poem: "In that place,
            the poems ran to the hills and hid.
            'All bets are off,' someone said,
            'only not-poems will live now.'
            That is what they said.
            And so we transformed ourselves—
            yes, our faces
            and our hands.

            We quickly grew six fingers
            and three eyes.

            We covered our mouths
            with clever lines from novels
            penned by dilettantes.

            We made the stanza
            merely a memory,
            while retaining allegory.

We scaled the walls
where freedom, once advertised,
no longer stretched.

We ceased worshiping
in all the poem holy places.

We replaced God
with the flag,
for freedom's sake."

Interviewer: "And so now you—"

Not-Poem: "Now
I am a not-poem,
still fearful of bullets,
uncertain of my lines,
content with no plot—
the plot they were certain,
beneath their flag,
we all possessed—

their darkest dream,
a poem. Any poem.

The unending line."

[VOL. XXV, NO. 2 / SPRING 2003]

P. F. Kluge

My Private Germany

Some are in prison, some are dead;
And none has read my books,
And yet my thoughts turn back to them.
—Theodore Roethke, *The Chums*

On a window ledge, above the desk where I grade papers, arrange notes, contend with a phone that does or doesn't ring, there sits a framed black-and-white photo that was taken fifty years ago: my parents, my aunts, and uncles on a day trip from northern New Jersey to Lake Mohonk, in the Catskill Mountains of New York State. Thirteen people, eleven of them German-born, stand on a trail above a lake, a stone cairn and a pine tree just behind them. They are my people, the ones in that picture. They are also my place: where I come from. They're the ones who knew me when I was small, who had hopes for me, and reservations. Now, they watch me work, their scholarship boy, half klutz, half wunderkind. Dead a long time, right on the edge of oblivion, they reproach me. Why haven't I written about them? You're not a kid anymore, they remind me. Fair enough. I'm older than they were, when our lives touched. I'm nearly as old as they were, when they started to die.

There's Pop, always the leader of the pack, standing out in white short-sleeved shirt, slacks held up by suspenders, as close to dressed-up as he ever got. My mother's nearby, smiling, holding up her hand, maybe to wave at the camera, maybe to shade her eyes. Was I the photographer? I was along that day in the Catskills but I'm not in the photo. "You were always someplace else, wandering around," my Tante Hede told me, when I asked her years later. She was my last link to the family past. She remembered holding my mother in her arms, both sobbing, listening to the screams coming from inside the doctor's office where I was being circumcised. Now she is someplace else too, her ashes scattered around a sycamore tree in our old neighborhood. Walter, Hans, Fritz, Rupert, John, Carrie, Paula, Else, Hede, Maria, Friedel, on the edge of time and memory, except for the stay of execution my words provide. American citizens, New Jersey residents. Residents, as well, of a dogged land which I've spent all my life trying to take the measure of, in them, in me: my private Germany.

"My Parents Before I Knew Them." In my family, I am the custodian of albums, loose photographs, diaries, letters, expired passports, birth and death certificates, all sorts of souvenirs and keepsakes. "My Parents Before I Knew Them" is an album I put together of family photographs taken before my birth, in 1942. Mom and Pop were both thirty-nine when I was born and I missed knowing them when they were young, during their "greenhorn" years in America. I missed a lot. So there is my father, a boy swimming in the Elbe, behind him ships at anchor. And my mother looking melancholy beneath a blossoming Swabian apple tree, homesick even before leaving Germany. And, farther back in time, there are whole generations—a grandfather in a spiked World War I helmet, a great-uncle with an Iron Cross from the Franco-Prussian War, a great-aunt who became mayor of Berlin. There are my grandfathers, a Hamburg coppersmith, a furniture maker in Stuttgart. South Germans and North Germans, wine drinkers versus beer drinkers, potato eaters versus noodle makers, converging on New Jersey, and in me. My mother came first, in 1922. In those days German nannies were still in demand by wealthy New Yorkers and there she is, just out of Ellis Island—she remembered the cockroaches living near where Zabar's is today, wheeling somebody's baby in Riverside Park. Served corn-on-the-cob for the first time, she bit straight into it as if it were a bratwurst. For my father, America's first magic was the oranges for sale on the streets of New York. No wonder, at the end of his life, he found his way to Florida. During the war, the British blockade, he'd subsisted on turnips. After he came to America, he never ate another turnip. My father was sponsored by the legendary Uncle Bruno, who brought over one greenhorn at a time, half a dozen at least, giving them brief employment as a janitor in a building where he was superintendent, at 125th Street and Seventh Avenue. My father slept in the basement, on a cot next to the boiler and, during his first days, couldn't resist picking things out of the garbage that came down the dumbwaiter, ladies' shoes with weeks of wear left in them, perfect for his sister back in Hamburg.

They met, I'm told, at a German picnic in Jersey City. The engagement celebration was at a Horn and Hardarts automat. They were a couple now, the bandy-legged, barrel-chested machinist, and the quiet, thoughtful housewife. They did not linger in New York, not even in the German-American enclave of Yorkville, with its beer halls, bakeries, and oom-pah-pah. They moved to Miami—married there in 1926—back to New York, to Philadelphia, then to New Jersey, twenty miles west of the Holland Tunnel, "out in the sticks." They were finishing up a house there, when World War II began and I was born, when I started to know and to wonder.

Start with my first memory, those long brown rolls of wrapping paper just inside the side door of our house, on the steps leading up to the kitchen, those assembly lines of neighborhood *tantes* joining my mother in expertly jamming soap, toothpaste, razor blades, coffee, Crisco, into five-pound "Germany packages" headed for bombed-out relatives who were—no double entendre intended—"on the other side." They took the packages to shipping firms in Yorkville, they drove to Philadelphia when the surrendered German pocket battleship *Prinz Eugen* arrived on its way to nuclear tests in the Marshall Islands and word came that the German crew was willing to carry packages back across the Atlantic. In Germany, a New Jerseyan in the occupying forces befriended a *tante* living outside Stuttgart and agreed to pass along packages addressed to him. He was a guest at New Jersey beer parties for years afterward. "We spent thousands and thousands of dollars on those packages," the neighbor *tante* told me years later, when we were both back in Germany. She paused a moment, looked outside the kitchen we were sitting in, out onto the cobblestoned streets, freshly plastered buildings, tidy gardens of a prosperous postwar Germany. "They wouldn't have done the same for us," she said. In private moments, they must all have wondered what gifts would have come their way, if Adolf had won.

What we got back were the "Deutschland pakete" that arrived when I sensed our Germanness the most, at Christmas. Our celebration was all on Christmas Eve; Americans waited till after breakfast to open presents. My presents were history by then. We gathered at dusk, my parents, the *onkels* and *tantes*, beginning at our house, moving on to two or three others. We sang "Silent Night" in German. That was mandatory, for kids. And the first gifts we opened were the ones from the other side. They didn't amount to much. Crinkly paper decorated with sprigs of pine, the needles long since fallen off. A necktie my father would never wear, some marzipan for me, some *schnappsbohnen*—whiskey-filled pralines—that had usually melted en route. An odd little ceremony before the unwrapping of the big ticket items began, a moment of silence for a hated nation where there were people my parents loved.

I wondered about the war years. My parents were loyal Americans, I was sure of that. My father had worked in a factory that shifted from locomotives to tanks. He'd shrugged off invitations to a prewar German-American Bund camp. Later, when asked whether German Field Marshal Hans Gunther von Kluge was a relative, he fired back, "Oh yeah, that's my uncle." And returned to work on tanks. My mother and aunt got dirty looks when they spoke German while shopping. Piddling stuff. But there must have been darker moments that I was too young to notice. How did they feel watching newsreels, hundreds of planes bombing their home cities? The world applauding while their relatives died? What about those slow-coming letters, routed through Switzerland, telling them that one of my uncles had been killed on the Russian front? "In Russland gefallen." I grew up wondering about the people on the other side. Were there any good ones? No heroes? The South had heroes in the Civil War. But not the Germans? Was there no one to mourn? I remember a rainy afternoon my mother and I spent sitting on the floor of my room, sorting through a box of loose photographs: trips to Florida, the building of our house, my brother's Boy Scout camping trips and then she was holding a picture of a handsome, sharp-featured fellow in a *Luftwaffe* uniform. She fell silent. My mother was thoughtful and reticent: the emotions she expressed were thrice-distilled. "That's your uncle Paul," she told me after a while. He'd died just two weeks before the war in Europe ended, while riding in a hospital train that had been strafed. He was her favorite brother and she mourned for him. "He was the best of us all," she said.

My mother saw her favorite brother for the last time in 1936. A photo of that trip sat in the living room. I see my mother, smiling, surrounded by three brothers and a nephew, all of them in uniform: Paul in Hitler Youth, Fritzle—later killed in Russia—and Walter in *Wehrmacht* uniforms, and Willi in the ominous black of the SS, a swastika armband above his elbow. I studied that picture for years. It fascinated me knowing that uncles of mine, beloved of my mother, could be part of something evil. It complicated my view of good, of evil, of heroes and villains, of war movies with monocled fascist officers, chuckling U-boat captains, hapless sentries quickly stabbed and garroted. I developed what I've never lost: an interest in the other side.

For sure, we were Americans in the New Jersey of the fifties. My mother cooked and gardened. She ate a piece of chocolate and read an article in *Reader's Digest* every night, and when she worried, it wasn't about war and loyalty. It was about me. School counselors had called her in and told her that I was something called "college material." She spent a lot of time wondering where that would lead. Outgoing, opinionated, physical, my father worried not at all. I picture him on Sundays, wearing shorts and, underneath the shorts, a pair of boxer underwear that always were an inch or so longer than the shorts. I see him in the yard, sweating and bare-chested, waving cheerfully to well-dressed churchgoers, then, when he finished working, sitting on the front stoop with a Ballantine Ale. He was an American success story by then. They all were, and I think of them as happy in America. He took me on camping trips, organized Boy Scout newspaper drives, paid union dues, voted Democrat, never missed the beautiful music on *The Voice of Firestone*. On vacations they went to Florida or went west to national parks, always traveling with *tantes* and *onkels*, recording mileage, meals, and gas prices along the way and never registering in a motel room until sending one of the women inside, to make sure the place was clean.

Still, Germany remained, for them and for me. It was in the language we spoke at home, so that I went to school with a German accent that caught the attention of a speech therapist: "washing machine, washing machine, washing machine," I was made to repeat. It was in the food, the roast pork with skin on, potato pancakes, herring salad, *rouladen*, unfashionable food that I'll never taste again. It was in the loud, smoky table-banging pinochle they played every weekday night for thirty years, hoots and gibes that roared into the living room where I sat watching Paladin and *Gunsmoke*. They played for money that no one won. Losers contributed to a savings account—a *sparkasse*—that financed the next trip back to Germany. But I never felt more German-in-New Jersey than at the beer parties we had in the summer. I still hear the crunch of cars coming down the driveway, *onkels* and *tantes* pulling in from New York and Long Island, carrying cakes and cold cuts they'd picked up in the city.

In the afternoon it was cake and coffee, it was garden walks and sitting in lawn chairs, American success stories posing in front of turkeys for pictures they'd send to the other side. As darkness rolled on, things got loud and a little rowdy. They drank beer, they sang old songs, German songs, some homesick, some political, and when they decided to dance, an *onkel* pulled out an accordion and they adjourned inside our garage, and those were the sounds I heard from where I was upstairs sleeping, drowsy from the beer they'd given me. Those were my lullabies.

In 1954, the poker-losings added up: we were going back to Germany, my parents, three sets of aunts and uncles and a great-aunt who'd known Lou Gehrig's parents when they were neighbors up on Amsterdam Avenue. "Lou was a nice boy," she said. There was another man, Hans, a German Jew whom members of a *tante*'s family had concealed in their cellar during the war. I was the "Kleine Amerikaner," the precocious diary keeper:

> We all said that we would not cry when we arrived in Stuttgart. Well there is where we made a mistake. We all cried except Pop as far as I could see. Most everybody I had ever heard of in letters was there and there were still some left over. I have never seen so much pure joy before and probably never will again. After that we went to a hall where we could be together for a while. I got a model ship from Tante Martha, the toy shop owner in Winnenden. It was very nice. I really like everyone. We slept at Onkel Walter's. When we were in Rotterdam Tante Helen threw up from seasickness even though she was no longer at sea.

Two of the uncles I studied for years were waiting for us at the Stuttgart station. Walter was a tall, genial man, a furniture maker — that was the family trade — who gave me chores in his shop, sweeping up woodscraps and sawdust. He'd been in the army, in ski troops, and had slipped out of a POW camp and found his way home. By 1954, Willi — the SS lieutenant — was a sweaty, high-strung corpulent man, an endlessly busy host, planning trips and meals a week ahead, meals in, meals out, big and

little, hot and cold. He was one of those Germans who came out
of the war eating and never stopped. Still, there were remnants
of the kind of masculine handsomeness you don't see anymore:
the dark, straight back hair, the heavy beard, the roustabout ad-
venturousness of a Clark Gable or Ernest Hemingway, a Jack
Dempsey or Max Schmeling. In a firmly Socialist family, he'd
rebelled and joined the Nazi Party early. Yet he was there for his
socialist brothers, intervening in their behalf when they got in
trouble with the new regime. It was always Willi to the rescue, I
was told. The stories were impossible to sort out. He'd refused
to participate in a firing squad. He had not joined the party
to kill Jews, he said, and these were Jews from Stuttgart. His
insubordination landed him in a punishment battalion — *strafs-
battalion* — on the Russian front, where he was gravely wounded,
shrapnel that he carried in his head for the rest of his life. It was
after this wound or possibly an earlier one, that Hitler, visiting a
hospital, gave birth to my best one-degree-of-separation story:
the Führer chucked him under the chin affectionately. In 1945,
Willi was in Berlin, swarming with Russians and — the story
was — he shed his uniform, put on a civilian suit, and made his
way through the lines carrying a wreath of flowers, pretending he
was on his way to his grandmother's funeral. "Babushka kaput,"
he told the Russians. The Americans came for him once he was
home, held him for a couple of years until he was cleared, sup-
posedly by the testimony of one of the Jews he'd spared. Were
these stories my parents made up to tell me? That he made up
to tell them? That he told himself? I'll never know. I can only
consider the possibilities, which is what my private Germany is
all about, the chance of good, of evil, of both, then and now, in
them, in me. Possibilities from here to the airport, the currency
of the realm.

From 1954, I remember the taste of hard cider, the coarse-
ness of toilet paper, the whiff of fresh bread at dawn, wafting
out of bakeries onto cobblestone streets. We visited all three of
Ludwig's Bavarian castles, drove across the Alps down to Venice,

my uncle wisecracking about the slovenly performance of the *Duce*'s troops in World War II, the same jokes that circulated in New Jersey's public high schools: "Want to buy a rifle that was owned by an Italian war hero? Never been fired, only dropped once." That was it: history into stories, jokes, and silence.

I wonder how we looked to them, we German-Americans who sent back pictures of the turkeys we ate at Thanksgiving, the cars we drove to Florida. I wonder what they thought of me, the chubby baseball fan who spoke broken German. I wonder, as with all reunions, which prevailed, the feeling of distance or connection. They never talked about the war, not when I was around and, I'd bet, not when I wasn't. No talk of politics or principles, no finding of fault, no measuring of private virtue and public crime. That's one vote for distance. But there were moments when we drove down bombed-out streets; there were pauses when they talked about the dead. There was the look on my mother's face when we visited the *Luftwaffe* pilot's grave, the date of his death just a couple of weeks before the end of the war in Europe. In that, in the unspoken love and poleaxed silence, there was a recognition that what had happened to them could have happened to us. We were family. One vote for connection.

If you grow up in New Jersey and have a knack for words, New York City is your Oz. Driving along wooded roads in the Watchung Mountains, parking in secluded cul-de-sacs on high school dates, I'd see that river of traffic down on Route 22, headed for the tunnel, that carpet of lights spread out below, shopping centers, factories, endless suburbs, my New Jersey alive and pungent, just stinking with promise. And, in the distance, the towers of Manhattan, where the future waited. And the past. When I moved there in 1970 to work for *Life* magazine, I was drawn to the old German neighborhood of Yorkville. I strolled 86th Street, where Germans once drank beer and danced. When I jogged around the northern end of Central Park, I nodded at the building where my father had slept in the basement, his first night in America.

In Riverside Park, watching the sun set over New Jersey's richly polluted skies, I imagined my mother pushing a baby carriage along these very paths, meeting up with other nannies sitting on this same bench. I felt close to them, sometimes. On Broadway, there was a barbershop, one of the last that offered shaves. The barbers were Italians of my father's generation, skillful and reserved. Stretched out in a chair, my face covered with a hot towel, I'd glance up at a stamped tin ceiling, a slowly turning fan. A baseball game was on the radio. Your world, Pop, I said to myself. Even as it was all slipping away.

"There goes another one," they used to say when they got a bad news phone call, when a Christmas or two passed without a card arriving. My mother was the first to go, laconic and heartfelt in her final words to me. With a friend waiting in the driveway, my ride back to graduate school at the University of Chicago, I ducked into her bedroom to say good-bye. She cried, whenever we parted. "See," she said to me, holding back her tears. "I've finally learned to say good-bye." The next minute I was gone and a month later so was she. My father never forgave her for ruining one last trip out West, one last trip to Germany. Before long, they all were making terminal moves. "This one will last me out," they said when they bought new cars. Unable to pay suburban property taxes after they stopped working, they moved to retirement communities in South Jersey, in the Pine Barrens near Lakewood, within jogging distance of the place where the *Hindenburg* had crashed. My father flirted with going back to Hamburg, of sitting in a beer garden above the Elbe, watching ships sail in from around the world. It appealed to him, being old where he'd been young. But in the end, Florida won: today's oranges over yesterday's turnips. I was halfway around the world when he died. So I had no last words. My brother was there at the end. Seeing my father in pain, he asked, "You want a shot, Pop?" "Yes," Pop said, "I'd like a shot." But it came in a syringe, not in the whiskey glass he'd wanted.

Before long, my private Germany was hard to find. It wasn't

in New Jersey, it wasn't in Germany. And certainly not in New York. The Germans didn't stick around the old neighborhood and once they were gone, their businesses were replaced by Irish bars, Korean fruit stands, discount clothing stores, and running shoe shops. You could see it in the parades on Fifth Avenue. Saint Patrick's Day was raucous and hard-drinking, Puerto Rican parades bristled with horn-blowing machismo, the state of Israel celebration with pride and clout. The German von Steuben parade was an orderly procession that disbanded on 86th Street in a neighborhood that no longer existed. Manhattan had more Ethiopian restaurants than German. It was over, almost everywhere. Except in me.

I could feel it, as the years passed. My old man was punctual. Dinner on the table at six o'clock sharp. If someone invited us for 8:30, Pop was on the doorstep on the dot, even if the host came to the door in a bathrobe. I'm like that now, too. And I share his obsession with work done on time, always a little bit extra, even if people laugh at you. I feel his admiration for smarts even if out of shyness, arrogance, whatever . . . I sense that some kinds of cleverness are not for me. I concur that a bill left unpaid, sitting on a table overnight, is as troubling as an unpulled weed in a garden and — this from my mother — that the morning after a rainy day is a perfect day for weeding. I garden more than I ever dreamed, listen to more opera, believe that any large withdrawal from my savings account is the first step leading to death in the gutter. And I can't bring myself to throw out an article of clothing that has "wear" left in it, however soiled and out of fashion it might be. And, incredibly, I'm neater. "Ein Platz für Alles, und Alles in sein Platz": a place for everything and everything in its place. The kid who spent years trying to convince his parents that messy was not the same as dirty, that kid puts his clothes away now! There are more serious things too. There's that inbred feeling for the other side, even though the other side — my father in this case — didn't support me. His commitment to the United States was firm. When I had my doubts about Vietnam, he treated me as if I were shirking garden work. "You think you can pick your wars?" he asked. That was the point exactly, I said, and Germans of all people should have learned by now. He wasn't impressed. Still, my private Germany resurged during the seventies, that interest in the other side. In my darkest moods, I pictured a war crimes trial, America's first taste of victor's justice. I didn't want to see it, mind you, but I had to wonder. I'd read endlessly about Nuremberg. How would Americans acquit themselves? Was Robert McNamara our Albert Speer, Westmoreland our Keitel? Who would feign madness like Hess? Discover religion, like Hans Frank? Who, like Goering, would bait and ridicule, knowing he had a capsule of cyanide hidden in his rectum? I couldn't help it. Being American, yet resident of a private Germany, meant that winners and losers, heroes and villains connected in me. I had ties to a nation that had known spectacular defeat and that gave me an edge on America in the seventies. Germans, in their awkward way, were ahead of Americans. Germans knew, Germans learned: that good men do bad. That lives are lost for nothing. In school I'd been taught that America never started a war. That was lesson one. And never lost a war. Lesson two. In Germany, wars were started and lost. And everyone with some German in them had traveled to a place no American had ever been, way out on the last frontier: defeat.

On the afternoon of my fortieth high school reunion, I head home. I turn the car I rented at Newark Airport down the street I know by heart, past where we waited for the school bus, past the neighbor's house, and I slow, I stop, looking in at where I lived. My private Germany, an American place in the last analysis. A miracle of love for America, of abiding concern for the people on the other side. They pulled it off quietly, cheerfully. They made less of it than I have. Two owners since the old man sold, but the trees he planted on weekends tower over the tiny house. I see the stoop where he drank his Ballantine Ale, the chicken coop out back, my bedroom window. The place is still there—the landscape of spruce and maples, the gravel driveway, the remnant gardens. It's the kind of golden-rich autumn afternoon that conduces to memory, that invites nostalgia. But no one's home. An empty stage inside an empty theater. The houses outlasted us all, the *onkels* and *tantes*, the people who built, sold, traded up, moved out into America. I've been missing them for years, that bunch, resenting every intervening day that separated them from me, leaving me to wonder about a chess set that Willi carved after the war while the Americans held him in Dachau; a dress sword with a swastika that belonged to Paul; a beer stein with socialist heroes, from Spartacus to Liebknecht, to Marx and Engels, a kind of Miller Time in left-wing heaven, courtesy of my father's father; a collection of letters—yellow and crumbling—logs from long-ago trips to Florida; diaries that end in death. And that reproaching photo across my desk, all these things with no one to claim them, after me. And yet, I was stopped cold by that remark in Saul Bellow's *Ravelstein* that, no matter what we say we think, despite all our tough talk, a part of us believes that we will someday talk with our parents again. Sometimes it feels that they are still out there, with their short-sleeved shirts and their big American cars, their small houses and spectacular gardens, waiting for me. "Sit on the table . . . eat your plate," they tell their kids at dinnertime. Rooting for the Brooklyn Dodgers, laughing at Jackie Gleason, and waiting for me. And my aunt was right: I was always someplace, always wandering off. For years they were drifting away from me, farther into the past, the way an island sinks beneath the horizon. But now I feel time rounding, I feel myself coming closer to them, a reunion imminent in my private Germany and many conversations we never got to have, along with beer and cake and the smell of cut grass and drowsy with Ballantine beer, I will fall asleep in my house, my room, hearing the songs of the other side as they escape into no-man's-land from time's dug-in trenches and go sailing out into the New Jersey evening.

[VOL. XXV, NO. 3/4 / SUMMER/FALL 2003]

Epithalamium

If you twist a rope
twist it and twist it
no matter how long a rope it is
after awhile you cannot make one more turn
without skinning your palms
and burning the backs of your knuckles
and if you lift one hand from the rope
to get a better grip
the whole thing springs back
toward its most direct shape
its original being
with the fury of a coiled spring
at having been diverted from its purpose.
Every fiber of its being
rolls over on its back
the way molecules according to science
align themselves magnetically.
It is instructive to imagine that
the atoms in a rope
know where they belong
when you see those sad pieces of twine
that retail clerks wind around
boxes of socks and drinking glasses,
from which broken strands seem to reproduce
and under which the box strains outward.
And it is comforting to acknowledge it

when the molecules of a husband align themselves
with those of a wife
and the iron filings on the desk
connect the two ends of a horseshoe magnet underneath
as the moon follows the earth
forever in darkness.

[VOL. XXVI, NO. 2 / SPRING 2004]

Alice Hoffman

The Witch of Truro

1801

Witches take their names from places, for places are what give them their strength. The place need not be beautiful, or habitable, or even green. Sand and salt, so much the better. Scrub pine, plumberry and brambles, better still. From every bitter thing, after all, something hardy will surely grow. From every difficulty, the seed that's sown is that much stronger. Ruin is the milk all witches must drink; it's the lesson they learn and the diet they're fed upon. Ruth Declan lived on a bluff that was called Blackbird's Hill, and so she was called Ruth Blackbird Hill, a fitting name, as her hair was black and she was so light-footed she could disappear right past a man and he wouldn't see anything, he'd just feel a rush of wind and pick up the scent of something reminiscent of orchards and the faint green odor of milk.

Ruth kept cows, half a dozen, but they gave so much into their buckets she might have had twenty. She took her cows for walks, as though they were pets, along the sand-rutted King's Highway, down to the bay where they grazed on marsh grass. Ruth Blackbird Hill called her cows her babies and hugged them to her breast; she patted their heads and fed them sugar from the palm of her hand, and that may have been why their milk was so sweet. People said Ruth Blackbird Hill sang to her cows at night, and that whoever bought milk from her would surely be bewitched. Not that anyone believed in such things anymore. All the same, when Ruth came into town, the old women tied bits of hemp into witchknots on their sleeves for protection. The old men looked to see if she was wearing red shoes, always the mark of a witch. Ruth avoided these people; she didn't care what they thought. She would have happily stayed on Blackbird Hill and never come down, but two things happened: first came smallpox, which took her father and her mother, no matter how much sassafras tea they were given, and how tenderly Ruth cared for them. Then came the fire, which took the house and the land.

On the night of the fire, Ruth Blackbird Hill stood in the grass and screamed. People could hear her in Wellfleet and in Eastham and far out to sea. She watched the pear and the apple and the peach trees burning. She watched the grass turn red as blood. She had risked her life to save her cows, running into the smoky barn, and now they gathered round her, lowing, leaking milk, panicked. It was not enough that she should lose her mother and her father, one after another, now she had lost Blackbird Hill, and with it she had lost herself. The fire raged for two days until a heavy rain began to fall. People in town said that Ruth killed a toad and nailed it to a hickory tree, knowing that rain would follow, but it was too late. The hill was burned to cinders; it was indeed a blackbird's hill, black as night, black as the look in Ruth's eyes, black as the future that was assuredly hers.

Ruth sat on the hillside until her hair was completely knotted and her skin was the color of the gray sky up above. She might have stayed there forever, but after some time went by, her cows began to cry. They were weak with hunger, they were her babies still, and so Ruth took them into town. One day, people looked out their windows and a blackbird seemed to swoop by, followed by a herd of skinny milk-cows that had all turned to pitch in the fire. Ruth Blackbird Hill made herself a camp right on the beach; she slept there with no shelter, no matter the weather. The only food she ate was what she dug up in the shallows: clams and whelks. She may have drunk the green, thin milk her cows gave, though it was still tinged with cinders. She may have bewitched herself to protect herself from any more pain. Perhaps that was the reason she could sleep in the heat or the rain; why it was said she could drink salt water.

Anyone would have guessed the six cows would have bolted for someone else's farmland and a field of green grass, but they stayed where they were, on the beach, beside Ruth. People in town said you could hear them crying at night; it got so bad the fish were frightened out of the bay, and the whelks disappeared, and the oysters buried themselves so deeply they couldn't be found.

It was May, the time of year when the men were at sea. Perhaps there might have been a different decision made if the men had been home from the Great Banks and the Middle Banks, where their sights were set on mackerel and cod. Perhaps Ruth would have been run out of town. As it was, Susan Crosby and Easter West devised a plan of their own. They won Ruth Blackbird Hill over slowly, with plates of oatcakes and kettles of tea. They took their time, the way they might have with a fox or a dove, any creature that might be easily startled. They sat on a log of driftwood and told Ruth that sorrow was what this world was made of, but that it was her world still. At first she would not look at them, yet they could tell she was listening. She was a young woman, a girl really, nineteen at most, although her hands looked as hard as an old woman's, with ropes of veins that announced her hardships.

Susan and Easter brought Ruth over to Lysander Wynn's farm, where he'd built a blacksmithing shed. It took half the morning to walk there, with the cows stopping to graze by the road, dawdling until Ruth coaxed them on. It was a bright blue day and the women from town felt giddy now that they'd made a firm decision to guide someone else's fate, what their husbands might call interference had they but known. As for Ruth, she still had a line of black cinders under her fingernails. There was eelgrass threaded through her hair. She had the notion that these two women, Susan and Easter, known for their good works and their kindly attitudes, were about to sell her. She simply couldn't see any other reason for them to be walking along with her, swatting the cows on the rear to speed them on, waving away the flies. The awful thing was that Ruth wasn't completely opposed to being sold. She didn't want to think. She didn't want to ask questions. She didn't even want to speak.

They reached the farm that Lysander had bought from the Hadley family. He'd purchased the property mainly because it was the one place in the area from which there was no view of the sea, for that was exactly what he wanted. The farm was only a mile from the closest shore, but it sat in a hollow, with tall oaks and scrub pine and a field of sweet peas and brambles nearby. As a younger man, Lysander had been a sailor, he'd gone out with the neighbors to the Great Banks, and it was there he'd had his accident. A storm had come up suddenly, and the sloop had tilted madly, throwing Lysander into the sea. It was so cold he had no time to think, save for a fleeting thought of Jonah, of how a man could be saved when he least expected it, in ways he could have never imagined.

He wondered if perhaps the other men on board, Joseph Hansen and Edward West, had had the foresight to throw him a side of salt pork for him to lean on, for just when he expected to drown, something solid was suddenly beneath him. Something hard and cold as ice. Something made of scales rather than flesh or water or wood; a creature who certainly was not intent on Lysander's salvation. The fish to whose back he clung was a halibut, a huge one, two hundred, maybe three hundred pounds, Edward West later said. Lysander rode the halibut like he rode his horse, Domino, until he was bucked off. All at once his strength was renewed by his panic; he started swimming, harder than he ever had before. Lysander was almost to the boat when he felt it, the slash of the thing against him, and the water turned red right away. He was only twenty at the time, too young to have this happen. Dead or alive, either would have been better than what had befallen him. He wished he had drowned that day, because when he was hauled into the boat, they had to finish the job and cut off the leg at the thigh, then cauterize the wound with gunpowder and whiskey.

Lysander had some money saved, and the other men in town contributed the rest, and the farm was bought soon after. The shed was built in a single afternoon, and the anvil brought down from Boston. Luckily, Lysander had the blacksmith's trade in his family, on his father's side, so it came naturally to him. The hotter the work was, the better he liked it. He could stick his hand into the flame fueled by the bellow and not feel a thing. But let it rain, even a fleeting drizzle, and he would start to shiver. He ignored the pond behind the house entirely, though there were catfish there that were said to be delectable. Fishing was for other men. Water was for fools. As for women, they were a dream he didn't bother with. In his estimation, the future was no farther away than the darkness of evening; it consisted of nothing more than a sprinkling of stars in the sky.

Lysander used a crutch made of applewood that bent when he leaned upon it, but was surprisingly strong when the need arose. He had hit a prowling skunk on the head with the crutch and knocked it unconscious. He had dug through a mat of moss for a wild orchid that smelled like fire when he held it up to his face. He slept with the crutch by his side in bed, afraid to be without it. He liked to walk in the woods, and sometimes he imagined he would be better off if he just lay down between the logs and the moss and stayed there, forevermore. Then someone would need their horse shod; they'd come up the road and ring the bell hung on the wall of the shed, and Lysander would have to scramble back from the woods. But he thought about remaining where he was, hidden, unmoving; he imagined it more often than anyone might have guessed. Blackbirds would light upon his shoulders, crickets would crawl into his pockets, fox would lie down beside him and never even notice he was there.

He was in the woods on the day they brought Ruth Blackbird Hill and her cows to the farm. Sometimes when he was very quiet Lysander thought he saw another man in the trees. He thought it might be the sailor who'd built the house, the widow Hadley's husband, who'd been lost at sea. Or perhaps it was himself, weaving in and out of the shadows, the man he might have been.

Susan Crosby and Easter West explained the situation, the parents lost, the house and meadows burned down, the way Ruth was living on the beach, unprotected, unable to support herself, even to eat. In exchange for living in Lysander's house, she would cook and clean for him. Ruth kept her back to them as they discussed her fate; she patted one of her cows, a favorite of hers she called Missy. Lysander Wynn was just as bitter as Ruth Blackbird Hill was. He was certain the women from town wouldn't have brought Ruth to the farm if he'd been a whole man, if he'd been able to get up the stairs to the attic where they suggested Ruth sleep. He was about to say no, he was more than willing to get back to work in the fires of his shop, when he noticed that Ruth was wearing red boots. They were made of old leather, mud-caked, but all the same, Lysander had never seen shoes that color, and he felt touched in some way. He thought about the color of fire. He thought about flames. He thought he would never be hot enough to get the chill out of his body or the water out of his soul.

"Just as long as she never cooks fish," he heard himself say.

Ruth Blackbird Hill laughed at that. "What makes you think I cook at all?"

Ruth took the cows into the field of sweet peas. Lysander's horse, Domino, rolled his eyes and ran to the far end of the meadow, spooked. But the cows paid no attention to him whatsoever, they just huddled around Ruth Blackbird Hill and calmly began to eat wild weeds and grass. What Lysander had agreed to didn't sink in until Susan Crosby and Easter West left to go back to town. "Hasn't this woman any belongings?" Lysander had called after them. "Not a thing," they replied. "The cows that follow her and the shoes on her feet."

Well, a shoe was the one thing Lysander might have offered. He had several old boots thrown into a cabinet, useless when it came to his missing right foot. He put out some old clothes and some quilts at the foot of the stairs leading to the attic. He'd meant to finish the attic, turn the space into decent rooms, but he'd had to crawl up the twisting staircase to check on the rafters, and that was enough humiliation to last him for a very long time. Anyway, the space was good enough for someone used to sleeping on the beach. When Ruth didn't come in to start supper, Lysander made himself some johnnycake, half-cooked, but decent enough, along with a plate of turnips; he left half of what he'd fixed on the stair as well, though he had his suspicions that Ruth might not eat. She might just starve herself sitting out in that field. She might take flight and he'd find nothing when he woke, except for the lonely cows mooing sorrowfully.

As it turned out, Ruth was there in the morning. She'd eaten the food he'd left out for her and was already milking the cows when Lysander went out to work on a metal harness for Easter West's uncle, Karl. Those red shoes peeked out from beneath Ruth's black skirt. She was singing to the cows and they were waiting in line, patiently. The horse, Domino, had come closer and Ruth Blackbird Hill opened her palm and gave him a lick of sugar.

In the afternoon Lysander saw her looking in the window of the shed. The fire was hot and he was sweating. He wanted to sweat out every bit of cold ocean water. He always built the fire hotter than advisable. He needed it that way. Sometimes he got a stomachache, and when he vomited, he spit out the halibut's teeth. Those teeth had gone right through him, it seemed. He could feel them, cold, silvery things.

He must have looked frightening as he forged the metal harness, covered with soot, hot as the devil, because Ruth Blackbird Hill ran away, and she didn't come to fetch the dinner he placed on the stair — though the food was better than the night before, cornbread with wild onions this time, and greens poured over with gravy. All the same, the following morning, the plate was clean and resting on the table. Every morsel had been eaten.

Ruth Blackbird Hill didn't cook and she didn't clean, but she kept on watching him through the window that was made out of bumpy glass. Lysander didn't look up, didn't let on that he knew she was staring, and then one day she was standing in the doorway to the shed. She was wearing a pair of his old britches and a white shirt, but he could see through the smoke that she had on those red shoes.

"How did you lose your leg?" Ruth asked.

He had expected nearly anything but that question. It was rude; no one asked things like that.

"A fish bit it off," he said.

Ruth laughed and said, "No."

He could feel the heat from the iron he was working on in his hands, his arms, his head.

"You don't believe me?" He showed her the chain he wore around his neck, strung with halibut teeth. "I coughed these up one by one."

"No," Ruth said again, but her voice was quieter, like she was thinking it over. She walked right up to him and he felt something inside him quicken. He had absolutely no idea of what she might do.

Ruth Blackbird Hill put her left hand in the fire, and she would have kept it there if he hadn't grabbed her arm and pulled her back.

"See?" she said to him. Her skin felt cool and she smelled like grass. "There are things I'm afraid of, too."

People in town forgot about Ruth; they didn't think about how she was living out at the farm any more than they remembered how she'd been camped on the beach for weeks without anyone offering her help until Susan and Easter could no longer tolerate her situation. Those two women probably should have minded their own business as well, but they were too kindhearted for that, and too smart to ever tell their husbands what part they had played in Ruth Blackbird Hill living at Lysander's farm. In truth, they had nearly forgotten about her themselves. Then one day Easter West found a pail of milk at her back door. As it turned out Susan Crosby discovered the very same thing on her porch—cool, green milk that tasted so sweet, so very filling, that after a single cup a person wouldn't want another drop to drink all day. Susan chose to go about her business, but Easter was a more curious individual. One night, Easter had dreamed of blackbirds, and of her husband, who was out in the Middle Banks fishing for mackerel. When she woke she had a terrible thirst for fresh milk. She went out to the farm that day, just to have a look around.

There was Ruth in the field, riding that old horse Domino, teaching him to jump over a barrel while the cows gazed on, disinterested. When she saw Easter, Ruth left the horse and came to meet her at the gate. That past night, Ruth herself had dreamed of tea, and of needles and thread set to work, and of a woman who was raising three sons alone while her husband was off to sea. She had been expecting Easter, and had a pail of milk waiting under the shade of an oak tree. The milk was greener than ever, and sweeter than ever too; Easter West drank two tin cupfuls before she realized that Ruth Blackbird Hill was crying.

It was near the end of summer. Everything was blooming and fresh, but it wouldn't last long.

"What is it?" Easter said. "Does he make you work too hard? Is he cruel?"

Ruth shook her head. "It's just that I'll never get what I want. It's not possible."

"What is it you want?"

There was the scent of cows, and of hay, and of smoke from the blacksmith's shop. Ruth had been swimming in the pond behind the house earlier in the day and her hair was shiny; she smelled like water and her skin was cool even in the heat of the day.

"It doesn't matter. Whenever I want something, I don't get it. No matter what it might be. That's the story of my life."

When Easter was leaving, Lysander Wynn came out of his shop. He was leaning on his crutch. He wanted something, too.

He wasn't yet thirty, and his work made him strong in his arms and his back, but he felt weak deep inside, bitten by something painful and sharp.

"What did she tell you?" he asked Easter West.

"She's afraid she won't get what she wants," Easter said.

Lysander thought this over while he finished up working. He thought about it while he made supper, a corn and tomato stew. When he left Ruth's dinner on the stair he left a note as well. *I'll get you anything you want.*

That night, Lysander dreamed he wouldn't be able to give Ruth what she asked for, despite his promise. She would want gold, of which he had none. She would want to live in London, on the other side of the ocean. She would want another man, one with two legs who didn't spit out halibut teeth, who didn't fear rain and pondwater. But in the morning, he found a note by the anvil in his shed. What she seemed to want was entirely different from anything he had imagined. *Bring me a tree that has pears the color of blood. The same exact color as my shoes.*

The next day, Lysander Wynn hitched up his horse to a wagon and left on the King's Highway. He went early, while the cows were still sleeping in the field, while the blackbirds were quiet and the fox were still running across the sandy ruts in the road. Ruth knew he was gone when she woke because there was no smoke spiraling from the chimney in the shed; when Edward Hastings came to get his horse shod, no one answered his call. Ruth Blackbird Hill took care of the cows, then she went into the shed herself. She put her hand into the ashes—they were still hot, embers continuing to burn from the day before. She thought about red grass and burning trees and her parents calling out for her to save them. She kept her hand there, unmoving, until she couldn't stand the pain anymore.

He was gone for two weeks, and he never said exactly where he'd been. He admitted only that he'd been through Providence and on into Connecticut. What he didn't say was that he would have gone farther still if it had been necessary. He had no time frame in mind of when he might return. He would have kept on even if snow had begun to fall, if the orchards had turned so white it would have been impossible to tell an apple tree from a plum, a grapevine from a trellis of wisteria.

Lysander planted the pear tree right in front of the house. While he was working, Ruth brought him a cold glass of milk that made him feel like weeping. She showed him her burned hand, then she took off her shoes and stood barefoot in the grass. He hoped what he'd been told in Connecticut was true. The last farmer he'd gone to was experienced with fruit trees, and his orchard was legendary. When Lysander had wanted a guarantee, the old farmer had told him that often what you grew turned out to be what you had wanted all along. He said there was a fine line between crimson and scarlet, and that a person simply had to wait to see what appeared. Ruth wouldn't know until the following fall whether or not the pears would be red, nearly a full year, but she was hopeful that by that time, she wouldn't care.

[VOL. XXVI, NO. 2 / SPRING 2004]

Samantha Simpson

Generations: An Excerpt from *Novella*

Let me tell you something, Berry Parker." Novella Wheeler took a drag on her cigarette and blew the smoke into his face. "There are two things I'll always have—a man and money."

Berry and Novella sat together on her father's porch under the dim light of the moon, smoking and drinking from his flask. She had complained of the heat and hiked up her skirt to her thighs. He pretended not to stare at her smooth, plump, brown legs. She smelled like a fresh orange. She held her cigarette between two fingers, like a movie star, and he noticed her sharp, shiny, red nails. She had powdered her face, and it looked pale in the moonlight. The light brown hair of her wig fell in soft waves against her back. He thought she looked like the most beautiful woman in the world—like Lena Horne or somebody.

She was nineteen years old, and she wasn't pregnant. He knew that because he understood she was the kind of lady who wouldn't manipulate a good man into marrying her.

When she turned eighteen in 1947, she went abroad, to Virginia, where her cousins lived. She made her return within six months of her departure. She didn't like the so-called big city. He couldn't know that. She gave him no reason to imagine the way she had walked the streets, newspaper in hand, squinting to look at the numbers on office buildings while people pushed past her. She had no luck finding a job as a secretary, and she didn't want to be a waitress or a maid. She just couldn't ruin her hands. The buzzing streetlights, the highways slick with rain, and the music leaking out of nightclubs frightened her. Men bumped into her and stared at her hips and her chest before mumbling insincere apologies. She had verses from her mother's worn Bible etched into her skull, and everything looked like sin. She sidestepped the drunken women with their smeared makeup. Here were the whores of Babylon and the Jezebels, cackling and laughing while they leaned against their men.

No one, especially not Berry Parker, knew how she trembled on the way to the bus station and all the way back to Leggett, North Carolina. In fact, when she stepped off the bus and greeted her bewildered parents, she looked like a good-time girl. She had painted a mole on her cheek and darkened the hair above her lip with a makeup pencil. She wore high heels with her flimsy-looking dresses.

Now she slapped at the mosquitoes feasting on her arms and pretended to ignore how handsome Berry looked in his Navy uniform. "Does your mother know you're out here trying to court me?"

"Don't be like that, Nora," he pleaded. Everyone called her that.

"I know that bitch don't like me. She said as much."

My grandfather flinched, but he had nothing to say to that. His mother didn't like Nora Wheeler. She was the kind of young lady who let two men court her at once. "Maybe if you didn't step out with —"

"That's my business," Nora snapped. "Anyway, I don't know about you. I don't know if I can depend on you for anything." She knew Berry had enough money from his time in the service to buy a house on her side of Leggett. She knew that her fiancé didn't have a head for business. He worked at the grocery store for eight hours a day and planned to live with Novella and her family until he earned enough to get himself a farm. She took an accounting class before she dropped out of high school to nurse her mother back to health. She knew her fiancé would never earn enough.

Berry took her hand, marveling at the softness of it. "I have a little — something, Nora. And I love you." He didn't lie, and she knew it. She had been banking on it.

This is, after all, a love story.

· ·

"Know what my mother used to say?" My mother tugged on the buttons of her dress. She hadn't worn it since her father's funeral in 1988.

I shrugged. "There are two things I'll always have — a man and money." I practiced the line. Unlike Novella Wheeler Parker's other grandchildren, I could say it without laughing. I knew she was a serious lady.

My mother rolled her eyes. "No. Do you know what she used to say about you?" She paused for effect, and I raised an eyebrow. "She said you have bad blood."

My grandmother was dead. She had never told me to my face that I had bad blood.

I sat on my mother's bed and watched her struggle with her most somber outfit. "I don't know that you can still fit into that dress," I observed.

"She said you had bad blood because I'd told her about your — " She paused to work on the next button. She tried squeezing her breasts together to make the task easier. "Your sickle cell trait. She thought you wouldn't be — " The button submitted to her will, and she began on the next one. "Healthy. She thought you'd be really sickly."

I laughed. "Why don't you just go get another dress? You look like you're about to pop out of that one."

She turned to face the full-length mirror. She had to suck in her stomach and hold her arms to her sides if she wanted the dress to look as if it fit. "I told her you were going to be fine. And you are. You're OK — all grown up. Not that she would have noticed before — or now."

I nodded.

My mother unbuttoned the dress and pulled it over her head. "I told myself to go see her, but I was too broke and too sick. And I didn't want to see her like that. Last time I saw her she couldn't even walk, and she didn't want to eat. I knew I wouldn't see her again. I knew it. But I should have visited her at least one more time." She made a sad face at the mirror. Her siblings would talk if she didn't look as if her heart were broken at the funeral. She smiled wistfully. "That stuff she used to say about her man and her money is kind of funny, especially—"

I stood and walked into the hallway. "I should get dressed. We have a long drive."

She started rummaging in her closet. "Yep." She pulled out another black dress. "This one's a size 18. I hate to admit that I've gotten this big. She pressed the dress to her body and turned in front of the mirror. "Oh, well." She sat on her bed and started pulling on her panty hose. "Anyway, I explained to her about how your sickle cell trait—I told her your blood wasn't bad. You weren't anemic. Your blood was just different. And she got that, you know. She liked to study biology in high school. She was a smart lady. That's why I named you after her."

I closed my bedroom door.

. .

The last time I saw my grandmother, she sat in her room at the rest home, staring out the window. My mother and my sister, Erika, tried to get her attention, but her filmy brown eyes remained trained on the parking lot. "Do you think she can hear us?" My sister's voice sounded too loud in the antiseptic-white room.

I sat down in a rocking chair and leaned back, bumping the back of it against the wall with a loud thump. I stood abruptly and apologized when my grandmother turned her eyes on me. "You," she mumbled. Her voice sounded sleepy and hoarse.

I waved. "Hi, Grandma. How are you?" I could always count on my voice to sound tiny and silly whenever I tried to be polite.

"You." She pointed at me. She struggled to get to her feet without success. "You're not nothing. You're nobody. You hear me? You ain't got nothing."

My mother gave me a sympathetic look. "The nurse told me she always says that. Don't worry about it," she whispered.

I didn't. "It's nice to see you, Grandma."

The old woman slumped in her chair for a moment. "You're young and they put you here to look out the window. That's what you do. See?" She stared out the window. "You're so young." She touched her face then looked at me. "You. Me. They don't let you have nothing. They make you sit here and look in the mirror or out the window. And you're so young."

She started humming a made-up song. I could see my reflection in the pane along with her blank eyes.

I spent the rest of the visit sitting in the cafeteria, watching the middle-aged nurses spoon-feed the other grandparents. I never wanted to see Novella Wheeler Parker again.

And I didn't.

The version of her who appeared at the funeral home looked distant and regal. They bought her a new wig with short, black hair, a new hat, and an expensive white dress. She wore clear fingernail polish and gloss on her lips that made them look flat. She looked nothing like a good-time girl.

I was disappointed.

Her children wept and snapped pictures of her at the same time. I sat in the back row, passing the time between fingering my car keys in my purse and checking my watch. None of Novella Wheeler's family and friends were supposed to notice the smell of mothballs creeping out of the floorboards; it would have been disrespectful to her memory. I wondered for a moment whether moths were interested in eating corpses.

I watched my mother bend to touch the forehead and the lips of her dead mother. She shed no tears. I decided to get a closer look. My palms were sweaty. She looked like a doll lying in a bed of pink satin. There were sequins on her dress that sparkled beneath the lights of the funeral parlor. Her gloved hands were folded over her chest, which seemed to puff out while the lower half of her body diminished. I tried to match the placid face in the coffin with the perplexed face of the woman in the rest home. I leaned forward.

Another aunt snapped a Polaroid, and I blinked. "Here, baby, you can have this one," she whispered as she dabbed at her eyes with her handkerchief. I took the photograph. There was my blurred hand hovering above my grandmother's face. I returned to my seat in the back, unable to take my eyes off the photograph.

••

There had to be a letter or a newspaper clipping or something somewhere.

They had buried her the day before. I watched them lower her white casket into the earth. I hated the sound the machinery made. It had to be quiet.

It was quiet in my aunt's house as I rummaged through her desk, trying to find a yellowing piece of paper, something as old as my grandmother. There were Post-it notes and grocery lists, old bills and doodles, but no letters written in my grandmother's handwriting.

I had never seen her handwriting, but I knew she knew how to write. She had graduated from high school, unlike my grandfather. I thought she might have been the kind to write stories, but never poetry. She wrote stories about wildlife adventures and detectives.

I had no way of knowing.

I slammed another drawer shut, not caring if I woke everyone in the house. I dropped onto a couch and pulled a blanket over my head. The sun was starting to come up, and I had been awake all night, trying to find some evidence that she had been alive, that she had existed beyond my memory of her humming and rambling in the rest home.

I said my own name aloud in the darkness, and my lips

brushed against the fabric of the blanket. "Samantha Novella Simpson."

That was all I had left of her.

．．

My mother never told me the story of how Novella Wheeler Parker used to spit in the Communion wine. Mother Parker just couldn't get enough of doing it, even after the deacons caught her in the act and made her swear on a stack of Bibles she would never defile the blood of Christ again.

She was older then. She didn't paint her face anymore, and her dresses were solid colors. She didn't care for sinful floral patterns and polka dots. Her Jesus wanted her to look decent. She didn't swear, even when her children—there were only five then—were getting on her damned nerves. She simply spit in their soup and mixed it with her finger. "Here's my sugar," she sang to herself right after she let the drops fall from her mouth.

She spit in the Communion wine for the first time after she thought she saw Berry making eyes at Catherine from the pulpit. He was a preacher, leader of a flock of lost souls, and he winked at that whore in the second row. She saw him do it.

She didn't cry. She didn't even raise her eyebrows in Catherine's direction. When it came time to pass around the bread and wine, she rose from her pew and made her way to the altar without stumbling. A deacon placed the cup holder in her gloved hands, and she stared at the miniature glass vials. She was so still, the dark juice didn't move. When the deacon turned his back, she furtively spit into a few of the cups. She then faced the congregation and lifted the wine in front of her face as her husband read from the Scriptures.

"I was only adding a little sugar," she would have told me, if she were still alive and had never been senile. "I can't see how there's anything wrong with that." I would have agreed.

No one in my family told me that story. None of them were willing to believe Nora Parker was anything more than a devoted wife and mother, an example to upright women across the county.

I had to know it on my own. I typed it out on my mother's old word processor while I fanned away the August heat. I looked down at the funeral photograph propped against the printer. Her face never changed. I counted on her to let me know somehow if what I had written about her was wrong. "I won't write it if it isn't right," I used to mumble. She never protested.

. .

Only now have I tucked the photograph in an old journal, out of sight.

I once carried it with me to libraries and used it as a bookmark. It helped me remember stories. I remembered her abortions. I remembered her labor pains. I remembered the satisfaction she got out of bringing an ax down on the windshield of Berry's new car. The photograph never changed. She had to approve of the stacks of printer paper dotted with her name. I didn't doubt it.

One summer afternoon I guided her through the lines of a Rushdie novel. She wouldn't have liked it. The people all had funny names, and the man didn't write anything about them going to church.

"Excuse me?"

I didn't look up. The blurred hand in the photograph hovered between the end of a paragraph and my grandmother's face. "Mmhmm?"

"Do you have the time?" The man's voice was gentle and high-pitched.

I heaved a sigh of irritation. "I don't know what time it is. There's a clock on the wall." I glared at him, and he walked away.

He returned with a thick book in hand. "Is anyone sitting here?" He indicated an armchair across from mine, and I shook my head. He smelled like cocoa butter, and his skin looked oily. The dots of his pores stood out on his cheeks.

"Do you see anyone sitting there?" I snapped. He looked hurt for a moment before he sat down. He stared at me, no doubt waiting for an apology. I returned to the novel and my secret photograph. They had found a way to smooth out the lines on her face. There were no creases in her forehead or around her lips. That couldn't be right.

I heard a loud sigh, and my heart began to race.

The man with the high-pitched voice still stared at me, but he wasn't waiting for an apology. He balanced his thick book on his lap with one hand and stroked himself with the other. Our eyes locked for a moment. He didn't blink or turn away. He just kept stroking and sighing to himself.

I closed the novel, and the photograph fluttered to the ground. I bent to pick it up, unable to escape his gaze. His hand moved faster, and he nearly dropped the hardcover book. I finally turned away, tucking my picture between the pages of my novel. Tears burned in my eyes, and the people I shoved past had no faces, no lines, no shapes. They were only colors bleeding together.

I expected the man to follow me into the lobby of the library. He did not. I stared out of the glass double doors at the downpour. I didn't have an umbrella.

I thought about turning around and saying something to someone, but I could think of nothing I could say. I pictured the librarians waiting impatiently for me to form a sentence while the man continued staring at me and sighing.

I didn't want them to know what I had done. Tears of rage crept down my cheek as I pushed myself into the rain. When I got home, I had to peel the ruined photograph off the damp pages of the novel.

··

My mother told me this one.

My grandmother set him on fire.

He had no business napping when there were rows to hoe,

and he had no business starting another family with that whorish Catherine on the other side of town. My grandmother dragged the big gasoline can out of the shed, careful not to let it hit her in the belly. This baby was going to be her last, and this husband was also going to be her last.

My mother watched her. She was six years old. She was sitting under a tree, making a grass doll, alone. Her siblings didn't notice their mother struggling with the tin can and swearing under her breath.

My grandmother didn't care if anyone saw her. Sweat drenched her tight dress, and the can slipped out of her hands and crashed onto her bare toes. She swore aloud, and her eight children turned their heads to see what was the matter. She glared at them and picked up the can again. Some of the gasoline had spilled from its lips and had begun to dry on the dusty driveway.

Novella Wheeler Parker stalked into the house, her neighbor's voice buzzing in her ears: "I seen him in that haystack with that no-good Cathy. I hate to tell you, but I seen him. And she said he was her oldest baby's daddy." He had made a fool of her, and everyone in Leggett knew about it. Her cousins snickered at her in church, and her sisters shook their heads when they saw her coming up their pathways. The white man who owned their farm knew about it and was laughing at her, too.

"Berry Parker, you no-good son of a bitch!"

He rested on the couch in their living room with the television on. He opened his eyes as she lifted the gasoline can. "Nora, what—?" His pants were wet—then his shirt. He felt the warm liquid dripping into his ears and eyes.

"You think I wouldn't find out? I gave up everything for you. I could have married a grocery store owner. And I shit all these children. And you do this to me?" She didn't look down at him, but spoke to the air around her.

"I didn't tell you to shit all those children, and what are you talking about?"

She tossed the can aside and fished a box of matches out of her pocket, and his eyes widened. "You're crazy."

She still did not look at him when she struck a match against the side of the box. He scrambled to get to his feet, but she tossed the lit match into his lap before he could make his escape. The flames illuminated the blank expression on her face in the moment before he tripped out the door and into the front yard, where his children watched him roll around in their sandbox.

My mother always ended the story there. She grinned when she saw the horrified look on my face. "What's the matter? You don't believe that story?"

She had told it to me dozens of times, and I couldn't believe in it and the doll-woman in the photograph, lying in her pink satin bed. I shook my head. I liked my stories better.

"She told everyone what she did, you know. And she didn't go to jail. Nope." My mother looked proud. "Everyone kept loving her. And my father kept loving her. He stayed with her until he was dead."

[VOL. XXVI, NO. 4 / FALL 2004]

Joanna Goodman

Beginning with a Line from NPR

Birds are returning to the city, and not just
pigeons. Last week, on the steps that flame the Met,
we saw a couple: glossed purple epithets
to the morning we'd mustered

together. Obscure wing bars.
They house inside cement — martins,
wide-gaped, thin.
Then through changed air they forge

circles in a glide, like star-
lings shoot straight, without a rise
or fall. A martin flies
direct. Unsure

where to sit, what to say: we
are most ourselves in
silence. The boy, alone, dumb, pretends
nothing in my story. Plucked clean

from human form, wrapped in silk,
he's thrown back
into a clapping
tree: the tree smokes; flick.

The kerchief's done
its trick and he's a bird, put
out to live. Just once I wore a mask to breathe. Sucked
air into the drowned

or almost drowned lace
of our daughter's heart. The beat skimmed clear
across the screen. Am I anywhere
you need? These birds are called escapes.

[VOL. XXVII, NO. 1 / WINTER 2005]

Brad Kessler

One Reader's Digest

Toward a Gastronomic Theory of Literature

The first novel I ever read with gusto was Pearl Buck's *The Good Earth*. I was a late reader and a slow reader and *The Good Earth* seemed, to a child at least, a particularly daunting book. The John Day hardback came with a brick-colored cover (mine had no dust jacket) with a typeface meant to mimic Chinese characters. The pages were yellowed and deckle-edged. The book looked exceedingly thick. *The Good Earth*—which won a Pulitzer in 1932—followed the fortunes of a peasant farmer named Wang Lung in prerevolutionary China. Somewhere at the outset of the story, Wang Lung and his family nearly starve to death. The rain doesn't come; the crops fail. Wang grows appallingly thin (we can see his bones). He digs a few moldy beans from earth and devours them—but the famine only gets worse. Soon there's no food at all. I remember reading these pages with a terrible appetite. I lay in the comfort of an American suburb, the cabinets filled, TV in the other room; yet for those moments, lost in the pages of Pearl Buck, Wang Lung's hunger seemed to leak off the page and lodge itself directly in my stomach, as if it were me, and not Wang Lung, who couldn't find a thing to eat. His hunger became *mine*. Some chapters later, when Wang finally eats a handful of hot rice, and then wheat bread folded around a sprig of garlic, I could barely contain myself. I ran to the kitchen, ravenous, ransacking cupboards for white rice, jasmine tea, bags of take-out noodles (anything that seemed Chinese) trying to fill *myself* with what Wang Lung lacked. I didn't know what to do next: read or eat.

Reading *The Good Earth* had a lasting effect. For since then, reading and hunger seemed somehow inextricably bound. What I didn't know then, was *how* they were connected, only that filling oneself up with words seemed almost an alimentary activity. The novels I gravitated toward, consequently, all had a lot of eating in them. They were books in which the author rewarded his or her figures every few pages with a supper or a light repast; where, every few chapters, characters broke from the hard work of being written about, and enjoyed a meal. How—and more important *what*—they ate seemed of paramount importance. And though I've read a thousand scenes in fiction since *The Good Earth*, the ones that stay in mind the most involve eating. Names of characters fade. Plots are forgotten (even the point of the novel itself). But the meals, strangely, persist. I recall absolutely nothing of Trollope, for example, except that somewhere, in one of his Barsetshire novels, a barrister or a clergyman (I have no idea which) sits down in a grubby establishment and orders a mutton chop and a pint of sherry. Likewise, most of Henry James has slipped from mind, except for a particular oyster saloon on Seventh Avenue in *Washington Square*, where the gold-digging Morris consumes a steaming bowl of oyster stew. These scenes—the plate of mutton chops, the glass of sherry, the oyster stew—remain as vivid as a still life by Chardin. Forever colorful. Forever fresh. Forever, seemingly, edible.

Characters in novels seldom require food to survive, E. M. Forster famously observed. They hunger, as we do in life, for each other, "but our equally constant longing for . . . lunch . . . never gets reflected." Fortunately, Forster overstated the case. For there've always been authors who "reflected" quite a good deal of lunch and dinner, breakfast, and dessert. Rabelais, Flaubert, Dumas spring immediately to mind (Dumas even wrote his own *Dictionaire du Cuisine*). But the gastrorealists weren't limited to the French. Cervantes fed Sancho Panza every few chapters.

Hemingway was never chary with the details of lunch (Nick Adams's thickly sliced onion sandwiches, flapjacks slathered with apple butter). Joyce's characters enjoyed squab pigeon pasties, porksteaks, nutty gizzards, and fried hencod's roes. Burnt kidneys, fried bread, and cold pig's trotters—the list goes on.

A friend once pointed out that every good novel she'd ever read opened with a food scene in the very first or second chapter. I doubted this was the case, but then, upon investigation, found she wasn't far off: many of the greatest novels did, indeed, have a banquet, a breakfast, or a dinner in the first few pages of the book. In *Madame Bovary* food appears on page ten (a baked veal); on page twenty-four (clotted cream and stewed pears); then three pages later (an underdone leg of mutton, old cider). But all this is just an appetizer for Charles and Emma's wedding feast, which appears a short time later, and whose comestibles are limned in full by Flaubert: fricassees, stewed veals, dishes of yellow cream "that trembled with the least shake of the table," a roast suckling pig "flanked by four chitterlings with sorrel."

Likewise, hardly has *Anna Karenina* begun, when Stepan Arkadyevich and the rather prudish Levin unfold their napkins in a Saint Petersburg restaurant. Stepan asks for not one dozen, nor two . . . but *three* dozen oysters. And what kind of oysters? he asks.

"Flensburg," the waiter tells him, "we've no Ostend."

"Flensburg will do, but are they fresh?"

"Only arrived yesterday."

Stepan then orders: clear soup with vegetables, turbot with a Beaumarchais sauce, a roast beef, capons, preserved fruit, and Parmesan cheese for after.

And to drink? Tolstoy's characters debate for a moment and finally agree: the Cachet blanc champagne with the oysters. A classic Chablis for table wine.

In *Moby Dick* food arrives in the first chapter as well (broiled, buttered fowl "judgematically salted and peppered"). Nine pages on, Ishmael eats his supper at the Spouter Inn (meat and potatoes, dumplings, and scalding tea), breakfast the very next morning (beefsteak), and finally, in Nantucket, before Ishmael and Queequeg *even set foot* on the Pequod, they enter the famous Try Pots (in a chapter called "Chowder") where they eat the soup of the same name. "It was made," Melville waxes, "of small juicy clams, scarcely bigger than hazelnuts, mixed with pounded ship biscuits, and salted pork cut up into little flakes! the whole enriched with butter and plentifully seasoned with pepper and salt." One gets the feeling, Melville was definitely a pepper man.

The point I'm trying to make is that all this eating happens quite early—the first chapter or so—which raises the question: What function do these early meals serve, if any, in the narrative? Are they merely *descriptive*? Do they simply set the scene? Or like an hors d'oeuvre, do they stimulate the reader's appetite for the larger meal ahead: namely the novel itself.

Food in fiction engages all the reader's senses (taste, touch, feel, sight, and smell). So putting a meal up front, early on, might very well stimulate the salivary glands. Food also lends a concreteness, a specificity, a round tactile feel, like an apple in hand. But what, if any, are the limits to eating in fiction? Could you put too much of it in? Would the reader suffer a syntactical indigestion? On the other hand, if you left eating out altogether, would you not starve your characters, and your readers in turn, and leave all parties peaked with hunger?

I want to mention one other example of eating in an early chapter, and this from *The Odyssey*. I'd like to pay particular attention to *The Odyssey*, because the epic is, in a sense, *the* Ur-novel, the template for all novels that came after. Unlike those other books of antiquity—the Old and New Testament—which were meant, less to entertain than to instruct or inspire (or browbeat), *The Odyssey* was primarily entertainment. It was music. It was poetry—only last was it inspiration, or counsel. Though *The Odyssey*, we're told, was sung aloud in dactylic hexameter, the architecture of the epic has the sensibility of a novel. Rather: all succeeding novels have vestiges of the epic still clinging to their pages (Borges called the novel a *degeneration* of the epic). At any rate, for my purposes, I'm claiming *The Odyssey* as a work of fiction, and true to the food-in-the-first-scene theory, eating begins early in the epic.

Hardly has *The Odyssey* begun, when Athena, disguised in human form, arrives in Ithaca at Odysseus' home. Telemachus, Odysseus' distraught son, invites the goddess inside for a meal, and before they speak, according to custom, Athena is offered food. The meal serves as both the entrée into the epic, and a kind of offering to the goddess, the muses, and the reader (or listener as the case may be), inviting them all to sit down to wine, meat, and bread, before they launch into the long poem.

But the eating in *The Odyssey* doesn't end there. Nor does it end in the next chapter or in the next. Or anytime at all, really. Some *forty-two* meals occur in the epic. Since there's twenty-four chapters, or "books" in *The Odyssey*, this averages almost two meals per chapter. Fielding called *The Odyssey* the "eatingest epic," and the meals there are no light affairs, no small Greek salads, or tiramasalata on pita. In *The Odyssey* they eat barley, oats, hot loaves of bread, honeyed wine. They eat barbecued backbones, beef, mutton, goat, venison, pork, wild boar. They eat sheep cheese, goat cheese, young porkers, roasted thigh bones, apples, figs, grapes, the famous goat sausages "sizzling with fat and blood" that Odysseus, disguised as a beggar, fights for upon his return to Ithaca. Even the adversaries eat in the epic: Polyphemus (the Cyclops) dines on human brains and bones and washes them down, alternately, with sheep milk and wine. The Lystergonians eat humans. The gods of course eat ambrosia.

The typical Odyssean meal involves not only descriptions of food, but also details of their preparation:

> They quartered (the heifer) quickly, cut the thighbones out, and all according to custom wrapped them round in fat, a double fold sliced clean and topped with strips of flesh. And the old king burned these over dried split wood, and over the fire poured out glistening wine, while young men at his side

held five pronged forks. Once they'd burned the bones and tasted the organs, they sliced the rest into pieces, spitted them on skewers and raising point to the fire, broiled all the meats. They roasted the prime cuts, pulled them off the spits and sat down to the feast while ready stewards saw to rounds of wine.

So the question is: Why so much eating? Did the meals serve as introductions to stories? Did they frame the scenes? Did they act as a spur, each meal leading to the next? Let's consider one theory. Almost all the stories in *The Odyssey* are told around the table. Only after his meal in King Alcinous' court, does Odysseus begin to tell his tale of the sea adventures (the Cyclops, Circes, the sirens, Schylla and Charybdis, etc). This is the heart, for some, of the epic, and we should remember it is told *en table*, as the banqueters sit spellbound for five chapters (76 pages) until Odysseus comes to the end of his saga. Afterwards, the diners decamp, in the early hours of the morning, only to return the next day for more food and more stories.

The table in *The Odyssey* acts as the locus, not only for food, but also for stories. The word "table" comes from the Latin *tabula*: a board, plank, a flat slab "intended to receive an inscription or an account." So the table, in its own etymology, is a place for recording, for inscription, for "accounts"—not only accounts in the mathematical sense, but accounts in the narrative sense as well. The board or plank turned horizontal is a dining table, and it serves the same purpose. The table is, at any rate, an ancient framing device for storytelling. The mead hall in *Beowulf*, the Round Table of the Arthurian tales, the inn of the *Canterbury Tales* all, in varying degrees, or by suggestion, serve as the frame for stories. The Passover table is the stage for either, or both, the Seder tales or the Last Supper narrative (depending on one's perspective, or religion). The link between table and account might well have something to do with *when* stories were told, or *when* it was deemed appropriate to tell them. For the troubadour and the bard and the harpist historically entertained after a meal, around the candlelight, when the body was sated and it was time to feed the imagination. (Interestingly, an old superstition in Iraq warns that, to tell a story during the daylight hours was to risk growing horns).

If we take the etymology of "table" one step further, we find its diminutive in the Old French, *tableau*: a striking scene, a picturesque representation, produced unexpectedly and *dramatically*. Here too, we find drama in the very meaning of the word "table." Certainly artists (painters, playwrights) have employed the table as a framing device and backdrop, the meal as the canvas around which figures come and go. Turgenev's novella *First Love* is told around the table between aging gentlemen. The principal action in Joyce's *The Dead* occurs around the Christmas table at the Misses Morkan (among goose, ham, spiced beef, red and yellow jelly, blancmange, Smyrna figs, custard, etc. . .). The dining table figures often in Chekhov, in both the dramas and the short stories. The table *and* the meal *is* the centerpiece of Isak Dinesen's wonderful *Babette's Feast*. Meals are magnets; they draw people together. They are dramas, in fiction as in life. They also follow a strict narrative logic, which roughly mimics Aristotle's rule for a three-act drama: beginning (appetizer), middle (entrée) and end (dessert). If we look at the meal from a metabolic standpoint, the Aristotle model might read something like this: development (eating), crisis (digestion), and denouement (defecation). Or this:

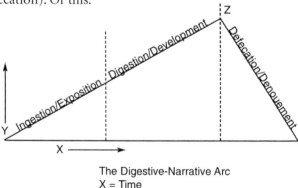

The Digestive-Narrative Arc
X = Time
Y = Drama

Few other writers in the twentieth century feature as many dinner parties in their fiction as does Virginia Woolf. Odd, it seems, since, on the surface, Woolf strikes us as a rather peckish author, a gastrominimalist to be sure. Some biographers (though not all) suggest Woolf was anorexic. Yet despite her personal eating habits—or perhaps because of them—the table for Woolf is a fertile place, a place where people imbibe mainly of each other. And while many of her books pass with slender a mention of food, she was too skilled a writer *not* to tell us, from time to time, what people actually ate.

Her two most celebrated novels, *Mrs. Dalloway* and *To the Lighthouse*, feature a meal at their very center. In *Dalloway* the novel's action builds to Clarissa's London dinner party, and in *Lighthouse* the action empties from the supper at the Ramsays' summer house in the Hebrides. In both cases, the meals serve as centerpieces, the place in which the drama is distilled.

The narrative in *Lighthouse* is told from many different points of view, from Mrs. Ramsay, Mr. Ramsay, the children (Cam, Prue, Andrew, etc.), Lilly Briscoe the painter, William Bankes the biologist, Charles Tansley "the atheist"—to name a few. We pop in and out of their heads, as they move about the house in the Hebrides, in the garden, the drawing room, the halls, the narrative passing from one to the other, like a baton, out to the beach, the bluffs, and beyond in the dunes, each character in his or her own orbit, separated by the nearly transparent membrane of his or her own consciousness. The whole action of the first part of *Lighthouse* can be read as a gradual movement toward the table, toward the meal, where the constellations briefly come into alignment and the disparate consciousnesses meld through the communion of the meal. What brings them all together is the main course, a Boeuf en Daub, Mrs. Ramsay's grandmother's recipe, cooked by the servants and overseen by Mrs. Ramsay herself. When the Boeuf en Daub is unveiled at the table, all the subterranean conflicts, intrigues, antagonisms, are briefly heightened, and then put aside, as each separate party partakes of the same flesh.

An exquisite scent of olives and oil and juice rose from the great brown dish," Woolf writes, "as Marthe, with a little flourish, took the cover off. The cook had spent three days over that dish. And she must take great care, Mrs. Ramsay thought, diving into the soft mass, to choose a specially tender piece for William Bankes. And she peered into the dish, with its shiny walls and its confusion of savory brown and yellow meats and its bay leaves and its wine, and thought, This will celebrate the occasion—for what could be more serious than the love of man for woman, what more commanding, more impressive, bearing in its bosom the seeds of death.

The "occasion" is the imminent engagement of two minor characters at the dinner table (Minta Doyle and Paul Rayley). But the occasion is also the engagement of all of them together, there in a house in summer in the Hebrides: By eating the roast, they become one body. For a novel that explores the separateness of consciousness, the table is the one place where all can commune, where all bodies connect, through food. The same might also be said for *Mrs. Dalloway*. For all the action in that novel leads to the dinner party, at the end of the book, where Clarissa and her old friends Sally Seton and Peter Walsh, and dozens of others (including the prime minister) come together to partake in each other, as well as chicken in aspic, salmon (underdone), soup, ice cream. *What* they eat is not as important as the fact that they *do* eat, that they manage, after all the aloneness and antagonisms and pain and separateness, they persist and find a way to put food in themselves. We know, for Woolf, this has special meaning, as there were times in her life when she couldn't eat at all, and was hospitalized by her illness. Just as she struggled with food and eating (and staying alive) she managed, like her characters, to find celebration, even beauty, in food and eating, despite herself.

"It is a triumph" the aloof scientific Mr. Bankes announces in *Lighthouse* after he has eaten the Boeuf en Daub. "He had eaten it attentively. It was rich; it was tender. It was perfectly cooked." The meat has melted his previous standoffishness toward Mrs.

Ramsay and the others. The meal, therefore, is as much social triumph for Mrs. Ramsay, as an epicurean one.

So what is this Boeuf en Daub that serves as the center-piece in *Lighthouse*? My *Larousse Gastronomique* has four reci-pes for Daub de Boeuf, and unlike Mrs. Ramsay's recipe, none call for olives. Larousse says a Boeuf de Daub is best prepared in a *daubiere*, which is a kind of casserole of stoneware or earth-enware or copper. It is, in other words, a pot for braising meat and vegetable, a melting pot, a kind of witches' cauldron, if you will. The feminist critic Alice Glenny suggests that the big round pot, with its mingled meats, represents a pregnant belly in which one flesh is indistinguishable from another. The stew pot alludes to the mother's gift— and specifically Mrs. Ramsay's gift—of feeding from her own body both the fetuses of her children, and all the sucklings around her, namely the communicants at the table, both male and female. Glenny argues that Mrs. Ramsay, in this regard, is a kind of fertility goddess, a Demeter, or Ceres, and the pot of meat suggests as well her sexual-marital unity with Mr. Ramsay.

That may be a lot to read into one pot roast, yet it is fair to say that food for Woolf, as with most other writers, is freighted with meaning. Just as in life, food in fiction signifies. It means more than itself. It is symbolic. It opens doors to double and triple meaning. The Invisible Man of Ralph Ellison's eponymous classic buys a hot baked yam from a stove cart on a cold night in Harlem, and the yam is as packed with meaning as it is with pulp. Eating it openly, on the street, is an act of defiance and liberation for the narrator. All the food in Ellison's novel has a semiotic quality, the cabbage soup in Miss Mary's house, the pork chop and grits breakfast he disdains (to prove he has risen above his poor southern black upbringing) while secretly longing. All of the food of his race haunts him as a kind of defeat, a humiliation. To shame his former mentor, the Uncle-Tomish Bledsoe, the nar-rator fantasizes about flogging him in public with a chain of raw chitterlings, shouting to the world that Bledsoe is "a sneaking chitterling lover," chewing hog jowls and pig ears and black-eyed peas on the sly.

On the simplest level, the yam and Miss Mary's cabbage soup serve as memory triggers in *Invisible Man*. The smell of the hot yam, bubbling in its own juice, floods Ellison's narrator with another time and place. ("I stopped as though struck by a shot," writes Ellison, ". . . At home we'd bake them in the hot coals of the fireplace, had carried them cold to school for lunch; munched them secretly, squeezing the sweet pulp from the soft peel as we hid from the teacher behind the largest book . . . candied, or baked in a cobbler, deep-fat fried, in a pocket of dough, or roasted with pork . . . the time seemed endlessly expanded.") For Ellison, food, as in life, is a transport, a vehicle for nostalgia. Smell, the librarian of the senses, stores in its stacks every odor we've ever sniffed, and leaves it there, preserved, unawakened, until we have cause to experience it again. In a way, when we talk about "craving" a certain kind of food, we're really talking about memory, about wanting to relive the past *through* food. The most celebrated unpacking of memory through food occurs, of course, in Proust. His madeleine soaked in a mouthful of lime-blossom tea awakens an entire world of memory—seven books worth. A madeleine is but a small fluted cookie made of flour, butter, eggs, and sugar (with the addition of vanilla or salt, depending on the recipe). Imagine what Proust could have done on a less meager diet, A. J. Liebling famously quipped. What kind of masterpiece might he have produced on a dozen oysters, a bowl of clam chowder, a pair of lobsters, a Long Island duck?

If food triggers memories in literature, if it can't help but be semiotic, what does it commonly signify? Carnality, appetite, desire—all the usual subjects. The perishability and baseness of the body. And, of course, sex. Eating involves putting things into our bodies, and usually when things get put into our bodies (through whichever orifice) or come out of our bodies (through whichever orifice) the activity is done in private. Eating transgresses the boundary. That it is done in public is a relatively modern phenomenon (in some countries eating in mixed company in public is still taboo). In fiction, as in life, people can be a bit squeamish about eating in front of others. It raises uncomfortable issues of body image, craving, sexuality; so it's not surprising that some authors are uncomfortable with the whole affair of eating. Some writers never have their characters eat, in public *or* in private.

Hardly anyone ever eats in an Austen novel, for example. Though there are balls and dinners and breakfasts aplenty, we never catch a Lizzie or a Jane or an Emma actually putting anything into her mouth. It's not that Austen characters are underfed; we're told about suppers all the time. But when they *do* eat, it's done furtively, hidden from the view of the reader. On the very rare occasion that Austen does mention food, it is something usually unappetizing, a plate of "cold meat" or a slightly putrified haunch of venison.

Most of the houses inhabited by Austen's characters have a specially designated "breakfast room." We hear about them in passing, in Netherfeld Hall, Northhanger Abbey, Mansfield Park, Longbourne, but we never actually *see* breakfast. Here is the closest we get, in *Northhanger Abbey*, when Catherine takes breakfast at the Tilney's:

> [Captain Tilney's] anxiety for her comfort—his continuous solicitations that she would eat, and his often-expressed fears of her seeing nothing to her taste—though never in her life before had she beheld half such variety on a breakfast table—made it impossible for her to forget for a moment that she was a visitor.

What, pray tell, did she behold on the table? Who's to know. When Austen illustrates a table, it's usually not the food she focuses on, but the china.

"The elegance of the breakfast set forced itself on Catherine's notice," Austen writes in *Northhanger Abbey*,

> . . . luckily, (the tea seat) had been the General's choice. He

243

was enchanted by her approbation of his taste, confessed it to be neat and simple, thought it right to encourage the Manufacture of his country; and for his part, to his uncritical palate, the tea was as well flavored from the clay of Staffordshire, as from that of Dresden or Sevres.

One clue to Austen's food attitude appears in *Emma*. Miss Bates confides that her niece has little appetite in the morning: "Dear Jane," she frets. "She really eats nothing—makes such a shocking breakfast, you would be quite frightened . . . how little she eats." As readers, we feel quite the same: frightened by how little *all* her characters eat. But the question remains: why does Austen never mention the particular "articles of plate"? Is eating inherently shameful, something best left off the page, like defecating, or changing underwear?

Certainly shame and eating have a long-linked history in Western culture. All the way back in Eden, when Adam and Eve ate the forbidden fruit (folk tradition has it as an apple) their immediate reaction was not delight or satiation, but humiliation: a crushing recognition of the exigencies of their bodies. Tellingly, they react by covering, not their mouths—the organs of their eating—but their genitalia. The connection at any rate is clear: Eating equals *shame*. Eating equals *sexuality*.

From Socrates to Descartes it's the same story: The body is bestial, unclean, base. The mind pure, spiritual. Socrates urged his acolytes to escape the body: ("as long as we have a body and our soul is fused with such an evil, we shall never adequately attain . . . the truth"). The body was to be conquered, controlled, governed; it was dangerous, unpredictable, a kind of *other*. Aristotle, for one, thought the body inherently female and the mind (surprise) as male. So women's bodies *especially* needed to be governed (because, among other things, of what they provoked in men). Denying the body through fasting was one path toward purity, just as celibacy was another. Christian iconography only affirmed that denial: Christ in all his imagery hasn't an ounce of adipose. (Contrast Him with Buddha Shakyumani, who is always portrayed as sated and content in his folds of body fat.)

The argument against the body found its full flowering in Victorian England. The critic Anna Silver maintains that Victorian upper-class women were supposed to appear unconcerned with food. They were to look sylph-like, and forced themselves into thinness through starvation, corsets, bodices, and stays. Slight, pale women were associated with the upper class (and spirituality), while large fleshy women suggested the lower class (and carnality). Silver argues that anorexia nervosa first appeared in upper- and middle-class Victorian households as a response to the idealization of the thin, etherealized woman. At the same time, rejecting the bounty of the table was one of the few avenues of protest open to young women: They could deny the patriarchy by simply refusing its food.

If Victorian women were supposed to display a demure appetite, it serves to reason that Victorian women *writers* would abstain from excess *writing* about food. It was one thing for Dickens or Hardy to wax about beefsteak or pudding, but quite another for George Eliot or Jane Austen. On the other side of the Atlantic, Emily Dickinson wrote over and over about her sacred hunger, but was quite happy to subsist, as she writes, on crumbs. And yet gastrominimalism, strangely, was not limited to women writers alone. How much food is ever eaten in Joseph Conrad, for example, or Nathaniel Hawthorne? Men stick cigars in their mouths all the time in Henry James, but rarely do they put anything else between their lips.

As for the characters in nineteenth-century novels, big eaters are generally associated with moral feebleness. Think of the gluttonous Gentleman of the Board in Dickens's *Oliver Twist.* Those who renounce food or eat sensibly — even better those who have no appetite at all (Kafka's Hunger Artist) — are superior, even noble. Chekhov employs food repeatedly to underscore the crassness and brutality of the aristocracy. At moments of great pique and passion, when his figures are on the brink of an enlightened thought or a grand emotion, Chekhov always has some brute stumble in and undercut the sentimentality with his stomach. There's the sexton in the short story "In the Ravine" who, "petrified with enjoyment," eats an entire jar of large-grained caviar (to everyone's horror) at a funeral. In the same story, a young woman has just lost her only child (scalded to death by a jealous rival); another priest "lifting his fork on which there was a salted mushroom" exhorts dismissively: "Don't grieve for the babe; such is the kingdom of heaven." In "Lady with Lapdog," after Gurev seduces the married Anna, he slips out of bed and greedily devours a watermelon while Anna sheds tears over what they've done. Later, when Gurev realizes he's actually in love with Anna, he's about to confess his great secret to a friend.

> "If only you knew what a charming woman I met in Yalta!" he
> confides after a Moscow dinner.
> "Dmitry Dmitrich!" the friend replies, surprised.
> "Yes," says Gurev.
> "You were quite right, the sturgeon was just a little off."

I want to look briefly at one more gastrominimalist: Let us sail swiftly now, across the Atlantic, toward another century and another author, who had an uneasy relationship with both food and women. We're in the 1930s, outside Jefferson, Mississippi, in a culture almost as coded and proscribed as Austen's. We could probably search high and low in almost any of Faulkner's works and find hardly a biscuit to nibble on, but I want to focus, briefly, on one of his best known works: *Light in August.*

It always puzzled me why an author as engaging of all the senses could get food (*and* women) so wrong. For such a descriptive author, Faulkner turns downright clamp-mouthed when food appears on his pages. To be fair, Faulkner does feed his characters, but he suffers, like Austen, from a nervous stomach. His characters smoke and drink with gusto, but eat grudgingly, almost as if it were a duty. And rarely, if ever, do we see *what* they eat.

There are several short meals in *Light in August*: the supper and breakfast the pregnant Lena eats at the Armstid's on her way to Jefferson; the bagged lunch Byron Bunch tries to offer Joe Christmas at the lumber mill; the dinner in the seedy luncheonette where Joe Christmas goes with his stepfather, Mr. McEachern. In each of these, we're never told *what* they eat. Here is a typical Faulknerian description of a meal:

> The food which McEachern ordered was simple: quickly prepared and quickly eaten . . . as soon as he laid down his knife and fork, McEachern said, come, already getting down from his stool.

Faulkner glosses over his meals because, among other things, food in his work is exclusively the domain of women. Women prepare it; women offer it; women eat it. Consequently, food seems beyond Faulkner's orbit of understanding. Yet food signifies something much darker for Faulkner. There are three women in Joe Christmas's life in *Light in August*: his stepmother, Mrs. McEachern; his waitress girlfriend, Bobbie Allen; his spinster lover, Joanna Burden. Each woman is a provider of food. But the food they provide comes with a cost. In each case, the food is sexualized, feminine, threatening, ("corrupting" *qua* Socrates). The act of desiring and eating woman's food is similar to the act of desiring woman's bodies. In both cases, the carnality is shameful.

The shame begins early for Joe Christmas. After a day of being whipped by his stepfather for not learning his catechism, the young Christmas is brought food by his stepmother, the preacher's wife. She steals into Christmas's bedroom with a tray of food "prepared in secret and offered in secret," made for the boy "against the will of the stepfather." The young Christmas takes the tray out of the woman's hands, walks to the corner, and dumps the food defiantly on the floor. He will not be feminized by the food. He will not eat the poisoned apple.

Later, Christmas lives in a shack behind the decaying mansion of the Yankee spinster, Joanna Burden. Christmas, who is half-white, halfblack, an orphan, a runaway, sneaks into the spinster's house at night, lured there like a feral cat, by plates of food left out for him by the older white woman. Night after night, he eats secretly, shamefully, until, emboldened, he creeps upstairs to Joanna Burden's bedroom. Instead of surprise or shock (or fear), Joanna Burden has expected him all along; for once Christmas has taken her food in the cover of darkness, he will take her as well, both carnal acts (eating and sex) equally secretive, equally shameful. Yet Christmas, in the end, must reject both food and women, and he does so violently. When he enters Joanna Burden's kitchen for the last time, he smashes plates of food against the wall, one by one. Interestingly, the only time we're told the specifics about the food is not when they're being eaten, but when they're being tossed. "Woman's muck" Christmas seethes, pitching plates across the room. "Ham, beans or spinach," he says, identifying each as he hurls them. "Something with onions, potatoes . . . beets." After he tosses the food, he smacks and punches Joanna Burden and then burns her house down. A dyspeptic moment to be sure. One wonders: was the food *that* bad?

Sometime after I discovered my preference for the gastrorealists, I began perusing cookbooks. If I wanted to read about food, why slog through all those scenes and plot twists in novels, just to find a sentence or two where someone actually eats? Why not cut to the chase? So I bought *Larousse Gastronomique*, the bible of French cookery, with its 1100 pages, and four-color photographs of *Hare Pâté* or *Eel en brochette*. I read Fanny Farmer and Irma Rombauer. I delved into *The Roman Cookery of Apicius* (the earliest acknowledged cookbook); I even read Platina, the Renaissance epicurean writer whose *On Right Pleasure and Good Health* was an eye opener (if not exactly a mouth waterer. His recipe for "Peacock Cooked So It Seems to Be Alive" is more decorative than appetizing). I read also the literary gourmands—Anthelme Brillat-Savarin's classic *The Physiology of Taste*, M. F. K. Fisher, Alice Toklas. Yet by and large the cookbooks themselves were disappointing. The plots were predictable (they always followed the same outline: appetizer, soup, vegetable, fish, meat, dessert). The characters (usually first person) were alternately charming, officious, or technocratic. Though cookbooks had a narratology all their own, they lacked the forward motion, the engine, the drama that food in novels offered. Oddly, the nakedness of the food itself in cookbooks, the frankness with which it was discussed, unadorned by plot or scenery, made the food seem scientific, clinical. It made the food, well . . . unpalatable. Meals limned in cookbooks did not arouse the same kind of appetite and longing that reading about them in fiction did. Was a meal surrounded by a story, then, more enticing? Did the narrative, the withholding, the slow striptease of plot and character, actually increase one's appetite? Did all the pages of noneating only make the eating seem more irresistible (as in *The Good Earth* when, after all those pages of hunger, Wang Lung, finally eats)? Either way, it seemed something enfolded or wrapped inside a narrative tasted better than simply the raw thing.

Besides, cookbooks read less like novels than collections of small, odd poems. Recipes, with their dramatic line breaks, their concern for metrics and timing (prosody), seemed to share more with poetry than narrative fiction. And a recipe, like a poem, has its own internal combustion, its own logic; a good one creates something greater than the sum of its parts. I read my *Larousse* that way, at any rate, as an anthology of odd poems translated from another language, each entry an ode. Enigmatic as a haiku. Here, for example, is a fragment (chosen almost at random) from a recipe for "Garden Warblers in the Manner of Father Fabri"—the line breaks are mine:

Garden Warblers in the Manner of Father Fabri

Put a piece of Foie gras
The size of a walnut
Studded with a piece of truffle
inside each warbler
Brown briskly in sizzling butter

simply to set the surface.

Another reads like this:

Irish Smoked Herrings

Wash and dry the Herrings
Cut off the heads.
Split the fish in half,
lengthwise.
Spread them very flat
in a deep dish,
cover with whisky and set light to them.
When the whisky has all burned away
and the flame extinguished,
The herrings are ready to eat.

They were wonderful recipes, at any rate, read side by side with the food poems of Frances Ponge, Pablo Neruda, Ogden Nash, D. H. Lawrence, or Gertrude Stein (all of whom were gastrorealists). Were the recipes in *Larousse* so very different from William Carlos Williams's "This Is Just to Say" (This is just to say / I have eaten / the plums / that were in / the icebox // and which / you were probably / saving / for breakfast // Forgive me / they were delicious / so sweet / and so cold.)?

A writer is forever trying to get his reader to taste. Taste my world, he says, smell it, ingest it. A novelist involves himself with the raw materials of the world just as a cook does with an onion, a carrot, an egg. Both the cook and the writer season and simmer their material for good long stretches, until they have accomplished something worthy (hopefully) of intake. Readers, alas, are finicky. They might taste a morsel, a sentence here, a chapter there. The trick is to convince them to stick around for the entire meal. The novelist's job (like the poet's) is to reduce experience into a fine distillation, what Rilke called "the smallest units of language." Just as a *sous*-chef reduces his stock, the writer must reduce his vision into a teaspoon of life, highly condensed, a tonic so potent that, when taken, it transforms us.

I think the real link between food and literature is that they both satisfy, not only an appetite, but a *hunger*. A hunger for words. A hunger for the lives of others, a hunger to transcend our own small selves and enter the bodies of others—different from us, yet the same—across the divide of centuries or class or culture or gender or race. Across consciousness itself. Food is the great leveler. We all need it equally as much as the other. When I read *The Good Earth* I didn't know it at the time, but I hungered not only for the food that Wang Lung lacked, but also for a connection to another time and place outside the proscribed suburb I'd grown up in. That was the transformative thing about the book, about any good book: that it transports us, that it fills in the voids, the emptiness, the terrible appetite in all of us.

"Ink runs from the corners of my mouth," the poet Mark Strand writes. "There is no happiness like mine. I have been eating poetry." But the same can be said about any good literature. We put a book inside ourselves and digest the edible bits, and jettison the rest, and if the story (or poem) is good, if it is honest, if it offers us some consolation or way of being in the world, it becomes, like bread, a part of us.

[VOL. XXVII, NO. 2 / SPRING 2005]

CARL PHILLIPS

Radiance Versus Ordinary Light

Meanwhile the sea moves uneasily, like a man who
suspects what the room reels with as he rises into it
is violation—his own: he touches the bruises at each
shoulder and, on his chest,

                  the larger bruise, star-shaped,
a flawed star, or hand, though he remembers no hands,
has tried—can't remember . . .

                        That kind of rhythm to it,
even to the roughest surf there's a rhythm findable,
which is why we keep coming here, to find it, or that's
what we say. We dive in and, as usual,

                      the swimming
feels like that swimming the mind does in the wake
of transgression, how the instinct to panic at first
slackens that much more quickly, if you don't
look back. Regret,

                like pity, changes nothing really, we
say to ourselves and, less often, to each other, each time
swimming a bit farther,

                  leaving the shore the way
the water—in its own watered, of course, version
of semaphore—keeps leaving the subject out, flashing
Why should it matter now, and *Why,*

                     why shouldn't it,

as the waves beat harder, hard against us, until that's
how we like it, I'll break your heart, break mine.

[VOL. XXVII, NO. 2 / SPRING 2005]

MAHMOUD DARWISH

Translated from Arabic by Fady Joudah

Don't Write
History as Poetry

Don't write history as poetry, because the weapon is
The historian. And the historian doesn't get fever
Chills when he names his victims and doesn't listen
To the guitar's rendition. And history is the dailiness
Of weapons prescribed upon our bodies. "The
Intelligent genius is the mighty one." And history
Has no compassion so that we can long for our
Beginning, and no intention so that we can know what's ahead
And what's behind . . . and it has no rest stops by
The railroad tracks for us to bury the dead, for us to look
Toward what time has done to us over there, and what
We've done to time. As if we were of it and outside it.
History is neither logical nor intuitive that we can break
What is left of our myth about happy times,
Nor is it a myth that we can accept our dwelling at the doors
Of judgment day. It is in us and outside us . . . and a mad
Repetition, from the catapult to the nuclear thunder.
Aimlessly we make it and it makes us . . . Perhaps
History wasn't born as we desired, because
The Human Being never existed?
Philosophers and artists passed through there . . .
And the poets wrote down the dailiness of their purple flowers

Then passed through there ... and the poor believed
In sayings about paradise and waited there ...
And gods came to rescue nature from our divinity
And passed through there. And history has no
Time for contemplation, history has no mirror
And no bare face. It is unreal reality
Or unfanciful fancy, so don't write it.
Don't write it, don't write it as poetry!

[VOL. XXVII, NO. 3 / SUMMER 2005]

BEI DAO

The Rose of Time

when the watchman falls asleep
you turn back with the storm
to grow old embracing is
the rose of time

when bird roads define the sky
you look behind at the sunset
to emerge in disappearance is
the rose of time

when the knife is bent in water
you cross the bridge stepping on flute-songs
to cry in the conspiracy is
the rose of time

when a pen draws the horizon
you're awakened by a gong from the East
to bloom in echoes is
the rose of time

in the mirror there is always this moment
this moment leads to the door of rebirth
the door opens to the sea
the rose of time

[VOL. XXVII, NO. 4 / FALL 2005]

RED HAWK

The Idea of Crocodiles

i have spent a good portion of my adult life
observing the connection between
thought and suffering,
between the mind's ability to imagine

and hold onto an idea in memory,
and the inherent fear which drives that process.
For example, we are in Lake Village on a bayou,
a body of water left by the Arkansas River

as it meandered toward the Mississippi then
changed its mind and took another route but
left behind this idea of a river, the memory of it.
We are preparing to swim in it when the old black man

fishing near us says, They's crocs in there.
How do you know, i quiz him?
Seen one once, he replies and that
is that. We

do not go in. i don't ask him how long ago
he saw one, it would not matter if it was 50 years,
and only one, and it long dead, because
the imagination has got hold of it and

now the crocodiles exist and
we are afraid of them.

[VOL. XXVII, NO. 4 / FALL 2005]

Reginald Shepherd

Kinds of Camouflage

For Robert Philen

1. Déjeuner, with Herbs

Then I am sitting naked on damp grass
(it rained in my yesterday)
while two white gentlemen
in black frock coats share lunch
around me, passing chèvre, cold andouille,
and baguettes, passing bon mots
in French, in someone's nineteenth century,
my muddled impression of one. I can't
understand a word. There must be
a picnic basket somewhere, lined with
a red-and-white-checked cloth,
some visual cliché, although
I know the cloth's pale blue, pale echo
of a sky that isn't there. They hardly
notice me (two men now passing apples, and
a bottle of medium quality red wine), or no,
I exaggerate, they don't see me
at all, my body naked to the breeze
too cold for noon although it may
be May; my skin responds
in kind and gets no answer, a situation
I am used to. Browned warmth of my flesh
tones is quickly cooling, and the day

is downcast, overcast: the basket's
been tipped over, grapes, peaches,
and some fruit I can't make out
spill over, shadowing green. I hate poems
about food. I am a painting
by now, varnish-smudged and darkening
in storage, and getting hungry fast.

2. Field Guide

Above the highway we drove home
between two hills of snow (from one
classical town to another), a bird
you couldn't recognize at first
when I asked, *What is that?*
Something trailing confused you,
threw you off track, a streamer,
scrap of dragon kite, festoon or
crimson plume. *Oh, it's a red-tailed
hawk, with something caught
I can't make out. Dinner, anyway.*
A piece of will defeated
in the wind, some little life's
fluttered surrender. Perhaps
a red squirrel, rare color
around here (you told me
that), I could have thought
but didn't. The hawk
won't be hungry for long, we're almost
home. It will be again.

[VOL. XXVIII, NO. 2 / SPRING 2006]

Cathy Song

Cloud Moving Hands

Cloud moving hands,
hand moving clouds —
in the water, boundaries shift,
the skin sheds its tight perspective,
stretched into a vast shimmering.
I enter the sea to the level
where my vision brims at the surface.
The position of swimmers and small
boats skim across the field,
supported by an imperceptible current.
On a platform a woman performs
a series of movements.
She seems to float yet remain
deeply grounded.
She appears to be walking on water.

With one kick,
I bob between earth and sky,
suspended in a blue globe,
gently rocking.
Everything is as it should be.
To leave the body
when it is time
must be like this,
nothing more than giving one's self
over to what is always
holding us, the soft lapping.

My mother lies on her back,
compressed into a pocket of bones.
At the appointed hour,
nurses flip her to one side
and then the other, to release
the pressure such tiny bones
leave on the skin, sores
that leak like grapes.
When they roll her over, her eyelids
flash open like a doll's.

I drift, and in drifting, think of her.
I surround her with a circle of light.
Out of this intention,
the girl who has smiled at me
from the picture on my desk
emerges, vibrant and lithe, just shy
of sixteen, a year before she is to meet my father.
She slips out of bed, hair curled, already
dressed, as if she has been waiting
for the signal.

She sheds the old body
like a nightgown she is sick of wearing.
She walks out the door,
down the sunlit hall, like a teenager
tiptoeing past her parents' room.
Once safely by the nurses' station,
she begins to run.
I am afraid in her haste
she will not remember me,
but she does.
She does remember.
She turns and waves.
And then, into the skylight

she leaves in earnest,
she exits,
swimming toward the surface.

Clouds move hands,
hands move clouds—
gently lifted, gently supported.
Everything is as it should be.
I stroke through air,
I fly through water,
I send my mother home.

[VOL. XXVIII, NO. 2 / SPRING 2006]

EAMON GRENNAN

Night

What to make of night, then, its caul of stars sequined and —
for all their fixture — unsteady as breath, able to be winked out
by the smallest cloud? Night, scratched at by traffic, a chirrup
or two from frog or dark-flying bird. Night with a dash
of cut grass, parched earth, the skunk that gave today his life up
to the blind hunger of trucks thundering up Main Street, his
aftermath tainting our air, making sure we won't forget his wild
flight and how we caught him short between one safe hedgerow
and another, left his ebony and vanilla body tucked into itself
beyond all remedy at the edge of the road, gathering the risen,
exploratory dust. Our cats know night for what it is — a dark
skinless beast with blazing eyes, a mouth soft as sleep but open
to swallow their ambition, a gigantic companion they can lie beside,
the one who covers for them and out of whose shadow they spring
to bring the little infant of night — field mouse or streaked
        chipmunk —
in their teeth, greeting its one last horizontal high-pitched cry:
Oh mother it is too late! Now night: last notes before the daughter
of the house calls it a day, closes the music, goes to bed, so when
the father gets home, he'll find the front door locked, a note
in an unknown hand pinned to the lintel: *Night comes down,
nothing to be done. Try again. Keep trying.* He looks around.

[VOL. XXVIII, NO. 3 / SUMMER 2006]

DON LEE

A Preference for Native Tongue

It's her last night in Tokyo, her last night with Junichiro, and although they have promised to see each other again, somewhere, sometime very soon, Elsa knows this probably won't be the case, and she thinks Jun knows this, too. Maybe that is why the evening is infused with such delicious melancholy, a well of yearning and nostalgia—false as it may be—that makes it hard to swallow, nearly bringing tears whenever one of them dislodges the blandest statement.

"The train is very crowded today," Jun says to her, and they almost crumble.

They are riding the Yamanote Line to Meguro, to a *tonkatsu* restaurant called Tonki. They've decided not to do anything particularly special tonight—well, with one exception—thinking it will be more meaningful to do what they've always done. It's the summer of 1982, the year of the Falklands War, the U.S. embargo of Libya, Israel's invasion of Lebanon, the deaths of John Belushi and John Cheever. The latter has affected Jun greatly. He loves Cheever's short stories. He is finishing his junior year studying literature at Todai—Tokyo University—and dreams of a career translating American fiction. For a few months this winter, Jun took private lessons with Elsa, who has spent the past year after college teaching conversational English at one of Tokyo's many *eikaiwa* schools.

As always, there is a wait at Tonki's, but they don't mind. It's all part of the experience. While they are in line outside, a waiter takes their orders—both opting for the *hirekatsu teishoku*, of course—and once they are inside the door, they sit among the chairs against the walls and happily watch the cooks working in the open kitchen. It's a wonderful bit of theater. The men rapidly bread and dip the pork no less than three times in batter, then deep-fry the cutlets in two different pots of oil, all with maniacal precision and the most profound solemnity. When Elsa and Jun are seated at the counter, they're served cold beers and peanuts, and, in less than a minute, their orders come—the *tonkatsu* and sauce and *miso*, the pickles and rice and shredded cabbage, the last two of which may be replenished at will. The *tonkatsu* is heavenly, crunchy on the outside, moist inside, so good they can't slow down to savor the meal, eating and eating. Still ravenous, they look at each other, laugh, and order an extra cutlet.

From Tonki's, they get back on the Yamanote Line for two stops to Harajuku, then meander down Omotesando-dori to walk off the meal. It's a stifling summer night—oh, the humidity. Within a block, Elsa's shirt is damp, and Jun is sweating rather heavily in his suit jacket, a Kawabuko knockoff. He's dressed in all black, as is au courant, making him a member of the so-dubbed *karasu-zoku*. The crow tribe. The jacket has upside-down pockets, sleeves that extend past his fingers, and looks as if it has been turned inside-out, frayed seams exposed. Needless to say, Jun—in contrast to Elsa, with her practical Midwestern tastes—is quite the fashion plate. He keeps tugging her to windows of boutiques along the boulevard.

Finally they make it to Minami-Aoyama, down a narrow alley that leads to a cramped, steep staircase, at the bottom of which is their favorite bar, North Beach. It's a funky neo-beatnik place modeled after Vesuvio's in San Francisco. Years later, Elsa will go to the real Vesuvio's with her first husband and see how close an approximation this bar is, down to the shambling wood chairs and café tables, the memorabilia and curios, the murals of Baudelaire, Rimbaud, and Bob Kaufman, even the sign from Jack

Kerouac Alley that reads "Beware pickpockets and loose women." And, of course, they have the drink here, Vesuvio's famous Jack Kerouac drink, tequila and rum mixed with orange and cranberry juice. Jun asks the waiter for two Jack Kerouacs after they find a table near the back, and then they relax in the air-conditioned dimness and talk, fingers twined.

"Tell me what you're going to do with your life," Elsa says.

"I am going to have many, many adventures," Jun says, and he vows that he will go to Harvard and get his doctorate and become friends with many writers, and then will live in the Village, where he will translate books, traveling frequently to Europe, occasionally accompanying authors to Tokyo on their tours. "What I like about American literature," Jun has told Elsa, "is that it is subversive. Japanese literature cannot be so subversive."

Now, in the bar, over the Coltrane playing on the turntable, he says expansively, "I will bring the infection of American books to the Japanese people!"

At first, Elsa — still the teacher — thinks "infection" is a malapropism, but then she reconsiders. It's the perfect word, a clever if unintended metaphor.

"Tell me what you will do," Jun says.

Elsa has so many plans. She is a humble, big-boned Swedish girl from Minnesota. Her father is a pharmacist, her mother works in an insurance office. Her brother manages conferences at a hotel. One sister is a housewife, the other fields calls at a mail-order company. Yet Elsa's parents, former campaign workers for Hubert Humphrey, have instilled in all their children a respect for public service, a passion for progressive, humanistic values, and Elsa will be going to the University of Minnesota for her law degree in two months. She wants to become a civil rights attorney. She wants to argue discrimination cases in front of the Supreme Court. She wants to help pass the Equal Rights Amendment.

"I will bring the infection of equality to the American people," she tells Jun, to which he raises his clenched fist into the air and says, "*Ganbatte!*"

"When we are fifty," he tells her, "we will meet and have an affair."

"I'll be fat."

"No, you will not."

They are a little drunk when they leave the bar. Elsa remembers her camera. She has taken so few photos in her year in Tokyo. Originally she wanted to go to Morocco, or Turkey, or India, somewhere truly exotic, but her parents worried for her safety, and her cousin, who once taught at the same *eikaiwa* school, reassured them that Tokyo, if anything, was safe. A little too safe, Elsa reflects, not challenging her comfort levels much, although maybe this is specious hindsight, a form of braggadocio. After all, before Japan, her only excursions outside the United States were family trips across the border to Canada.

She poses Jun on Aoyama-dori and snaps a shot with the flash, after which he pretends to have been blinded, shuffling toward her with outstretched arms.

They catch the subway at Omotesando for the short ride to Akasaka and walk up the hill to Palace Wales. Jun lives at home, and Elsa has been staying at a *gaijin* house in Suginami, so this love hotel is an indulgence of privacy. Palace Wales indeed looks like a British castle on the outside, but inside they have their pick of themes. In the lobby, they examine the lighted panel of room photos, and after careful consideration they press the two-hour "rest" button for Sunset Strip, an homage to art deco. In the room, it's all pastels and black marble. There are zebra-patterned velvet wing chairs and George Nelson bubble lamps, spelter sculptures of women and gazelles, lacquered wood screens. A reproduction of Tamara de Lempicka's *Sleeping Woman* hangs over the bed, and the glass-blocked bathroom features a huge claw-footed tub, which, despite its faux-antiquity, incorporates hidden pressure jets.

They get into the tub, and, facing one another, they do things beneath the surface with their feet, smirking. When they dry each other off with the hotel's plush towels, Elsa admires Jun's body.

He's her first Japanese lover, her first lover ever, in fact, who is not white. Except for his head and the profusion of coarse, straight strands in his armpits and on his genitals, he is completely hairless, his skin smooth and unblemished, paler than her own. His body is muscular but without definition, without shape or protrusion, thin and rectilinear, an unearthly, exquisite plank. He has only one distinguishing mark, a birthmark that looks like an indigo inkblot on his lower back. Jun has told her it's called a Mongolian blue spot, common among Asian babies. The spots, which can resemble bruises, usually shrink and disappear by adolescence, but Jun's never quite did, leaving a vestige the size of a nickel. Many years from now, this information will prove useful to Elsa. A Korean client will take her baby to the hospital because of a fever, and a callow intern will summon child protection services after seeing the blue spots, thinking Elsa's client has been abusing the baby.

They sprawl onto the French bed, which has scalloped head- and footboards made of burr walnut. There's no mirror on the ceiling, thank God, with which the hotel equips most of its rooms, but as Elsa and Jun begin to make love, they discover, to their shock and hilarity, that their room is rigged with lasers that shoot over the bed when one of them moans.

"Turn it off, turn it off!" Elsa laughs as Jun scampers about, looking for the sensor switch.

"*Kuslo*," Jun swears, starting to lose his erection. He locates the control console and says, "*Hayaku, hayaku,*"—hurry, hurry—and, grinning, leaps back onto the bed.

Years and years later, Elsa will find the photograph of Jun on Aoyama-dori that night, grinning at the camera. Because of the flash and his black clothes, he will be disembodied, only his face and right hand, raised in a victory sign, visible. She will, of course, wonder what has become of him then. They will have stopped writing to each other long ago. She will know that he studied for a brief time at the University of Texas, and though he enjoyed the music scene in Austin and was popular with the girls, he felt dislocated. He will have moved back to Tokyo and found a job at a publishing company, albeit not involving literature, and then quit and begun working in advertising for the fashion industry, and that will be the last Elsa hears of Jun.

He scoots down on the bed for what she likes best. He has a special technique that dements her. After repeated inquiries, he revealed what he does down there. With his tongue, he is lightly tracing the *hiragana* and *kanji* characters that comprise the translated opening for *The Great Gatsby*: "In my younger and more vulnerable years . . ."

There is so much that Elsa doesn't know yet. She does not know she will never leave the Twin Cities. She does not know about her father's Alzheimer's or her best friend's son being blown apart by a rocket-propelled grenade or her sister's car getting T-boned by a drunk driver and leaving her a paraplegic. She does not know about the mindless infidelities and small heartaches and everyday betrayals — ordinary tragedies that abuse and ravage one's faith, yet constitute a life. She will never file an appellate brief or work for the ACLU or the Southern Poverty Law Center. She will be an attorney, part-time, for a small nonprofit legal aid center in Minneapolis and specialize in immigration law, most of her clients Hmong, Laotian, Somali, Mexican, and Russian. It will be noble, important work, but a drudgery in many ways, processing applications for green cards, work permits, deportation stays, asylum claims. She will marry and divorce twice. First a public defender (African American), then a photojournalist (Chicano), with whom she'll have one son each. During the second birth, she will nearly hemorrhage out, and then two months later will almost die again because of a missed piece of placenta. They will tell her that, because of the scars in her uterus, she will never be able to conceive again, which will make her pregnancy with twins eight years later a bit of a surprise. She will not marry the girls' father, an ESL teacher (Japanese American), skittish about the institution, but will live with him, reasonably happy, hoping she is doing some good, doing her part, however small it might be. But occasionally, although she will try not to, she will be struck more by what she hasn't done than what she has. She will forget sometimes that she also knows about love, the virtue of patience and forgiveness, and about joy, the pleasure of being with those closest to her, family, friends, comrades, these beautiful children no one ever believes are hers, picnicking with them alongside Lake Harriet on a warm, clear, breezy day, hearing their easy laughter, the reassurance of their safety.

Jun senses where she is and presses a little faster, harder. She wants it to last forever, this feeling—youth, time, glory, everything still before her, waiting, her extraordinary life—but she feels it rolling over her and gives in to it.

"Oh, that was good," she says. "That was so good."

[VOL. XXVIII, NO. 3 / SUMMER 2006]

Life Expectancy

Coach Theo Burke was standing outside his classroom during break when he noticed Josie across the hall, pinned up against a locker. One of the varsity basketball players, Jatarius, was doing the pinning—his near-seven feet making Josie seem almost short in comparison, big hands straddling her shoulders, too-handsome black face leaned in to kissing distance. The worst thing—the thing that felt like a punch in the gut—was the look on Josie's face, a look Theo knew. Her head was tilted, and she was smiling, but just a little: that smart smile, that sexy half-smile with the bottom lip barely caught under her front teeth, an expression that Theo recognized as the smallest bit calculated but mostly genuine. Mostly the only way Josie knew how to be.

He strode over, hands shoved so deep in his khakis that his watch got caught on one side. He cleared his throat.

"Jatarius," Theo said.

"Yeah." A slow breath, dusky, directed on Josie and not at him.

"Move it along."

Jatarius pulled to a slow stand, languid, his skin gleaming as if oiled. "Just talking, Coach," he said, and Josie giggled. Theo turned to her, and she looked away.

"You're supposed to be swapping books now, not talking," he said, realizing as he said it how ridiculous—how *old*—he sounded. Josie was losing interest in him, and all he had to cling to was his authority as her teacher and her coach. Her better. And how false that felt, watching her, knowing what her breasts looked like beneath that T-shirt and hooded sweatshirt: small, spread apart—a tall girl's breasts.

Jatarius pulled his bookbag up over his shoulder. "See ya," he told Josie, and she fluttered her fingers at him as he sauntered off.

"What are you doing?" Theo whispered, looking around to make sure nobody was watching them.

She tried to laugh again, but her voice caught a little, and she stopped. Her eyes were over-bright, her shoulders stiff, but she smiled—for him, for the group of girls crossing behind him. "I'm pregnant, Coach," she said. She opened her mouth, then closed it again. She shrugged.

The bell rang, and Theo turned to his classroom, to twenty-six sophomores waiting to learn about the Fertile Crescent, the first bloom of civilization.

• •

Abortion, she told him. Soon, now, so I don't have to miss any game time. Right away. Yesterday.

"All right," Theo said, fanning the air with his palms, that implied *calm down* that he gave students when they freaked out about a bad test score or got into fights. He and Josie were in his coach's office. He'd let practice out early that day, after only an hour. Josie had seemed normal—made her warm-up sprints at top speed, missed only a single basket as they ran figure-eights—but he could barely concentrate enough to follow the action or to guide the girls to the next drill. They looked the same out there in their practice jerseys and white high-tops: lanky girls with brown ponytails and acne. Only Josie stood out, her gold hair alight under the gym's fluorescents. Only Josie seemed real. "All right, slow down. Give me a minute."

She looked at her hands, as if she were counting off the seconds. "Antibiotics," she said finally. "I was sick over Christmas break. That's what did it."

Theo was thinking: *baby*. He had a baby, and a wife. His

273

baby was eleven months old, and they called her Sissy, short for Cecily. Five months ago they found out that her breathing problems were caused by cystic fibrosis, which turned the name—their affection—into a lousy pun, a cruel joke. "Wait," he said. "What? Did what?"

"The antibiotics affected the pill," she said. "I looked it up on the Internet. At least I'll know better from now on."

"From now on?"

"Jesus," she said. "I'm eighteen. I'm not going to stop having sex."

"I'm just saying," Theo said. He wondered, despite himself, if she would want to have sex with him again.

She pulled a package of gum out of her purse and unwrapped a piece. "I'm just ready to get this over with," she said, now chewing. "I've got a lot to worry about. School and all."

"Of course," Theo said. She was going to WKU in the fall, a full ride. He had helped her get it. He had posed with her, her mother, and Western's basketball coach three months ago when they signed the letter of intent, and the photo ran in the *News Leader*. "Cute girl," his wife had said when she saw it. And Theo—who was already meeting Josie for fast screws in his office and his car and a few times at her house, when her mother was pulling seconds at the sewing factory—only nodded.

Now Josie sat in the chair opposite Theo's, the desk between them, and played with the end of her thick, yellow braid, wanting, he saw, to put it into her mouth. He'd done his best to tease her out of that habit, seeing it as the one solid piece of evidence between them—other than the obvious facts of their positions as teacher and student—that being together was scuzzy and wrong, an embarrassment to them both. Because in so many other ways, it hardly seemed like a problem at all. She'd turned eighteen in December, and she was about to graduate. She was mature. She had a good future ahead of her. There was the infidelity, but Theo tried, with some success, to keep his home life and school life separate, and it seemed to him that he was

OK—getting by, at least—as long as he was able to do what had to be done in both lives. He was an average teacher, but better than most coaches: he liked his World Civ sections, tolerated Kentucky Studies, and at least he wasn't just popping a movie in the VCR every day like Mathias, the boys' basketball coach, who famously screened *Quigley Down Under* for his freshman geography students during their Australia unit. He thought that he was a better than average father, at least most of the time. He'd hoped for a son, sure—pictured a boy all those years he and Mia were trying and failing to conceive, a boy to play basketball with and to fish with, all of the clichés. But he'd been happy with his girl, and if her delicacy dismayed him a little—how could it not?—in so many ways, it only made him love her more.

Some days, driving home from work, he thought, *I have a house*, and was instantly filled with pride. House, yes—he was a man, all right. *I have a wife. I have a child.* Before coming in the front door, he could picture all three, house, wife, daughter, as they ought to be: clean, happy, healthy. *This is my life*, he'd think, and then he'd open the door.

"My mom probably wouldn't be too upset if she knew," Josie said. "She likes you. She doesn't get hung up on stuff like you being a teacher. She'd take care of it if she had the money to, but she doesn't."

"How much?" Theo asked.

Josie shook her head. "I don't know yet. I'm not sure what to do."

"I'm not either," Theo said. How much was an abortion? Two hundred dollars? A thousand? He tried to imagine withdrawing that much money from the checking account without Mia noticing. Mia was in her own world a lot of the time these days, but she could surprise him with her sudden sharpness, awareness.

"But you'll take care of this, right?" Josie said. She was going to cry, he was sure. *Put the braid in your mouth*, he thought. *Do it if that'll shut you up.* "Right?" Josie said.

No less than five hundred, he bet. But he could scrounge it up. Mathias might loan it to him out of his pot fund. He could pay it back slowly that way, twenty this week, fifty the next. There wasn't any question, though; it had to be done. His job paid for shit—and he'd have to work tobacco this summer, probably, just to make ends meet—but it was all he had, and the insurance was good. He couldn't lose that. Not with Sissy to worry about.

"OK," Theo told her. "You get the information and set it up, and I'll pay for it."

"And drive me," Josie said. "I can't ask Mama to do that."

"I'll drive you, too," Theo said.

She pulled the rubber band off the end of her braid and raked her fingers through the thick weave of her hair, setting it loose. It ran over her shoulders, halfway down her back, wavy and almost iridescent. Rapunzel hair, he'd always thought. Her nose and cheeks were freckled, and she had that balance between strength and delicacy that most of his girl athletes lacked. Miraculous.

"We could have sex," she said, almost with resignation.

He nodded.

. .

When Sissy's cystic fibrosis was confirmed, the doctors threw a lot of numbers at Theo and Mia, too many to make sense of. Life expectancy. Percentage of cases in the U.S. Chances of this, chances of that. But the fact that stayed with Theo—the data that confirmed for him everything wrong with his marriage and his life—was this: a child could only get the disease if both parents carried a defective gene. Defective, the doctor's word. Dr. Travis—the first of several—told them this in his wood-paneled office with the dark green carpeting, and Theo could remember thinking he, Mia, and Sissy, who was too small at six months but still porcelain-pretty, were lost in the woods together. He and Mia, two unknowing defectives, had somehow found each other, beaten the odds, and brought forth a child who was drowning in her own chest because the two of them should never have been together in the first place.

When he came home that night, Mia was in the old recliner, Sissy in her lap, and they were rocking, watching TV. Mia's bare foot bobbed above the floor, keeping time. The house was filthy, and Theo was nauseous at the smells that assaulted him as soon as he walked in the door: soured food stuck to the dishes that were piled up on the kitchen countertops; the heavy metallic tang of piss, where the toilet hadn't been flushed; and shit, too, he was sure of it. Maybe the baby's, but probably the dog's. Mia took care of Sissy to the point of obsession, but she seemed to forget that they had a dog—a Beagle mix they'd gotten for free from an unplanned litter—though bringing him home was her idea. She'd read in some magazine that dog owners had longer life expectancies, and cancer patients with dogs more often went into remission or had spontaneous recoveries. He didn't ask her how the cancer thing was supposed to apply to their daughter.

"Smells like crap in here," Theo told her, setting his briefcase and duffel bag down by the front door.

"I hadn't noticed," Mia said. "Baby-Girl's clean." As if in support, Sissy erupted into one of her chants: *ma ma ma ma ma MAAAA!* Theo picked Sissy up and kissed her clean neck, trying to fill his nose with her scent. She hooked her small hand and paper-thin fingernails into his ear and twisted. "Ma," she said again.

"I hear you," Theo told her.

"Might be the dog," Mia said. She kept watching TV, and Theo knew what she was thinking just as clearly as if she'd spoken out loud: *You'll take care of this, right?*

Theo put Sissy down, his stomach already starting to churn. "I'd say that's the most likely option." He whistled and walked around, trying to find the source of the smell. "Joe!" he yelled, whistling again. The odor, thick, sickly, seemed to be everywhere at first; then he rounded a corner, and it hit him like an arrow, coming from the bedroom. He got down on his knees and looked under the bed.

"Christ," he said. "Fuck."

Joe was in the corner, far from the bed as he could get, and Theo could see the fast rise and fall of the dog's stomach. "Hey, boy." The dog cowered at first — his eyes, so eerily human, rolled up at him warily — then let Theo lift him. He packed Joe into the living room like a baby.

"Dog's sick," he told Mia.

She nodded.

"Did he get into something?"

"I don't know. He was out back for a few hours. Maybe he got into the garbage." She was watching the TV around him. "Poor boy," she said without interest. "Should we take him to the vet?"

"Probably just needs to finish his business," Theo said, and he put the dog out. In the low light, he could see Joe make a slow circle in the backyard, then lie down. He went back inside and tried his best to clean up the mess, using every chemical he could find under the kitchen sink, moving the bed and pulling up the corner of the carpet so he could get to the pad and sub-floor, too. The smell lingered, and he opened a window.

In the living room, Mia hadn't moved. He sat on the couch and watched what she was watching: a cooking show. Not a regular show, though, like his own mom had watched on PBS when he was in high school — *The Frugal Gourmet* or that one with the old Cajun guy, Justin Wilson — the shows where somebody stood behind a counter and cooked the food regular-style. This show had a fattish woman with brown hair, and she looked to be in her own house, because the sunlight seemed real and not put on. The camera zoomed in as she dropped an egg into a mixing bowl, which you didn't see happen on Justin Wilson.

"What is this?" he asked her.

"My favorite show," Mia said. Her voice was dreamy. "This woman owns a restaurant in New England. She cooks very simple foods. She doesn't use margarine, only butter."

"Margarine's better for you," Theo said.

"Not true," Mia told him. They watched as the woman dipped a fancy silver measuring cup into a bowl of sugar. *This dish is fragrant and delicious*, the woman was saying.

"Margarine is a trans fat, which doesn't break down in your system. Natural foods are better," Mia said.

"Why do you like this so much?" Theo asked. The woman was grating lemon peel.

Mia stroked Sissy's arm as she talked. "Her hands. She has such clean hands and fingernails. And her sugar, it doesn't just look like sugar."

Her medication. She'd been a mess since Sissy's birth — postpartum depression, her doctor had said — and she had just started to come back, to be herself again, when Sissy was diagnosed. Her meds were a square dance at this point: Prozac helped for a while, then made her worse than ever. Paxil worked, but they couldn't get the dosage regulated, and the doctor warned them that taking her off it early would result in a major crash. They'd gone on a date a few weeks ago — left Sissy with Mia's mother, tried to dress up and make a night of it — and at the movie, *Million Dollar Baby*, Mia had stared, emotionless, through all the parts that would have had her sobbing a few years before. Theo had asked her what she thought of it on their drive home, and she seemed confused by her own answer — or not even confused, exactly. Perplexed. Like the changes in her were a cause for a scientific kind of curiosity and nothing else. *I don't know what I thought of it,* she'd said. *I could see that it was sad, but I didn't feel sad. It was intellectual. Is this what being a man is like?*

"Looks like sugar to me," Theo said now.

"Figures."

"You could try making that," Theo told her. "Doesn't look hard. I bet it's real good."

Mia kept rocking. "No, I couldn't do it," she said.

Theo left her and went to the kitchen, unbuttoning his shirt cuffs and rolling up the sleeves to his elbows. He started organizing the dishes and cleaning the counters, pitching empty Lean Cuisine boxes and a Tropicana carton and Ramen noodle bags into a Hefty sack. He couldn't get Josie out of his head, not even for a second. Too easy to think of her, to feel her warm hips between his hands even as he plunged his hands into scalding dishwater. He pictured her in the hallway that morning, with Jatarius, and tried to remember the exact look on her face. *You'll take care of this, right?*

He noticed the wet circle in the driveway as he was taking out the trash, but the detail didn't click into place until he was closing the lid of the garbage can, and he realized that Joe wasn't there to meet him. It occurred to him that there *wasn't* any strewn garbage out back, any sign of disturbance at all, and he remembered the wet spot then — not oil, not water, but anti-freeze, leaked out while his car was warming up that morning. He peered into the dark shadows of the far corner of the yard, where the security light didn't hit. "Joe," he said. "Joe, old boy."

There was a tire propped up against the toolshed — Theo had been meaning to take it to the rubber yard for months now — and he found Joe curled up in the space between it and the concrete wall, the thin scrim of green foam on his jowls barely visible in a sliver of moonlight. "Joe," Theo said. He looked at the still body. "Joe," he said again.

· ·

The first time he kissed Josie was in August, two weeks before Sissy's diagnosis. Someday, he might be able to blame the whole affair on his difficult home life, on the fear of losing his baby girl before she could have a home and family of her own. Someday, he might be able to forget that those two weeks existed.

When it happened, though, he wasn't thinking of Sissy, or of Mia. He'd known Josie for four years by then, pulling her from Jayvee when she was still in eighth grade — she was that talented — and letting her start power forward on her first game as a high school student. He had recognized in her that quality which would later attract him: the blend of rawness and refinement, power and grace. In the beginning, though, she'd only seemed a grand kind of experiment. What could he turn her into?

The girls came in for mandatory weightlifting in the summer and through September, before real practice started, and the kiss came after one of these late-afternoon sessions. She was telling him about her father—how he left her mother in June to move to Nashville with his new girlfriend, a thirty-year-old wannabe country singer. How her mother had been struggling since then to make ends meet. She wasn't crying, but Theo could tell she wanted to, and the desire he felt for her—until this moment hypothetical and even harmless, like a childhood crush—was overwhelming. So he kissed her. He did it because she looked like she needed it. He did it because he knew he could get away with it.

Now, two days after the dog's death, Theo was determined to make it through a full practice without stopping early or fading out mid-speech, which had been his habit since Josie dropped her news. Some of the girls were beginning to look at him strangely, though he actually wondered more about the ones who weren't. He wondered if Josie had told a friend about them, and if that friend had told a friend. She had always promised him complete secrecy, but he'd worked with young girls long enough to understand how unlikely that was, especially among teammates. Before the news of her pregnancy, he and Josie had fallen into a strange sort of complacency with one another, an ease that he was now terrified to remember. How careless they had been—with the sex, of course, but also with too-long looks, knowing smiles, risky, ridiculous moments between classes when they passed in the hall and let their fingers brush. They should have been caught already, he knew. They would get caught.

On the court, the girls were running a pass drill. Josie caught the ball, made it around Lisa in three easy strides, and pistoned upward, sinking a two-pointer. She landed hard, and Theo felt his heart wallop. "Josie?" he said.

Her expression was bewildered. "What?"

"Are you OK?"

"Yes," she said testily, already dribbling again.

He'd buried Joe in the backyard, not far from the spot where he died. Mia cried, which was more emotion than Theo could remember seeing from her in a while. He'd dug the grave; then, still sweaty and dirt-streaked, he'd hosed the greasy patch in the driveway, watching the liquid blur, blend, then run off into the grass, indistinguishable from a light rain. *I couldn't have known he'd gotten into that,* Mia had said, and Theo had only stripped off his old UK sweatshirt and blue jeans, wadding them into a ball and throwing them in the hamper. His muscles, once so long and powerful, ached now. *Sissy was coughing again, and I had my hands full. You know how it is.* He'd nodded and started the shower running. *It was your car, for fuck's sake.*

The girls thundered down the court, mechanized, rehearsing a series of dribbles and passes: Sasha to Rebecca, Rebecca to Carrie, Carrie to Josie. Josie was in top form, her gold braid snapping behind her with each lunge and jump. Her breasts quivered under her jersey and spandex sports bra, and each time she landed—each time the ball connected with her hands, rattling her—Theo felt his chest tighten. If he and Mia ever had another child—as if they'd want another child together—there was a twenty-five percent chance that it would have CF, like Sissy. *Chance, chances.* A gamble. Josie was a gamble, too, or maybe just a stupid risk, but she was carrying their child, and Theo felt—no, he *knew*—that their baby wouldn't be sick. Their baby would be OK.

Josie caught the ball and Lisa slid into her, knocking them both out of bounds. Theo ran over, and Josie quickly jumped to a stand. "I'm OK," she said. She still had the ball.

"I think you should take a break," he told her. The gym was suddenly very quiet.

"I'm fine," she said, tapping a nervous rhythm on the orange skin. She started to dribble and put a hand out to block Lisa. "Come on, babe. Let's do this."

Theo leaned forward and knocked the ball out of the way, mid-bounce. "I told you to take a break," he said. The ball rolled across the floor, and he imagined that every eye in the gym was following its path. "So take one, unless you'd rather be running laps."

Josie stared at him, face bright with sweat, then bounced on her toes. "All right," she said. She started to jog, and the rest of the girls looked at each other, then Theo, and he knew he had to go on with practice or lose them all completely. He clapped his hands two times. "Back to the court," he said. He pointed to Amanda, who was on the bench. "Take her spot."

The girls resumed their drill, and Josie ran laps. Theo lifted his eyes every time she rounded the corner and passed in front of him, and her speed actually seemed to be increasing instead of slowing. Her braid trailed behind her.

"Pace yourself, Jo," Theo yelled.

She didn't look at him.

They started a new drill, and while he tried to focus as the players ran lay-ups, he watched for Josie in the periphery of his vision, sure that she would lose steam and stop at any moment. But she kept going. Thirty minutes passed this way, and though the practice shouldn't have been over yet — they had a big home game coming up against Franklin-Simpson — he called it to a halt. The girls, who normally would've been happy to have a long evening ahead of them, hovered mid-court, looking at him. "Hit the showers," he told them.

"I'd like to get a little more time in, Coach," Carrie said. "I don't feel ready for Saturday yet."

"Practice at home," he said, and pointed to the locker room. "Go on, now."

The girls jogged off court, and Josie continued to run. Her face was dripping, her hair dark now with sweat, and her pace was finally beginning to flag. Her big leg muscles trembled with every jolt against the polished wood floors.

"Stop now," Theo yelled to her. "Practice is over."

She shook her head.

"Do it, goddammit!" he said. "Unless you want to ride the bench Saturday."

That did it, as he knew it would. She lunged off a final three or four steps, then hunched over, grasping her knees. She coughed, the sound seeming to rise from the bottom of her stomach, scraping her insides raw. Theo ran over and put a hand on her neck.

"Get the fuck off me," she gasped, knocking his hand away. Her freckled face was scarlet across the nose and cheeks, ivory on her forehead and chin. Her neck was red-streaked, too, welts that could have been made by a claw.

"You happy now?" Theo asked. He could hear a couple of the girls sneak out of the locker room behind him, could feel their eyes on his back, on Josie, who had lain on her side and was pulling her knees to her chest.

"You're going to kill that baby," Theo said, keeping his voice low and steady, more steady than he felt. "You're going to bleed him out right here on this gym floor you love so much, if you aren't careful."

"Good." Her eyes darted to his and away, childlike.

"You stupid bitch," he said, thinking, absurdly, of Joe. He hadn't wanted a dog—hadn't seen the sense in committing to another responsibility—but Mia had insisted, and he'd gone along. And the dog was all right. Not man's best friend, exactly, but good enough. Joe didn't get walked much, but when the walking got done, Theo did it. Joe was always full-steam-ahead, too. Didn't matter where they were going, or coming, he wanted to dig into the ground with his toenails and drag, mush, himself forward. Joe didn't care about the destination, so long as he was moving. "Maybe you don't know what's good for you," he told Josie.

She looked up at him, her face now bleached, the freckles like tiny bullet holes in her fair skin. "What do you mean?"

"Have you made an appointment yet?" he whispered.

She stood up and brushed off her shorts. "I was going to tell you after practice."

"Come to my office," he said.

He could still hear showers running in the locker room, so he closed and locked the door behind them, hoping anyone remaining would assume he and Josie had both gone home. Unlikely, given the public nature of their weird argument, but he couldn't think about that right now. "What did you find out?" he asked her.

"It'll be four hundred," she said.

He nodded, relieved but detached. This wasn't as bad as it could be.

"I found out about this clinic in Louisville on-line," Josie said. "So I called them, and they told me I'd have to come in for counseling, then wait twenty-four hours, because of some law. The closest day I could get was next Friday for the counseling, then Saturday for the other."

"Saturday's the Todd County game," Theo said.

"We'll just have to miss it."

He rubbed his forehead and laughed. "You can miss it, maybe. But I can't, hon. What would people think, both of us gone? It wouldn't look right."

She was very still. "It would look a lot worse if I started to show."

She was right, of course. But part of him was picturing his future, *their* future, and how quickly a thing like this—her one remaining semester of high school, the fifteen years between them—would blow over in this town. People would probably be more upset if they found out about Mathias's little stash in the head coach's lounge, the nicer office near the boys' locker room, with the windows. People in this town would understand that there's a difference between taking drugs, being purposefully incompetent, and falling in love with the wrong person. Because he *did* love Josie, he was sure of it. He wanted to do right by her, and he wanted to hold on to her. People here would understand that, too. And if they didn't, so what? There was always Bowling Green or Lexington or somewhere else.

"I don't know, Josie," he said.

Her face crumpled — that was the only word for it — but she still didn't understand him, still didn't realize what he was proposing. She drew an invisible line on his desk with her finger, trembling, and then the action turned loopy, and her face drew into her old sexy look that Theo knew so well, and he was fascinated by how he could follow her thought process with that one nervous finger, like she was a planchette, divining messages from a supernatural power.

"We could make a whole weekend out of it," she said. "We could go early, you know? Maybe go to Kentucky Kingdom—"

"They'll be closed," Theo said. "For winter."

"Aw, that doesn't matter. Not there, then. We'll have dinner somewhere nice. And I can wear something for you. Real special."

"What would you wear?" Theo asked. He sensed his cruelty, but he was also following her, imagining with her. Honeymoon: the word seemed silly, ridiculous, even, but he thought it anyway.

She tilted her head. "You know," blushing, "like a nightie or something. The night before won't matter. We can really live, right? It'll be the best time."

"I hear you," Theo said.

She stopped tracing with her finger. "You're screwing with me, aren't you?"

"No way," he said.

"You're not going to take care of this."

"I'm going to take care of you," he told her. "I just don't know that this is the way to do it."

She started to cry, the first time he had ever seen her do it. "You bastard. You selfish asshole. I'll tell. I'll tell the principal."

"Tell her," Theo said. She wouldn't, he felt sure. She had as much at stake as he did. He thought about Sissy, his insurance. *I don't care*, he told himself. *None of that has to matter anymore.* There were other schools, other jobs — positions at factories, right in this very county, that paid better than teaching did.

Josie picked his cup of pencils up off his desk and threw them against the wall, but the sound was small, lightweight, and Theo could tell that the gesture embarrassed her. "I'll tell my mom!" she yelled.

"Calm down," he said, waving his hands at her, open palms patting air.

"My scholarship," she whispered.

"Honey," he said, "you can still use it. We could do this."

She ran out of his office. He didn't follow her, but he felt certain she would come around. He wasn't being reasonable, exactly, but this was the right thing to do. His adrenaline was high—he hadn't felt this way since college, when his own feet pounded the court, matching his heartbeat.

.．

When he came home from that night's practice, Mia was in the kitchen, scrubbing the counters, and Sissy was in a bassinet across the room. Much as he'd been disgusted by the state of the house for the last several months—and the dog, the dog had been the most senseless, irresponsible kind of loss—it hurt him to see her like this: so ardently domestic, so desperately sorry. She raised a finger to her lips when he walked into the kitchen, and he wondered if he were supposed to play a part in this scenic little moment: tip-toe across the linoleum in his sneakers, silently plant a kiss on her forehead, then her mouth. She had an apron on, for Christ's sake; should he untie the neat bow, unbutton her clean blouse? He remembered her as she'd been before the burden of Sissy's birth and disease had landed so heavily on them both: not his soul mate, maybe, but a woman to feel proud of. A woman to feel good about coming home to. Mathias had called her "eleven different kinds of fine" just after Theo came to RHS, and that was maybe the best compliment he'd ever been paid. She'd been dark-haired and lively and lovely. She'd been a thing worth beholding.

Her eyes now, though, were just as empty to him as they'd

been the night Joe died. She smiled and turned back to the counter, yellow rubber gloves brushing the bends of her elbows as she scrubbed hard water stains out of the grooves around the faucet, SOS pad rasping against the stainless steel. Maddeningly single-minded. He went to the bassinet, leaned over his daughter, and brushed his lips against the satiny skin of her temple. She was gorgeous, tiny, doll-like. Mia took good care of her. Theo worried for them both — and already, the thrill of deciding to be with Josie and raising their child was ebbing, becoming entangled and complex. Sissy sighed in her sleep: a luxurious sound that made Theo ache. He wished he could have done better by her. He'd spent the first few months of her life resenting her, despite himself; he'd expected hard work and lost sleep, but he hadn't been prepared for the sudden changes in Mia, who cried so often that her face always shined and who told Theo one night, with a calm that chilled him, that she was thinking about swallowing a bottle of pills. He understood that what he and Mia had was fine in the good times, when they could rent movies and eat out and shop for a new car together. Hard times were another matter. Then Sissy started getting sick, and he realized at some point that he wasn't thinking of her as a child anymore, or his daughter: she was a hypothetical, a baby who may or may not live to see thirty, and if he expected too much, or loved her too much, he'd be disappointed. Her weakness dismayed him, but he was weaker. "Night, baby," he whispered, and Sissy sighed again. He went to bed.

Mia slipped in beside him an hour later, skin still faintly redolent of Windex and Lysol. "I do the best I can," she whispered against his back, and the sensation stirred him, surprised him. She ran her fingers lightly across his ribs, tickling.

"I know you do," Theo said. He rolled over and kissed her, slipped his hand into the open neck of her gown, touching the familiar slope of her breast — the first time in a long time, and maybe the last. He traced the line of her collarbone, making a chart in his head, two-columned: *Mia, Josie.* One bigger in the chest, one taller. One with lines at the corner of her eyes, one with acne clustered around her temples. He thought about songs they liked — songs he thought they liked — and the way they wanted to be touched. One of them liked him to flick his tongue lightly across the nape of her neck, where her real hair turned into the fuzzy, baby-down of soft skin. One liked him to breathe into the cup of her ear, not words, just heat. He couldn't remember which was which. Sissy slept, and as he pushed the gown up around his wife's hips, raking his boxers down at the same time with his knees and then his feet, he imagined the wet gurgle of her chest as she drew in air, mobile of stars suspended above her, the moon a smiling crescent in neon.

..

They won the game against Franklin-Simpson. He and Josie had never been so in synch. If he thought an instruction, seemed like, Josie reacted: cut quickly to the left, passed the ball to Lisa, who was open, took the chance at the three-pointer and made it, sealing the victory. At some point in the game, he looked up at the bleachers, and in a throng of black and gold sweatshirts and flags, he thought he saw Mia. She used to come to his games, unannounced, before Sissy was born, when she was still teaching special ed at Stevenson. She'd sit closer down, though, just behind his row of benched players, and it seemed to him now that some of the best moments in their marriage had been unspoken, when the Panthers would score, the crowd would erupt, and the band would kick into "Land of a Thousand Dances," all the sounds punctuated by the occasional slide-whoop of one of those noisemakers the Band Boosters were always selling in the lobby. Amid all of this — his favorite kind of chaos — he'd turn around, savoring his moment, and see Mia just a few paces away; they'd smile at each other, and he'd know that she understood him. That she was feeling the same way he was.

This woman he thought was Mia, though, was up pretty high, just short of the second tier of bleachers that only got full at the boys' games, and she didn't smile or wave when she saw him, and why would Mia be at the game anyway? She'd no sooner bring Sissy than she'd don sequins and dance to "Tricky" with the cheerleaders at halftime. He turned away from the woman in time to see the other team score, and when he looked back, she wasn't there anymore. A guilt hallucination, he was sure. He wasn't made of stone, after all.

The game ended, and Theo felt someone sidle up beside him, shoulder hitting his shoulder.

"Theo, man," Mathias said.

Theo glanced at him, then back at the court. The girls were filing out, and Josie was already gone. He scanned the crowd for her.

Mathias stuck his hand out and Theo shook it, hesitantly. Mathias wasn't in the habit of coming to girls' games, even when his boys played the occasional Friday night game and the schedules didn't conflict. Theo had always been sore about that, but now he wanted Mathias to leave—to high-tail it back to his bachelor's pad and his dope and his easy life.

"Good game," Mathias said.

"Yeah." Theo looked over his shoulder, where the Mia look-alike had been. "Yeah, the girls did good."

Mathias crossed his arms. He was almost a foot taller than Theo, broad through the chest, and he had a presence—as a player so many years back, now as a coach—that Theo deeply envied: the reason, he knew, that Mathias was coaching boys, though they'd joked a few times together that the boys' team didn't have Josie-style perks. Uncomfortable joking.

"You're out, friend," Mathias said. He didn't lower his voice at all, but parents and teenagers were a churning mass around them, and the words felt muted, unreal. But Theo understood them.

"Out," he repeated.

Mathias looked at the court. "I guess things got around. You know—some parent, then a teacher got involved. Then Rita Beasley."

"Well, don't draw it out, for Christ's sake," Theo said. "What's going on?"

"They're having an emergency school board meeting tonight, and I expect that you'll get a call by tomorrow. That's what Noel Price told me." He sighed, and Theo could smell Listerine. "They'll let you resign. They won't want a big stir."

Sissy. Theo couldn't breathe.

"You OK?" Mathias said.

Theo laughed out loud. "She's pregnant, Matt."

"Mia?"

Theo shook his head.

"Goddamn," Mathias said.

"She's going to leave me," Theo said — out loud, but to himself. Saying it, he realized that she probably already had: *Things got around.* Mia had been in the bleachers, watching him, and now she gone: to her mother's, with Sissy. He would come home tonight to an empty house, to the lingering smells of Joe's sickness and Sissy's baby lotion, and the rest of his life would begin. He didn't know what kind of life that could be.

"I'm sorry," Mathias told him.

Theo went to the locker room, where the girls were gathered for his wrap-up talk — Josie, nowhere to be seen — and he said the nonsense things he always said — "Good game, good teamwork, let's focus on defense at practice this week" — watching the girls' faces, wondering who among them knew. All of them, of course, but they made their expressions innocent and blank, and he appreciated them for it. He said a prayer with the girls and called it a night, and he could hear, leaving, their talk shift from *amens* to discussions of parties — Chad's house or Tresten's? — prom dates, and *man, we were so fucked up!* It occurred to him that Josie had a second life, too. On game nights, when Theo went home to Mia, changed a token diaper, and made himself watch Sissy sleep for thirty minutes, she was over at some kid's house, nursing a bottle of Boone's Farm that somebody's older brother had charged her eight bucks for. She studied for tests, asked her mother for money. In another month or two she'd start shopping for prom dresses, and whatever she'd find would look awkward and hopeful, and on prom night she'd stand out in the middle of this very gymnasium wearing too much eyeshadow and lipstick, unsure for once, graceless.

He saw her as he was walking to his car, the February night air like novocaine to his bare arms. She was with Jatarius in the parking lot and the light from a security lamp fell over them softly, the scene picturesque, staged. She was still in her jersey—she'd never showered—and Jatarius was working his big hands up and down her bare arms, warming them, and in a moment Theo knew that they would kiss, that Josie was just waiting for him to see it. He could get in his car and follow them—she'd let him, she'd make sure Jatarius slowed down, using any excuse that came to mind; and he'd do it, do whatever she asked, spurred on by the promise of her. He'd do it, because Josie was a girl—a woman—who would, Theo was understanding, have her way: with his help, without it. Now, no more than thirty feet away, she lifted her chin, and Jatarius lowered his, and they were a single dark shadow outlined in a hazy yellow nimbus. She was gone already and he had been a fool to think otherwise.

Later, he could turn off on whatever country road they turned off on, drive a little past the thick of trees where they'd park, and pull his own vehicle over to the shoulder, quieting the engine, shutting off the headlights. His overcoat was in the passenger seat. He'd put it on, creep back down the road, take a spot behind the trunk of a leafless water maple. And they'd watch each other through the rear windshield of Jatarius's car: Josie's slow undress, her mount, her gentle rocking, baby between them.

[VOL. XXIX, NO. 1 / WINTER 2007]

FADY JOUDAH

Ladies and Gentlemen

... the easiest pain is someone else's,
And even the Hittites

Kept their nuclear weapon a sole possession
For as long as they could.

But it's been a bit much to take since then,
One exodus after another,
Like getting used to the life of

Frequent flyer miles
Without ever cashing them in.

Ladies & gentlemen,
Life will get old soon
And death has long been part of the treatment plan.

What's the use of a flag
Without a land that believes
In poetry and no more

Contused waters to cross?
It's nothing special this waiting
For what will never be

One's own twice.
A flesh wound merely,
An eggplant bruise of a myth.

Ladies & gentlemen, my friends
Of the jury, if you were born in Tokyo

Would you be Japanese?
Or Athens, Georgia, or Rome, Ohio,
Or the land of cactus wind

Where the one-eyed are many: *Why
Do they call the Black Sea, black?*

Because it's always mourning the Dead one.
What doesn't evaporate burns.

[VOL. XXIX, NO. 1 / WINTER 2007]

Cake

Annette the facilitator pretended to be Kate, a woman in our chronic pain support group who killed herself. We went around the circle, Annette in the middle, each of us given the opportunity to tell "Kate" what we were feeling.

Gail with fibromyalgia: "How could you give up?"

Stephanie with the botched spinal fusion: "You should have reached out for help!"

Liz with diabetes-related neuropathy: "What about your children?"

There were a lot of tears. A lot of hugging. Then it was my turn.

"I have a question," I said.

"For Kate?" Annette asked. "Or for me, Annette."

"Makes no difference," I said. "Is it true she jumped off the San Pedro Bridge?"

"Yes. But—"

"Is it also true that she landed on a Maersk cargo ship headed out to sea?"

Annette shifted uncomfortably. "Claire, we should focus on our feelings—"

"And is it also true that Maersk sent back what was left of her body in a Rubbermaid cooler, that the cooler was stuck in customs for a week before Kate's husband could take custody of it, that the cooler was stolen on the way to the funeral home because a homeless guy thought it contained a picnic?"

Annette looked around the circle at the horrified faces. When she looked back at me, she nodded.

I started applauding.

"Why are you clapping?" Annette asked, her big fat cow eyes filled with confusion.

"For a job well done. Personally, I hate it when suicides make it easy on the survivors."

· ·

When I got home, there were two messages. On the first one, Annette said the group had stayed late after I left, that it had been a difficult session for everyone and she didn't want to minimize my feelings, but—

She and the others feel it's in everyone's best interest if I find another support group—perhaps one specifically to deal with my "anger issues."

The second message was from my ex-husband, Jason. He said he wanted to come by and pick up the last of his things. He asked me to call his assistant with a time when I won't be home, because he feels it's prudent that we don't see each other right now.

I'm sure his mother told him exactly what to say on the message because he never used to say things like "prudent." He always was a big mama's boy.

With all the excitement it was no wonder I was experiencing breakthrough pain. Breakthrough pain is my worst nightmare because it means the meds aren't working right.

Imagine the most excruciating thing you ever experienced. A migraine. A kidney stone. Giving birth.

All of these I've experienced, by the way.

Now try to imagine that the nerves involved in that pain are being pulled out by a sadistic fuck, one by one. No matter what you scream to make the sadistic fuck stop, he won't. The sadistic fuck just keeps laughing at you because he's enjoying your agony.

That, in a nutshell, is breakthrough pain.

· ·

Guess who got a private room at Cedars with her very own morphine drip?

Morphine is like being wrapped up in warm towels fresh from the dryer. Morphine is like your mother rubbing your back when you have the flu. Morphine is like drinking cold water from a hose on the hottest day of the summer.

Who am I kidding? Morphine's even better than all that.

Thank you morphine.

Thank you.

Thank.

You.

Morphine.

· ·

Drug Induced Hallucination #1:

There was a boa constrictor slithering under my sheets. The snake tried to convince me that *As You Like It* is Shakespeare's most unjustly criticized play. I stared at the mound under my sheets and didn't move a muscle for hours. I knew if I made any movement the snake was going to stop arguing literary theory and devour me.

· ·

Drug Induced Hallucination #2:

A group of young kids was standing outside my room, talking loudly. They didn't go away. I got angrier and angrier.

I finally rang the nurse and told her to tell those fucking brats to move it somewhere else, if that wasn't too much fucking trouble. Or was I interrupting her goddamned fucking break?

That's when the kids started throwing a basketball against my door.

"Don't you hear that?" I asked the nurse.

She pulled the drip out of my arm and started jabbing the needle in her eyes. "I can't hear a thing."

· ·

Drug Induced Hallucination #3:

Kate walked into my hospital room carrying a cake with a bunch of candles on it. I told her I liked her new look.

"Thanks," she said. "I wish I could say the same about you."

"The morphine makes it kind of hard to fix myself up."

"You're probably wondering about the cake."

"I didn't want to be rude, but yes."

"Remember that time when Annette asked us what our dream would be if we didn't have chronic pain?"

"I always hated her drippy little exercises."

"You said your dream involved the Brazilian soccer team." Kate crinkled her nose in disapproval.

"And you said you wished you could bake your kids a birthday cake."

Kate lit the candles. "Everyone in the group cried after I said that. You didn't, though."

"I had my reasons."

"I know that now."

"To be honest, I wasn't that impressed with the whole Saint Kate thing."

"Saints don't jump off the San Pedro Bridge onto a Maersk cargo ship."

"Nice touch."

"I thought you'd like it."

Kate brought the cake over to me. "Make a wish," she said.

I closed my eyes and blew out the candles, even though I couldn't think of anything to wish for. When I opened my eyes, Kate threw the cake out the window and jumped out after it. There was a sickening thud and someone started screaming from the street below. A nurse ran into my room.

It took me awhile before I realized that the person screaming was actually me.

• •

The remote didn't work so my TV had been stuck on the Discovery channel the whole time. No wonder I was having nightmares about fucking boa constrictors. I told the mousy Filipina nurse to change the channel manually.

"No problem, your highness," she said.

"Ooh," I said, "somebody developed a spine while I was out of it."

She left the TV on the History channel after I told her to turn it to HBO. Touché, Imelda.

I watched a documentary about the demise of drive-in theaters in America. Apparently there aren't any left in California except for one in Barstow.

Jason took me to a drive-in theater when we were dating, back when we were both in law school at UCLA. He'd been mortified when I found the *Carpenters: Greatest Hits* in his glove compartment. I teased him about it, until he cued the tape up to "Close to You." He held me in his arms while we listened to the song—I'd never felt as safe as I did at that particular moment.

It was only the second time I'd ever gotten drunk. Captain Morgan's Spiced Rum and Coke, on top of a large carton of buttered popcorn. After I threw up, his car smelled like sour cinnamon toast. He gently stroked my hair and told me everything would be OK.

I was stupid enough to believe him.

• •

When I got home, I made two phone calls. First I called Rosalva, my cleaning lady, and asked if she had a driver's license. When I found out she did, I asked her if she wanted to make an extra couple hundred bucks.

Then I called Jason's office. I told his assistant to tell him I was going to be out of town tomorrow, so he could come by the house then.

I told her to tell Mama's Boy I'd changed all the locks, but I'd leave a key in the bottom of the deep end of the pool for him.

• •

For the road trip:
1. Vicodin.
2. OxyContin.
3. Methadone.
4. A nasal opiate from Glaxo that's still in the trial phase.
5. The phone number and Mapquest directions for a pharmacy in Barstow. Just in case.
6. A fifty-dollar ergonomic travel pillow I bought at Sharper Image.
7. A two-hundred-dollar lumbar support pillow I bought off the Internet.
8. Orange juice.
9. Chips.
10. My sunglasses.
11. A change of clothes. Just in case.
12. A bottle of Captain Morgan's Spiced Rum.
13. A six-pack of Coke.

• •

The drive to Barstow should normally take two hours, not five. I had to get out every twenty minutes to stretch. I felt like my breaks were starting to get on Rosalva's nerves.

"No, no, no, Mrs. Fine. Is OK," she said.

I told her I was still freaked out by the crow we killed near San Bernardino, the way it dived head-on into our car like a kamikaze pilot.

Rosalva acted like she was about to cross herself. "No more please."

"Sorry. We don't have to talk about the crow." I offered her some chips and a Coke and that seemed to improve her mood.

· ·

The pain got bad near Apple Valley. That annoyed me. It also annoyed me the way Rosalva looked at me when I took my pills.

"Could you do me a favor?" I asked.

"Yes, ask me what you need."

"Don't call me Mrs. Fine," I said. "I'm divorced now so I don't want to be called Mrs. Fine."

"But what to call you?"

"How about Claire. That's my name."

"OK, Mrs. Claire," she said.

With a sweet smile. Oh, fuck it. She'll get it right one of these days.

· ·

Rosalva loved *The Passion of the Christ*. I found it kind of weird to listen to all the torture through the small, tinny speaker. I started chipping off the polish on my toenails.

"You must be seeing this," Rosalva said, her eyes filled with tears.

"I *am* seeing this," I told her, as chunk number forty-five flew off Jesus' body. "I'm also seeing we're out of Coke."

She seemed relieved when I offered to go to the concession stand so she could keep watching the movie. It's OK, I get it: The Jews killed Jesus, so we should have to go to the concession stand during *The Passion of the Christ*.

· ·

The desert night sky is dreamy this time of year—a deep purplish blue and stars that look like Christmas lights. The cold air hurt my lungs, but in a good way.

I crawled under the low wire fence behind the concession

stand and walked through shrubs and gravel down to the train tracks.

What would Jesus do? I think if he were in my shoes he would lie down and wait for the next Union Pacific freight train.

. .

When you think you're going to die imminently, you choose your final thoughts carefully. I tried to think of beautiful things, like Michelangelo's *David*. A Bach cantata.

That got me thinking about the *Nutcracker Suite*. When I was a little girl, I danced as a mouse two years in a row. It's still one of my favorite pieces of music.

My thoughts turned to Jason.

I hated to admit it, but I did understand what he meant when he said I wasn't the only one suffering—right before he handed me the divorce papers he'd personally drawn up. It was hard at the time to react graciously to what he said, because, after all, he'd walked away from the accident with only a sprained shoulder.

But now—I can see.

I can see that we were both the wrong kind of people to deal with this kind of situation. Problems that could be solved by money: *that's* the most we could handle. Not the loss. Not the pain. Not all the thousands and thousands and thousands of pills.

Too bad Jason's such a mama's boy that he'd never take methadone, because it really does help take the edge off life.

I felt the low rumble of a train. Then I heard a voice, getting closer and closer.

"Mrs. Claire! *Ay Dios mío!* Mrs. Claire!"

I struggled to sit up and saw Rosalva scrambling towards the tracks. I tried to gauge how far the train was in relation to her distance from me.

"It's OK, it's OK," I said, "I just got tired and needed a rest."

··

During the drive back Rosalva kept looking at me like I was going to jump out of the car.

"Knock it off with the attitude already," I said.

She scolded me in Spanish. I think she said something about how it was a good thing Jesus told her I went "loco."

I was thinking of the most profane thing I could say when the car started making a grinding noise. Right before the "service engine" light went on.

··

The guy at the garage in Barstow said it was going to take at least three days to fix the car. He tried to explain the problem to me.

"I don't need to understand what a head gasket is," I said. "Just make the arrangements for a rental car."

Blank stare.

"OK," I said, "maybe you don't understand Triple A. I have the *platinum* coverage that gets me a free mid-size rental if repairs are going to take more than twenty-four hours."

"There's nothing open now," he said.

"Why? Is it a holiday?"

"It's nearly midnight. People have to sleep."

Now it was my turn for a blank stare.

··

Inside a dark Greyhound bus, strung out on opiates, traveling through the high desert in the middle of the night, I started to feel like I was in a rocket flying through outer space. I stared at Rosalva while she slept next to me. She opened her eyes.

"Gracias," I said.

"Why?" she asked.

"For putting up with me," I said. "I wish I knew how to say that in Spanish."

"Sleep, Mrs. Claire." Rosalva closed her eyes again.

I heard muffled laughter from the back of the bus. I turned around and saw a group of teenagers passing around a joint. Everyone else on the bus was asleep. I waited a few minutes, the smell of pot becoming stronger.

I made my way to the back. The leader of the group, a girl with a bad tattoo of a python on her arm, glared at me.

"Toilet's broke, bitch."

Her friends laughed.

"I don't need to use the toilet."

She sneered. "Then beat it."

Her friends were enjoying the show. I leaned down into her face.

"I used to be married to a federal prosecutor in L.A. Even though I hate his guts, I have no problem getting on my cell phone and asking him to send a marshal to the bus station."

The sneer disappeared.

I pointed to the joint in her hand. "Is that just pot or did you morons cut it with something else?"

• •

I'd hoped the girl—Becky, a runaway from Idaho—wouldn't want to talk, but once we started on the second joint she wouldn't shut up.

"I want to be an actress," Becky said.

"Can I give you some unsolicited feedback?"

"Hell no."

"You're going to end up doing porn. Or worse. That's what happens to girls from Idaho like you."

"Gross! I won't do porn!"

"Right. Do any of these stars ever say in an interview, 'I ran away from Idaho when I was sixteen and ended up doing Hollywood movies'? No. That's what porn actresses say. Not Hilary Duff."

"I hate Hilary Duff," she said.

"If I had your body I would too."

"At least I don't look like you." She pointed at my face and arms with a vicious little smile.

"Give it time, honey. You'll get your own scars some day."

I asked if she had another joint.

"I hope you know these weren't free," she pouted.

I pulled out a hundred dollar bill. "Let's skip the soul baring. It's starting to get on my nerves."

• •

Becky finally passed out. The bus was absolutely quiet as we went down the Cajon Pass. The sun was just coming up. The San Gabriel Valley glowed from under an ozone shroud.

Rosalva woke up. She panicked when she didn't find me next to her. I waved from my seat next to Becky.

"Who is this?" she asked, eyeing Becky's tattoo.

"I'm starved. I want a yellow cake with lots of fudge frosting."

"I make one tomorrow."

"I want one the minute we get home."

"Mrs. Claire, I must go to my home. Later I come to your home."

I realized I had no idea where Rosalva lived.

"Downey," she answered. "You do not know this place I am sure."

"Isn't that where the Carpenters were from?"

"I have not met them."

When we sat down in our seats, Rosalva pulled out a brush and started combing my hair. I began to sing.

"Why do birds . . . suddenly appear . . ."

Rosalva smiled. "This is very pretty song."

"Every time . . . you are near? Just like me . . . they long to be . . . close to you."

• •

At the L.A. bus station I sent Rosalva to Downey in a cab. While I waited for my own cab, I noticed Becky's friends had deserted her. She walked up to me with a shy look on her face.

"What are your big plans?" I asked. "Oh that's right, you're going to be a star."

"Shut up."

"Want to make an easy hundred?"

She gave me a look of disgust. "I knew you were a dyke."

"I don't want to fuck you. I just want you to bake me a cake."

"You're a freak. You know that, right?"

"Can you follow directions on a package, or are you illiterate?"

"Am I what?"

"Jesus. Can you read? Do they still teach that in Idaho?"

A cab pulled up. I opened the door and waited for Becky. She studied my face, trying to decide if I was a good risk or not. I felt bad for her until my legs started killing me again.

I sighed. "Do I look like someone who could hurt you?"

"You're mean enough."

"You outweigh me by at least fifty pounds."

"Fuck you."

"Fine."

I got inside and gave the cabbie my address. We were driving off when I heard Becky's voice.

"Wait!" she yelled, running after the cab.

I didn't look at her when she got in the car. "Offer's fifty now."

"What?"

"You heard me."

"That's not fair."

"Life's not fair. Any more lip and it goes down to twenty-five."

· ·

Becky decided to make the cake from scratch. We were at the grocery store right by my house, in the baking section. I'd become distracted by the Disney-themed birthday candles.

"Do you have baking powder?" Becky asked.

"I'm not sure." I was starting to lose focus. "Is that the stuff you put in the fridge to keep it from smelling?"

Becky rolled her eyes. "That's baking soda."

"Then I don't think I have baking powder."

"Who doesn't have baking powder?"

"People who order out, that's who."

"You're pathetic," Becky said, while were standing in the checkout line.

"You're only just now realizing that? God, you *are* stupid."

"What about booze?" Becky asked.

"Can you handle liquor? I don't want green puke all over my carpet after you drink a whole bottle of Midori."

"Why are you such a cunt?" she hissed.

"Paper or plastic?" the clerk nervously asked.

··

While Becky made the cake, I went through the house. The last of Jason's clothes were gone. All the tools were missing—not that I'd ever use them. All his books were out of the den. With his collection gone it really exposed my intellectual laziness—Clive Cussler no longer propped up by *The Collected Works of Shakespeare*.

I found the picture on the desk, the framed photo of Jason and me and the twins. We'd hired an expensive photographer, a guy who does fashion spreads for *Los Angeles* magazine. The year before the accident, for our holiday greeting card.

I picked it up and studied our faces, until none of us was recognizable. I thought I'd made it clear to Jason he could keep the picture.

I called his office.

"Mr. Fine's not in. Would you like to leave a message?" his assistant asked.

"Tell him he won."

"Won what?" The assistant sounded nervous.

"He'll know," I said, before I hung up the phone.

• •

I took so much methadone I just barely made it to my bed. Becky yelled from the kitchen.

"Where's the fucking booze?"

"Be resourceful!" I yelled back. "You need to be resourceful!"

My last thought before I passed out was that maybe primitive cultures are right—I think the camera did steal my soul.

• •

When I woke up, Rosalva was wiping my face with a cold washcloth.

"What time is it?" I asked.

"Too many hours," she said.

"Is the girl still here?"

"No. I think she stealed."

Rosalva helped me get up. We discovered that Becky had taken my purse, all of my jewelry, all of the liquor, and the entire stash of pain medication, including the methadone.

How did she find the methadone? I'd completely underestimated her.

"I call the police," Rosalva said.

I stared at the frosted cake on the kitchen counter, covered in plastic wrap. "No."

"She does wrong when you are sick! This is bad girl!"

I dabbed my finger on the top of the cake and tasted it. Homemade fudge frosting. A little on the sweet side, but definitely homemade.

..

It's impossible in L.A. to find out where someone lives if they haven't given you the information. The white pages are useless; 411 is a fucking joke. I needed to talk to a human being and not Verizon's annoying computer, so I called Annette.

"And how are we doing Claire?"

"We're doing *great*."

"Well, that's super. Did you find another support group?"

"Funny you should mention that. Ever hear of Gloria Allred?"

"Uh, well, yes, I have."

"Because I've decided to sue you for discrimination."

"Goodness. A lawsuit?"

"Just kidding. I'm calling to get Kate's address."

"I don't think I'm allowed to give out that information. Was there something else I could help you with?"

"That's hardly possible."

"Well, I'm certain I can't give you that information. I'm sorry."

"Remember when I said I was kidding about the lawsuit?"

"Uh huh."

"Now I'm not kidding."

..

The address was in Palos Verdes, for a house that looked like the bastard child of a mansion and a small hotel. Rosalva, bless her heart, drove me there in the mid-size rental. I told her to wait for me in the car.

"I help you, Mrs. Claire."

"Thanks, but I need to do this by myself."

I wonder what Kate's husband will say. I have to remember his name before I ring the doorbell. Ken? Ben?

Fuck it. I'll just mumble something.

I hope he doesn't freak out and think I'm a crazy person for bringing a cake with cheap Disney-themed candles. Will I actually tell him it was something Kate had wanted to do for the kids?

Jesus, I hope he doesn't start crying, or worse, ask me to come in to meet the family.

I stand outside the front door, my hand ready to press the bell. I hear children's voices inside. Lots of children.

I take a deep breath.

[VOL. XXIX, NO. 1 / WINTER 2007]

G. C. WALDREP

Bergson's Arrow

Rain in the holly, rain on the
                              shelf of self.
Many things may be blamed on the fall line:
        the mechanization of flour
        and weapons production, the rise
                              & ultimate wreckage
of Richmond's Jackson Ward.
              A surgical procedure was pending:
              I had developed
        striations in the passageways of my
                incli-
                        nations,
              stress fractures
along the waterfront vistas
                              of semblance,
        those pleasing prospects, those
                        gay promenades.
No further tickets would be issued,
              no more booths at the Tri-County Fair
                      nor natives on the far shore
waiting to express
              their complete confidence
                        in what could only
              be degrading.
        A clearer praxis
                        would involve,

e.g., turn in on itself
& then away. There should, perhaps,
be a museum of numbers
　　here, at the liminal juncture,
　　　　in place of this museum
of trains & palaces. We have not received
　　any coded messages.
　　The possibility of love remains
real
　　though relegated to foot-
　　　　　　notes, first
　physician of race & gender:
Heal thyself. Some implement
　　　drawn from the suture
　　　　(again).
　To stay on the subject. To be
　　thrown under, and yet remain.

[VOL. XXIX, NO. 1 / WINTER 2007]

EAVAN BOLAND

To Memory

This is for you, goddess that you are.
This is a record for us both, this is a chronicle.
There should be more of them, they should be lyrical
and factual, and true, they should be written down
and spoken out on rainy afternoons, instead of which
they fall away; so I have written this, so it will not.
My last childless winter was the same
as all the other ones. Outside my window
the motherless landscape hoarded its own kind.
Light fattened the shadows; frost harried the snowdrops.
There was a logic to it, the way my mother loved astrology—
she came from a valley in the country
where everything that was haphazard and ill-timed
about our history had happened and so it seemed natural
that what she wanted most were the arts of the predetermined.
My child was born at the end of winter. How to prove it?
Not the child, of course, who slept in pre-spring darkness,
but the fact that the ocean—moonless, stripped of current—
entered the room quietly one evening and
lay down in the weave of the rug, and could be seen
shifting and sighing in blue-green sisal and I said
nothing about it, then or later, to anyone and when
the spring arrived I was ready to see a single field in
the distance on the Dublin hills allow its heathery color
to detach itself and come upstairs and settle in
the corner of the room furthest from the window.

I could, of course, continue. I could list for you
a whole inventory of elements and fixed entities
that broke away and found themselves disordered in
that season, its unruly happenstance, without
a thought for laws that until then had barred
an apple flower from opening at midnight
or lilac rooting in the coldest part of the ocean. Then
it stopped. Little by little what was there came back.
Slowly at first; then surely. I realized what had happened
was secret, hardly possible, to be remembered always,
which is why you are listening as rain comes down
restored to its logic, responsive to air and land
and I am telling you this: you are after all
not simply the goddess of memory, you have
nine daughters yourself and can understand.

[VOL. XXIX, NO. 2 / SPRING 2007]

CAMPBELL MCGRATH

September 11

1.

Morning, stretching sore muscles on the floor by the bed,
sifting the night's quota of thoughts, images, tasks,
half-remembered insights, odd lines of poetry stranded

by the ebb and flow of the mind. So it is an ocean,
then, this Sea of Consciousness
mitigating, filtering, accommodating everything?

A child's unfinished alphabet puzzle on the sunporch
overlooking the reconfigured beach after the hurricane,
the beyond-dazzling shimmer of light across water.

Twenty-six letters, *a* to *z*, fingerable, adept.
Is it possible to intuit from these simplistic characters
Leaves of Grass, the *Duino Elegies*?

Who, shown a hydrogen molecule, would envision the sun?
As from leaf to rain forest, as from ant to biosphere,
as from a single brick to imagine Manhattan,

as from a human instant the totality of a life,
of lives interwoven, families and affiliations,
the time-trawled nets of societies and cultures.

So the arc of creativity is an ungrounded rainbow,
and cause for hope. Why distrust the universe?
We are engines burning violently toward the silence.

2.

Frigate birds in high wind over the inlet, enormous chains
of the construction cranes rattling like rusty wind chimes,
current running hard out through the channel,

schools of quick minnows along the rocks while midstream
the big fish wait for a meal, silver-gray flashes
of their torpedoing bodies — tarpon, bluefish, snook.

Heaps of seaweed on the beach, rim of clouds on the horizon
to mark the trailing edge of the storm pinwheeling
north to ravage the Carolinas, while along the jetty

Cuban fishermen with cruciform tattoos
are hand-netting baitfish to dump in old roofing buckets
like needling rain or schools of silver punctuation marks,

liquid semicolons seething in paratactic contortions,
prisoners seeking to deny a period to their sentence.
Surfers by the dozen — this is what they live for,

the cyclonic surge — waxing their boards,
paddling out, rising and tumbling.
Three fish on the sand, Jackson says they are cowfish,

one still breathing, we throw it back.
A few other families picking through the flotsam,
eel grass, purplish crenellated whelks,

a brittle-shelled starfish,
his little polyp feelers probing our palms,
estrella de mar, estrellita,

butterflies lit by chimerical sunlight on orange-fingered
sea fern fronds, the smooth black coral trees
we use as Halloween decorations,

tubular mangrove seeds, coconuts, and buoys,
blue and yellow tops of soda bottles,
pink cigarette lighters, a toothbrush, a headless doll.

3.

That they were called *towers,* the irony of that
ancient fortress word, twin strongholds, twin keeps,
that they fell and the day was consumed

in smoke of their ruination, in dust and ashen iota.
And the next day came and still the towers were fallen.
That morning I went for a long, aimless walk

along the beach, listening to *Blonde on Blonde,*
watching the sunlight stroke and calibrate the waves
like the silvery desire in Dylan's voice

as the skipped heart-beat cymbals declared closure.
Later I met the gods emerging from a topaz-faceted sea,
their long hair flashing in the wind,

and the gods were beautiful, bold, and young,
and one called out to me as they arose and came forth.
Come and see the world we have created

from your suffering. And I beheld a city
where blood ran through streets the color of raw liver,
stench of offal and kerosene and torched flesh,

tongueless heads impaled on poles and severed limbs
strung on barbed wire beneath unresting surveillance cameras,
industrial elevators shuttling bodies to the furnace rooms,

and speakers blaring incongruous slogans, the tinkle of a toy piano,
maudlin and inane, and vast movie screens depicting
the glittering eyeballs of iron-masked giants,

and beyond the city hills of thorn trees and people in shanties
talking softly, awaiting their time in the carnage below.
No, no, laughed the god. *That is your world,*

the world we created is here— .
And I saw rolling hills carpeted in wild flowers,
tall grasses swaying in the wind,

no trees, no streams,
just grass and wind and endless light.
These fields are watered with human tears.

4.

Images of the aftermath: smoke and rubble,
gothic spire of a wall still standing, ash-white paper
blizzards of notary calculation like the clay tablets

of the Sumerians smashed and abandoned.
They seem, now, already, distant and historicized,
like Mathew Brady's Civil War photographs—

the dead sniper at Little Round Top, the Devil's Den,
blasted trees and ravaged fields of the homeland.
And the camps of the Union Army,

numberless crates of supplies at the quartermaster's depot,
acres of wagon teams like the truckers
hauling debris away from Ground Zero, how Whitman

would have lauded their patriotic industry,
carting the wreckage of empire,
as he praised the young soldiers in their valor,

"genuine of the soil, of darlings and true heirs,"
as he cared for them in the army hospitals in Washington,
bringing to the wounded small, homely comforts —

apples, tobacco, newspapers, string,
pickles and licorice and horehound candy,
pocket change to buy a drink from the dairy-woman

peddling fresh milk cot to cot in the field wards,
a comb, a book, a bowl of rice pudding
for Henry Boardman of the 27th Connecticut —

the democratic simplicity of his compassion,
whatever the erotic charge of its currency,
whatever its voyeuristic aspect,

discovering in the moment of material attention
the salve for a wounded life, and in the lives of the wounded
a serum for the injured nation. Meaning, by *compassion*,

his unique, coercive, actively embodied brand of empathy,
his conspiratorial love of self and other
intermingled, undivided, prelapsarian and entire,

his simple kindness, his tenderness,
Whitman's tenderness is everything, the source
of his greatness and the key to his enigmatic soul,

the agent that calls sentimental platitudes to task
and elevates his grief into lasting eloquence,
the force that disavows anger for love

even amidst the inconceivable
carnage of that war, the suffering of those men,
the magnitude of that national trauma.

But *Leaves of Grass* does not negate Gettysburg,
lilacs could not return Lincoln
to a grieving people,

no poem can refute the killing fields,
art will not stop the death squads
sharpening their machetes in the village square before dawn,

the militiamen, the partisans, the cutters-off of hands,
boy soldiers in new barracks playing dice,
the child nailed to the hawthorn tree and the parents

beyond the barbed wire forced to admire the work of the nailers,
the nails themselves, iron ore and machines to quarry it,
mills and factories, depots and warehouses,

the distribution software,
the brown truck and the deliveryman,
wheelbarrows of lopped hands burned in pits with gasoline,

pretty smiling girls favored by the rape brigades,
the believers, the zealots, sergeants at arms, gangsters,
ethnic cleansers and counterinsurgency units,

tyrants, ideologues, defenders of justice,
technological sentinels in hardened bunkers
scanning infrared monitors for ignition signatures,

mass graves and secret facilities,
scientists chained to the lightning of matter,
the atoms themselves,

neutrinos and quarks, leptons
refracting alpha particles as words reflect
the stolen light of truth or revelation,

the faces of the terrorists as the airplane strikes the tower,
the faces of the firemen ascending the stairwell,
the faces of Stephen Biko's torturers at the amnesty hearing

while the dutiful son listens impassively
as if attending Miltonic lectures on human suffering,
the real, the actual, the earthly, ether of bodily want,

love and its granules pouring from the crucible,
rain to bathe the ingots, a gray horizon of muddy shoals
where ocean-going freighters are taken to pieces

by half-naked laborers wielding hammers and blowtorches,
a wrecking ground reverberating with gong-sounds
and the screams of yielding metal,

black and white photographs to document
that place, that labor, human history,
the work of men.

5.

Strange that we are born entire, red-faced and marsupial,
helpless but whole, no chrysalis or transformation
to enlarge or renew us, unless — who is to say that death

might not signify a wing-engendering reanimation
such as believers in the afterlife propose?
Is it a dream, then, this beach of seraphic sunlight,

silos full of clouds, monarch butterflies
flown from Mexico to roost on storm-uprooted trees
as a school of stingrays weave their way

through a realm of water which is their own,
the breaking through, the crossing over,
wing-tips in the wave-curl

impinging upon us as ghosts or angels might,
cracks in the crystal spheres through which perfume
floods unending into our world?

Which passes, as lightning or a waning moon drawn
above the Atlantic, my Atlantic,
rose petals poured from silver goblets into molten glass,

nectar of apples and papayas,
shoes composed of wampum and desire,
my own Atlantic — but, why are you laughing?

Not at you, no.
Then with me?
No . . .

Clouds more enormous than souls,
more sacred, fatal, devoted,
saints climbing pearl-inlaid stairs into the burning sky,

saints or golden ants, but no —. *No?*
Are you sure? And the god smiled,
and picked up his scythe.

6.

Odor on the breeze of sea foam and decay,
the stars' genuflections,
subsidence, forgetfulness, the tides.

And beneath the still surface,
what depths?
And the creatures in the chasms below the waves?

All night I dreamt of mermaids caught in fishing nets
and now, jeweled with sargassum in the surf,
the body of a mermaid, drowned.

[VOL. XXIX, NO. 2 / SPRING 2007]

Atar Hadari

Why the Dead Have Lives

John Donne
Anne Donne
Un-done.

This was a bit of doggerel the poet and later preacher John Donne wrote and sent to friends in the aftermath of his elopement, while a young and ambitious courtier, with the daughter of his patron. Anne's father, in a fit of temper he later came to regret, got Donne thrown out of his appointment at court and for some long years the poet lived in limbo, unable to return to court, unable to make a living to support his wife and growing family, until he finally gave in to the demands of the king, converted to Protestantism, and accepted the only offer the king would make, priestly office. He became the Dean of St. Paul's, the most prominent pulpit in the land, and many of the phrases he is known for, phrases which have entered the language, come not from his poetry but his rolling and thunderous sermons: "The sun also rises . . . ", "Do not send to ask for whom the bell tolls, it tolls for thee. . . ." Ernest Hemingway would have had a difficult time with titles if John Donne had not run away with his patron's daughter and so lost a promising civil service career. The language would also have missed quite a few phrases if he'd been allowed to remain just a comfortably court-ensconced, part-time poet, circulating poems to his friends.

324

In my twenties, a few years after taking all the poetry work-shops I was ever going to take, I began to read biographies of poets. These were no random poets either—and not necessarily figures I admired—but rather people who had made a career in a particular way—William Carlos Williams, for instance, earn-ing his living as a doctor, as well as Dylan Thomas, who did it by writing for radio and touring the poetry circuit. What I was looking for was guidance as to how the poetic enterprise ticks on once you are no longer bubbling along with a crowd of also-striving mini-bards. I was looking for a view of how people do this thing, really. I was looking for the shape of a poet's life.

Why was I looking for such a thing, you ask? Surely, live fast and die young is the classic recipe—hopefully leaving a beauti-ful book, or three. Well, I was already older than Keats when he died, and had been studying with Derek Walcott, who had just set about his masterpiece at age sixty, and also had a sneaking admiration for Chaucer, who'd only settled to his own master-work around sixty, so I believed there had to be a way of going about this over the long haul. Finally, I was, like any young man starting a job, looking for a manual to see me through. Poets have not, with the possible exception of Robert Penn Warren and his daughter Roseanna, generally produced poet offspring. Novel-ists' children clutter the shelves—Amis, Cheever, Dubus, just to start the alphabet—but poets don't grow up in a house, usually, watching Mum or Dad carve out the time or peace or paper re-quired for a life in poems. To learn how to do that you have to read the lives of poets.

One set of books I was given by my father (a businessman) was a battered green four volumes of the 1830 edition of Samuel Johnson's *Lives of the Poets*, which he picked up at auction. (My father was a bookaholic and always brought some amount of books home with him. I can simply say I learned to read brows-ing his shelves. It was only in my thirties, later, that I learned he'd had a failed career as a writer himself before turning to business. That was why I was looking for role models outside the house in the first place. As Kurt Vonnegut notes, a writer's ambition is usually cross-generational; it comes from someone else, further back.) I promptly ignored the books my father gave me, as I had ignored Dickens's *Great Expectations* when he tried to urge it on me when I was twelve, but they sat on my shelf and some years later I read the "life" devoted to Alexander Pope, a favorite of mine from high school English literature classes.

Johnson had the advantage over many modern biographers in knowing, often intimately, either his subjects or their friends. He never met Pope, having narrowly missed running into him at a mutual friend's bookshop, but he knew Pope's world like the smell of his own sheets. Here is Johnson on Pope's famous creation, an underground grotto in the garden where light filtered dimly from above and the sound of water played from artificial springs:

> A grotto is not often the wish or pleasure of an Englishman, who has more frequent need to solicit than exclude the sun; but Pope's excavation was requisite as an entrance to his garden, and as some men try to be proud of their defects, he extracted an ornament from an inconvenience and vanity produced a grotto where necessity enforced a passage. (95)

Johnson was a poet as well as every possible kind of man of letters, and what this all but epigrammatic passage illustrates is what he brings to the commercial endeavor of life-writing about the great dead: the literate imagination to convey, by means of an image drawn from his subject's life, a deeper truth about his subject's character. He draws, out of the scraps and memorabilia of a poet's estate, the shape of a career, the habits of a gift. Bear in mind that Pope was deformed by an early disease and a Catholic in a country that denied office to anyone but Protestants, and the observations about being proud of a defect start to have reverberations about the life, not just the garden.

Another book from my father. He, too, liked Alexander Pope and for his birthday, again sometime in my twenties, I gave him Maynard Mack's thousand-page tome *Alexander Pope: A Life*. I inscribed it, "A book about the first poet to make an independent living, from your son, who to your great distress has yet to become the second. All my love. . . ." My father duly howled that I would not see another penny from him, and after a decent interval, say one or two days, I made off with his book to my own shelves. Mack's life was actually the standard work—though probably much less widely quoted than Johnson—and this is a relatively early passage:

> In any case, it would inevitably be a soberer existence from now on. Many of the friends with whom he had been merry in younger and more hopeful days were dead or gone now. . . . Pope would make new friends—was making new friends: Burlington, Bathurst, Peterborow and many another. Still, there is a glow about one's earliest companions during those short days when Time lets us play and be golden in the mercy of his means that is never quite re-capturable. He was thirty, going on thirty one. His youth had passed. (343)

What Mack does here is take a date and a series of deaths and departures in the poet's life at that time and make of them—what? Poetry? If not poetry then certainly the kind of wistful pain that poetry often comes from. He evoked, again, out of a poet's life, the shape of life itself. That image of Pope, alone at thirty, also stayed with me—this was Mack's legacy, his sympathetic projection of his subject's life into a not-quite myth, something more real than myth—the outline of a heroic path. Not a romantic death, you understand, nothing half so simple, just a view of the road as it unwinds ahead, not so much the path less taken as the path you didn't realize you would travel alone, or fall back from.

Another man of letters and another Life. When I was eighteen or so, T. S. Eliot's centenary came up and his newly reissued *Collected Poems* was accompanied by the first full-length biography, by Peter Ackroyd. I understood and retained very little about Eliot or his life from Ackroyd except this remark about a drama fragment of his I much admired:

> Eliot himself believed that *Sweeney Agonistes* was the most original of his compositions, but he was never able to finish it and, characteristically, refused to speculate on what it might have been like if he had done so. (146)

This is Ackroyd to a T—distilling data into ringing critical observations, chattily made and neatly turned to move the page along. There's not much sense of pain, or at least nothing you can conjure up in the mind's eye when you close the book. Some years later I encountered Lyndall Gordon's two volumes on Eliot and, despite my prejudice to agree with the poet's own view that his best work was done, so to speak, in volume one of his biography, I also read the latter part, *Eliot's New Life*. What most moved me was the sense of isolation—of a public poet's role gradually drowning out the sound of the man, of outside noise finally extinguishing the voices heard at night. There's nothing like this in Ackroyd:

> Almost all accounts of these years sound curiously empty, as we are regaled with anecdotes of people who "knew" or interviewed Eliot. The man is simply not there. Did he go dead in the late forties, as he saw himself in his relation to Emily Hale, or did the prophetic soul live on, burning, inscrutable, behind the facades? The whole truth depends on holding a balance of two almost antithetical selves. There is the man who was burnt out, and accepting fame to the further depletion of his vitality; and there is a public hermit who recognized that the time had come to take up, once more, the task . . . still uncompleted: to sound a message that could pierce the worthless chatter of the sycophantic throng. To command its attention he did need fame, yet to live as a celebrity cut him off still further from the human heart. . . . Many letters to Mary Trevelyan or to . . . a priest in New York, suggest that sensations now tapped their beaks in vain against the hardening shell of the elder statesman of letters. (192)

Perhaps, also, I'd been reading about the Hebrew national poet Bialik, who died when Eliot was just getting going. He, too, was a very famous poet whose voice drowned in the adulation of the cheering mass. Eliot reminded me of Bialik, or at least Lyndall Gordon's human being in distress did. It was the first poet's life I read that taught clearly the need to be careful of fame. Years earlier I had asked the poet George Macbeth, who taught a workshop at the University of East Anglia, if it was not rather easier to write your poems before you became famous or knew you would sell them. He replied that it was not easier to do before but rather harder to do after, and getting known made it not easier but less spontaneous. You were better off before your name was made. Wrote more, cared less.

Gordon is a woman who freely admits having been ferociously in love with her subject during the writing of the two biographies. She does successfully bring across the plight of the various women in Eliot's life whom he drew into intimate friendships — sometimes lasting fifty years — and then dropped quite suddenly, quite absolutely. These women are quite apart from the first wife, Vivienne, whom he consigned to a lunatic asylum. Another thing you can learn from poets' biographies: how not to behave. It may seem merely morally judgmental, but it's also a question of artistic good business — as the most recent English language poet to win the Nobel, Seamus Heaney, attested: the vigorous laughter of a first wife and old friends are a great preservative in the face of fame.

Bankers rarely leave behind the letters and poems that illustrate how a marriage worked: poets do, and if their marriage and life produced many poems, then both will be worth perusing. You may not be able to emulate their marriage, let alone their poems, but you may benefit in both cases by knowing such things can be done.

A major example of another poet with unconventional life-style choices and a biographer who knew him well, is Philip Larkin. He was fortunate, perhaps, to share a university and a friendship with a younger poet and award-winning biographer, Andrew

Motion, to whom he started making remarks, Motion says, "as if he was addressing posterity." Indeed, Motion's *Philip Larkin: A Writer's Life* is littered with footnoted quotes, which upon investigation in the back pages you'll find attributed: "PAL to author." (Philip A. Larkin being the subject, which is to say: "He told me so.") That is the highest authority, in some ways, but also restricts the biographer's point of view. Perhaps, unlike Samuel Johnson, he shares the poet's world but is not free to depict it, to interpret its images metaphorically, as he sees fit. But Motion is a canny, sympathetic writer with a considerable eye for the drama in facts and objects (his first biography was of a painter). Here is a scene I can't forget from the end of the Larkin biography. Monica is the companion Larkin had avoided living with almost until the end, and also the other source providing authentic flesh to much of Motion's account:

> As Friday wore on Larkin grew steadily weaker. In the evening, trying to get into his chair in the sitting-room, he fell to the ground and picked himself up with difficulty. Monica, not strong enough to help him herself, rang for a neighbour. Later Larkin collapsed again in the downstairs lavatory, jamming the door shut with his feet. Monica was unable to force the door open. She couldn't even make him hear her—he had left his hearing-aid behind—but she could hear him "Hot! Hot!" he was whispering pitifully. He had fallen with his face pressed to one of the central heating pipes that ran around the lavatory wall. (522)

Everybody dies—but it is something of a metaphor, I now realize, for a man who's kept the women in his life at bay for most of his days, to end those days fallen in a toilet, keeping the door jammed shut with his feet to keep one out. A starker image of the isolated poet's life I can't imagine.

(For those with less lurid and more textually oriented tastes, *Larkin at Work* is a study of Larkin's many drafts, which he meticulously filed in shoe boxes, and the story they tell of how his poems were made. This tells you more than most biographies ever can about the actual poems. This tells you, actually, what biographies promise but can't give—an explanation of "what the poems meant." No one could tell you that—not even the living poet—but the word he discarded, having grasped for it first, may tell you a great deal of where he was going, or trying to go.)

A year or two ago, when my father died, I decided to read Allen Ginsberg's exchange of letters with his poet father, Louis, *Family Business*. I read it, as one reads any book, to reflect my own emotional concerns at the time, but the book remains probably a better portrait of Allen than any of the glitzier, hipper, more star-struck actual biographies. As well as giving an account, blow by blow, of his initial rise, it also includes the best single piece of advice I've ever read on putting together a first collection, and it is all the more moving because the star son was giving it to his eclipsed poet father:

> I repeat, please select the very best for [the publisher]—they can be reprinted in a collected works, or a hardback volume later if you're not satisfied with [his] sales and splash. But the book won't make a splash if you give him secondary work and hold out your gems for some future fantasy publisher because publishers are (1.) hard to get (2.) stupid. Have a ball with this book. Forget about tomorrow. (133)

The collected letters as a whole, skillfully selected and annotated by Michael Schumacher, is another very nuts-and-bolts look at the poetry business, which I would recommend to anyone interested in the *business*, not the glamor, as well as a very moving account of two very different men and how their love for each other survived career declines and ascents, political and moral disagreements, and, finally, death. We should all have a chance to part from our fathers, poets or businessmen, as Allen Ginsberg did.

And it is perhaps to hunt down that other father figure of my own experience that I got around to reading another book only last year. It's the only one I can judge the tone of in any way from direct knowledge, having known the subject Derek Walcott for a year in 1989 when I was studying with him at Boston University. And here we reach the basic problem with biographies of anybody famous, even poets. One of the definitions of fame is that everyone wants a piece of you—which means you talk to fewer and fewer people in a natural way. Hence the subject matter of the biography—the life, not the work—shrinks in direct proportion to the fame of the subject.

Why did I want to read a biography of a poet I knew myself? Why does anybody read a biography? To know more! And Bruce King's *Derek Walcott: A Caribbean Life* is not disappointing in many ways—it gives the dates, the degrees, the marriages and—more important—the financial details of how Walcott's career—in poetry, plays, film, and finally the Broadway musical—progressed to the Nobel and beyond. King is very good at giving an overview of the literary business at the highest level—how Joseph Brodsky took over from Robert Lowell as Walcott's mentor, for instance, coaching him to act more "coolly" to build a stately and dignified manner, as befits a major contender, and even arranged a major Italian literary prize for him, to be awarded only after Brodsky's death. And there are traces in the book of the man I knew, but only fleeting snaps—he isn't quite alive.

When Walcott taught his poetry class at Boston University in 1989, Brodsky came to sit in one day, a hawk-nosed Russian man, stocky, with wispy red hair straying off his balding pate. I remember being highly offended when he turned to us in the class and said, "You are all—what?—twenty-two? You don't know anything yet. . . ." I shifted in my seat, thinking: "I'm the same age Keats was . . . I've actually learned quite *a lot.*" But he was certainly right in what he said. What we learned we learned later, after we stopped studying.

In the restaurant "The Kangaroo," right across the street at the time from Boston University, Walcott used to take the class to lunch, though he only once, that I remember, actually paid. He brought along Brodsky to eat lunch with us, and as the bill was split and Brodsky rummaged in his corduroy slacks, bringing up a handful of change to throw over the bill, Walcott said: "Joseph, is that what's left of the Nobel Prize money?" Brodsky gave him a look. The next year Walcott finally won the Nobel and started fooling around a little less.

There is not so much of that sort of thing in King's bio, and I miss it, knowing it could be there — there are many stories — but that's a problem, again, of fame and of writing the life of a poet still famous and still living. King has a photo of Walcott pulling a face, as a young man, with the caption: "Derek Walcott being amusing, St Lucia, early 1950s." It is one of the rare moments of genuine affection that can be felt between author and subject, though the subject is very much still warm. Until you're dead, people don't want to retell your jokes, or your embarrassments, in case they lose what access they have to that fame, lose that little bit of the poet they know for real, and give it up to the public, to the microphone of posterity. People never tell their best material on mike; they know that's when they're not "being themselves."

Brodsky was right. You know nothing when you're twenty, and you try to learn it from books. You learn little. But you learn, over time, and what you learn is your own life of a poet, that's what you come to know. And some day, if you haven't lived too foolishly, and haven't let your talent waste away — someone may write your life, sniffing around your tracks. And some twenty-year-olds may read it, looking for their own way to be real. And you, some time or other, have to stop looking for fathers and start being one yourself, however ill-prepared. I was asked to teach a poetry workshop recently, to graduates of an M.A. program, some of them already sixty themselves. And I teach it, and I quote Walcott, but often as not I say what I know from my own flesh, by sending out poems, and then I back it up with things from poets' lives.

I'll mention one last bio — not even a full life — Ian Hamilton's *A Gift Imprisoned: The Poetic Life of Matthew Arnold*. It's a short book, written by a poet who spent his life on journalism and biography, about another poet who gradually got blocked and spent his life as a critic and school inspector, not as the author of "On Dover Beach," the famous poem he wrote just after his marriage:

> Ah, love, let us be true
> To one another! for the world which seems
> To lie before us like a land of dreams,
> So various, so beautiful, so new,
> Hath really neither joy, nor love, nor light,
> Nor certitude, nor peace, nor help for pain;
> And we are here as on a darkling plain
> Swept with confused alarms of struggle and flight
> Where ignorant armies clash by night.

At a similar point in life to the beginning section I quoted from Mack's life of Pope, Hamilton's life of Arnold has this:

> By 1851 he had—he might have said—renounced renunciation. True enough, he had been forced to, in order to get married. On the other hand, he knew that his free time had more or less run out, that now a different kind of battle must be joined. He had no strategy, could not distinguish friend from foe, and certainly could entertain no hopes of a heroic triumph. He was simply ready to bear arms, and prepared also to concede that his young dream of the poetic life might have to be among the early casualties. (147)

It's a very readable, terse and affecting book, but more important, I'll tell you this: if you ever notice a few months going by without your writing a poem—pick up that book. It'll scare you so much you may write a poem so as to be not like Matthew Arnold, but yourself.

Works Cited

Ackroyd, Peter. *T. S. Eliot: A Life*. London: Hamish Hamilton, 1984.

Bald, Robert Cecil. *John Donne: A Life*. Oxford: Oxford UP, 1970.

Gordon, Lyndall. *Eliot's New Life*. New York: Farrar, Straus and Giroux, 1988.

Hamilton, Ian. *A Gift Imprisoned: The Poetic Life of Matthew Arnold.* London: Bloomsbury, 1998.

Johnson, Samuel. *Lives of the Poets. Vol 3.* London: John Bumpus, 1830.

King, Bruce. *Derek Walcott: A Caribbean Life.* Oxford: Oxford UP, 2000.

Mack, Maynard. *Alexander Pope: A Life.* London: Yale UP, 1985.

Motion, Andrew. *Philip Larkin: A Writer's Life.* New York: Farrar, Straus and Giroux, 1993.

Schumacher, Michael, ed. *Family Business: Selected Letters between a Father and Son, Allen and Louis Ginsberg.* London: Bloomsbury, 2001.

Tolley, A. T. *Larkin at Work.* Hull, UK: U of Hull P, 1997.

[VOL. XXIX, NO. 3 / SUMMER 2007]

DOLEN PERKINS-VALDEZ

The Clipping

The scrap of newspaper is shaped like an unfamiliar country. The edges are blunt where the paper has snapped off with age: "ANOTHER NEGRO BURNED. The eyes were burned out and hot irons rolled all over his body. Both testicles were removed before the pleading Negro was set afire." The ones who pick him up promise his wife that there will not be trouble. They are there to protect. He leaves behind a screaming, sobbing woman and two teenage boys whose eyes are haunted with collective memories they have not yet lived. The unstable house leans forward, anxious, as if ready to tumble into the fragmented remains of his past. He never looks back as he follows them. Obediently. Silently.

Curtains drop in neighboring windows as the sound of slamming car doors echo in the street. He is helped into the back of a pickup truck, shouldered between two roughnecks gripping rifles and across from a sloe-eyed man holding nothing but anger in his fists. He keeps his eyes on the bed of the truck and jabs his own hands into the pockets of his overalls. Headlights light up the truck as if it is a moving stage. It swings out wide, pitching the men to the edge as it turns around in the street. The procession takes its time, two parallel lines of twisted faces flashing gleeful smiles in his direction as they pass. Up, down, up, his head bobs along with the truck, a floating ball abandoned in the water.

That history might be all but forgotten were it not for the

clipping, this reminder of a past horrible enough to intentionally erase. I keep it safe, tucked away in a small, private place where I can get to it if I ever need to remind myself of a crisp, autumn night when a man trying desperately to be a man squeezed his wife as he slept, finding temporary peace in a six-hour knot of work-worn exhaustion, only to be awakened by a casual knock on the front door.

This is not something our family often speaks of — the only words needed are those on the page, void of oral engravings, sketches of heroic endurance, empty libations for someone none of us living can remember.

But my great-grandfather's fortitude is something that those of us on my mother's side who know of it call upon when misfortune strikes. When my grandfather was told that he had the debilitating disease that most likely was what had taken his birth mother, we whispered prayers that blessed the grave of "the one who was killed." When my father was struck by a bus and lay in a coma for two days straight, the right side of his torso decorated with scars, my mother cursed my great-grandfather's attackers and all of the gods that allowed such things to happen. When my childhood cold turned into pneumonia, then turned into bronchitis, my mother pressed the clipping to my feverish cheek as if it were an amulet. My great-grandfather's death is our religion, the clipping our scripture, and the memory our sanctuary.

My mother covets her sons, an unnatural longing that has resulted in my two younger brothers, twins, still occupying the bedrooms of their teens. I am not far off; I live two blocks over in a small, but newish apartment that my mother decorated. Nine months of the year, I teach first graders at the same school where my brothers and I spent our early, awkward years. Now that it is summer, I spend my days watching television and looking out the window at skinny white girls napping by the pool. At night, I chat on the Internet, random associations that allow me to change, metamorphose into the faces of my imaginings, where I can emerge potent and invincible.

I have read how genes often skip a generation: amber eyes, freckles, complexions, even birthmarks appearing as echoes of ancestors, near and far. I have heard that when a man is hanged, he loses consciousness instantly. But I have also heard that sometimes he doesn't, and he feels his eyes spring out of his head, feels the loss of control of his tongue, feels his neck splitting as he kicks and struggles to summon one more breath.

.•

Octavius Benedict is newly married, having lost his first wife to a disease improperly diagnosed by an animal doctor from neighboring Brownsville. After a year of guilt for not paying the colored doctor who had graciously offered to come at a reduced fee, a year in which Octavius drank so much that his young sons were forced to grow up fast, a year of waking visions filled with her emaciated, accusing face, he married again to a seditty nurse from Memphis. Perhaps he had been attracted to the fact that she was in a health profession. Or perhaps it was that she believed in him enough to figure that he wouldn't do the same to her. She trusted him and the boys trusted her, so Octavius decided within weeks of meeting her to make her his wife.

He makes a living farming another man's land in Bolivar, the boys are back in school now because their new mother insists upon it, and she works as a caretaker for a rich, elderly woman. They make do enough to buy a small excuse for a house. Eventually, Octavius falls so deeply in love with this mild-mannered woman that he wonders if his first wife's death was not just a clearing for the second. She even learns how to cook the country way, the way he likes it.

The older son will grow up and move to Memphis. He will marry a high school girl he meets there who he will intentionally get pregnant in order to win her over. They will have one girl-child who will use all of her parents' savings to get the education that they didn't.

The younger son will disappear at the age of seventeen after leaving the house one evening for a box of yeast. He will never return, and his new mother will make herself so sick from worry that this time, this loss will kill her as the first one threatened to.

The article about Octavius Benedict's murder will cause such a stir that it will be printed in the *Commercial Appeal*. His wife won't read it, but the older son will cut it out, save it in his birth mother's Bible. He will hold on to it for his daughter after the doctor delivers the news that the infection has gone bad, and his young wife must have her womanly insides removed, depriving him of the sons he craves so. That daughter will save it for her firstborn son.

She knows me as "Theone." She is simply "Marie." We have been meeting online for over a month now, and most of our exchanges have been quick, mutual masturbations. She lives with her ex-husband, who doesn't know that she can use his computer. He drives a truck most nights. She gets a check.

I know these things because we are beginning to talk more, get to know each other. She tells me that her ex is a user and that she fills fake prescriptions under various names. I tell her that I am a twenty-four-year-old virgin. The screen is blank for a long time after that, and I go fill a glass with orange juice while I await her response.

> Marie: Why?
> Theone: Why what?
> Marie: Why R U still a virgin?
> *Long pause.*
> Theone: Just cause.
> Marie: U never had a girlfriend?
> Theone: Of course I've had a girlfriend.
> Marie: And?
> Theone: And it just never happened that's all.
> Marie: My son. He did it with a girl already.
> Theone: You have a son?

Marie: He's 12.
Theone: I'm sorry.
Marie: Me 2.
I take a sip.
Theone: He's so young.
Marie: What can I say. He's mannish.

I don't know why, but I want to end the conversation right now. I worry about seeming rude. Even so, I log off without saying good-bye. She will understand. This is the nature of these things.

The story that the clipping doesn't tell is what actually happened between Octavius Benedict and Edna Wyatt. Unlike the details of the murder, that part of the history has not been passed down, so I have sketched it in for myself. I imagine that some people reported that Mrs. Wyatt was a low kind of woman and that she and Octavius had a thing going on for some months prior. Others probably said that Octavius bided his time, working for Mr. Wyatt for all those years and watching the old man's wife through the back window of the house nearest the field where he and the others worked. And they probably said that when that conniving bastard finally got the chance, he took it. And maybe there were others in the town, the publicly silent few who whispered behind doors and windows that Octavius was too in love with both of his women to have a lustful eye for a middle-aged shrew like Edna Wyatt.

This is what I think of after the conversation with "Marie." I sleep dreamlessly, but I wake up to the same thoughts of the night before.

Even without looking up, he knows which direction he's headed in. He knows every road in this backcountry, even the ones that he never travels. The wind whistles messages in his ear, and he can tell by the odor of the night air that tomorrow it will rain, bringing welcome nourishment to his thirsty crops.

He struggles to remember her voice, the voice of the first one who made him feel that he could own the land he worked. Instead, he recalls the musky scent of her womanhood and the way her girlish body filled out until her belly swelled with their love. He remembers how he kissed her bump of a navel, trailing his tongue around and around it until she exploded in a ticklish fit.

The paved road turns to gravel and then dirt, cloaking them in a battery of dust. It stings his eyes. The truck lurches over dried craters in the road; branches crackle beneath its wheels. Trees flank them on each side, extending their limbs and meeting above like arms embraced, erasing the full moon. Hollering reaches him from the car behind, and he knows that they are far enough away from the nearest house that the men can now reveal themselves. Deeper, deeper they go until they reach a glade. Massive clouds edge across the sky, leaving the blink of lonely stars in their wake. Insects twitter. Trees sway, a chorus of hands rubbing together in anticipation.

The truck stops and the cars form three points around it. Octavius scans the scene in a quick, but thorough survey. Three cars, four men in each. The truck has one in the cab, three in the back. Sixteen total. Too many. They begin to turn out of the cars, some with rifles, others with sticks or broken off broom handles, and one swinging a long, black object that he doesn't recognize in the darkness.

The first son came so easily. The woman who helped birth him said that it was the easiest delivery she'd ever witnessed. In the dark of the kitchen, they'd placed his boy on the piglet scale. Nine pounds even.

The man sitting across from him says, "You the one. You the one done that to Mrs. Wyatt."

Although he says it quietly enough that the others can't hear, Octavius knows that this is the juried pronouncement, the verdict of the vigilante.

Octavius concentrates on the distant chatter of a magpie. And it arouses his memory of her voice. Yes, that's it. He can hear it now. Leaned toward the high register, but incorporated rich, bass notes when she was serious.

The butt of the gun knocks the voice out of his head.

It's the twins' birthday, and my mother is planning the type of party that you'd give a child. Foil balloons float through the house, wrapping paper rustles behind her closed bedroom door. My father has been standing over the grill all afternoon, flipping slabs of ribs, foot tapping to Bobby Womack, wet, runny face grinning through the smoke. He is holding court with our neighbor, another man his age, reliving his bad motherfucker past and getting badder the more beers they have.

The twins are upstairs competing, so concentrated on their video game that their mouths make strange, grimacing movements as they maneuver gun-toting characters around the television screen with their control pads. They barely look up when I greet them with a "wassup" from the doorway. I envy the nonchalance of their manhood.

The sprawling house feels empty. An impersonal box. I wander through the oversized rooms, seeking a place where I can camp out, remain unobserved. My mother views the size of the house as a tribute to the triumph of our family. To me, it is repressive, confining.

I dread meeting with the usual crowd, my parents' circle of overly affectionate friends who will endlessly remark on how big the twins have gotten and how they are still as identical as ever, as if they can think of nothing more interesting to say to two college dropouts. Then they will ask me about school and how they think male elementary school teachers are darling and when will I have a child of my own. Later, after the twins have devoured as much meat as they can, run thoughtlessly through their gifts, after they have taken a swim in which they race each other until they are bronzed and breathless, their friends will arrive hours late to the party and they will all leave without telling anyone. This will happen just as my parents and their loud-talking bunch bring the party inside and set up a card table.

Octavius manages to respond to the command by pushing himself off the ground to a stand. When everything slows, he observes the man before him, a face that he knows, recognizes from the feed store. The self-appointed leader. Other faces, too, recall scenes, reminders of something that now feels strange. But there is no mutual acknowledgment. The transformation has happened. These men are now remnants of the selves they occupy outside of this secret space, closeted by trees so thick that it seems as if there is no yesterday, no tomorrow. If he strains, Octavius can hear their rapid, uncontrolled breathing over the quieting wind. Their bodies flex with desire.

"Don't you have nothing to say? An explanation for your cowardly act."

Octavius waits without speaking. He will not give that to them. He will not arouse them further.

The man looks past him, and Octavius cannot suppress the urge to turn around. He had not noticed it before, but there is one tree near the edge of the circle with a single, lone branch jutting in his direction, a finger pointing.

Both of his sons had been easy births. He feels good about the older one because he is strong. Bullheaded, but cool. He knows how to keep his temper in check. It's the younger one that he worries most about. He's only thirteen, but Octavius can already tell that he will not fare well in this world. The boy doesn't understand because of his immaturity, but he refuses because of his spirit. Like the time that Octavius told him not to be taking that shortcut through Donnie Pryor's field. And then the whipping he'd had to stand by and watch the old man give his boy when he was caught. Or the time when their cat was found cut open wide, and the younger one again, barely of school age, convinced that he knew the culprit, had thrown a rock at the suspected offender's dog, leaving the mongrel with a crooked, sideways walk and one eye running from the other. Octavius wonders if he should have beat him more. He hadn't laid a hand on either one of his boys since their mother died, and now he wonders if he should have. Thinking of this grieves him.

Someone kicksweeps him and he collapses. The follow-up kick in his ribs knocks the wind out of him.

"You think you can just have any white woman you want, don't you. You think you can just stick your thing in any of our women anytime you get ready, don't you."

The voices run into one another. They kick him in the stomach, the back, and put a boot to his neck. He tries to protect himself by cradling his head. But it leaves other parts exposed, and they swing at him with their homemade weapons, weapons easily disposed of in a backyard bonfire. One of his eyes pulsates and it goes dark on that side.

"Teach . . . you . . . we'll . . . teach you."

They drag him by his feet, and the ground burns his back, ripping the skin. Unconsciousness threatens, but he fights it. He cannot think, can only react instinctively in a litany of Jesuses in his head. Then even the words stop, and he is reduced to that which they make him.

The muffled sounds of partying seep through the closed door of my former bedroom-turned-home office. The screensaver on the computer monitor is no doubt my mother's idea, an African mask with a white, elongated face and high, regal forehead. I log in as "SweetWillie" and become a lurker, watching bits of conversations play out in public chatrooms, people struggling to connect amidst a myriad of voices so that they can later Instant Message one another in private.

"Hey you."

I jump and turn around, instinctively pushing the button that will close my active window and uncover a Web site for a popular newsmagazine. It is the fluid motion of one who is practiced enough to always be prepared to hide his computer activities.

"Hey," I say. I know her. She is the daughter of that judge, whats-hisface. We went to high school together. I remember that her name is Salina. I remember that she had a certain reputation.

"Your mom told me you were probably up here. I'm bored down there."

"Oh."

"I can come in, right?"

"Sure." I fumble for a moment as she pushes the door open. Even though it is now an office, I still feel territorial about it as if it is still my bedroom. She sits on the wine-colored loveseat, and drapes an arm across the back. The room fills with her presence, and her eyes refuse to give me a moment's relief.

"You look the same," I say. This is my attempt to say that she looks good. Pretty. Sexy. Dangerous. She still sports the same short natural haircut from high school. But her outfit is grown up, modest, loose-fitting. Even so, I can make out her curves because she is plumper than she used to be. It is hard to hide so much thigh, so much breast. I catch her eye and she appears to be watching my mouth, as if she expects me to be on the verge of saying something important. I sit suspended between her and the computer screen, frozen in utter inadequacy.

"You look good. Better." She nods at the screen. "What were you doing?"

"What?"

"There." She points at the screen.

"Nothing. Just . . . surfing."

She stands and walks toward me. I am transfixed by her jiggles. She leans over me and takes the mouse beneath her fingertips. Something grazes my cheek. I stiffen.

"Let me show you something," she says. She types in an address that I cannot see past her bulk.

She stands back. Able to breathe again, I wait as the Web site comes up. It's her personal homepage. SALINA scrolls across the top of the screen.

"Do you like it?"

"Why do you have a homepage?" I ask.

"I want to be an actress. This Web site is for my publicity shots. Look at them. You're not even looking at them."

"In Memphis? How are you going to be an actress in Memphis?"

"Why not? You can act in Memphis. You're not looking." She clicks on her face.

"But why not move to L.A.? That's where you need to go."

A picture of her wearing an orange bikini comes up on the screen. Then it fades into another picture, in a different bathing suit. Picture after picture of a near-naked Salina.

"Because I'm good enough to make it here." She melts into my neck.

My body responds against my wishes. My arm girdles her waist. I pull her to me until she is sitting on my lap, and I am surprised by the confidence of my touch. I am now "SlickWillie" and she is the temptress of her pictures. We lean back in the office chair as far back as it will go. She takes my face in her hands and says "it's OK, it's OK" over and over, as if she is granting me permission. Then I get nervous. I start to shake and when she tries to kiss me, I push her back so hard that she falls off my lap.

"Honey?"

Salina scrambles to her feet at the sound of my mother's voice. My mother stands in the doorway, one hand propped against the doorjamb. I know she has seen what we were doing, but she acts as if she hasn't. Her attention is elsewhere.

"Sweetheart, please excuse us, please excuse us for a minute. Would you? I need to talk to my son."

Salina exits without a word, without even a glance in my direction. The looping slideshow of her in bathing suits continues to run on the screen. I don't move to stop it. I just sit there, awash in a puddle of shame.

My mother sweeps into the room, silky fabrics swishing with the stale scent of perfume, fingers covered in gold rings, neck draped in clunky plastic jewelry. It is hard to know where her outfit ends and she begins. Her bracelets rattle as she reaches for my shoulder.

"I need the clipping."

Her voice is hoarse with anxiety. I know what is to come before I even ask.

"Why?"

"Because I'm giving it to your brothers for their birthday. None of that other shit meant anything to them. I'm going to give them something that means . . . you know . . . something that means . . . something. You know."

I am stunned. I did not expect this.

"No, Mama."

"You still got it, don't you? You still got the clipping?" The side of her face jumps and her words now carry the southern drawl of her youth, a secret that she rarely shares.

I remove her hand from my shoulder and stand to face her. I want to tell her about my fear. No. I want to slap her. I want to hurl my pain at her. But she does not see me. She is looking at my face, but not at my eyes. Nothing I say will matter.

"Come on now. Maybe it'll help them get back in school. You still got it, don't you?"

"No, Mama." I speak, shake my head, and move out of the room all at the same time. I rush down the hall and ignore her calling me back. When I turn the corner, I walk right into a soft mass of flesh. Salina corners me. Her eyes glint threateningly.

"What the hell was wrong with you back there?"

I push past her without answering and run through the laundry room out the back door. The sound of glasses clinking and B.B. King picking the guitar grows fainter behind me as I pick up speed, running past boxlike hedges, away from the house, away from my family, away from our history.

He is running, pushing through tangles of trees and brush. His sense of direction is completely gone, but he thinks he knows enough not to circle back. And the animals are helping. He can hear the ripping shouts of the men behind him, the firing of their rifles as they mistake the movement of night creatures for him.

My. Sons. Oh. Woman.

His thoughts come back as one-syllable words. He has just come as close to death as any man ever has, but he still thinks only of his family. He can no longer feel the raw wounds of his seared flesh, the broken fingers, the torn rectum, his mind shattered into enough pieces to tell him to fight through sixteen men, grab the hot iron, swing it at one of them so hard that he could hear the skull crack, and run into the trees.

And the woods welcome him, brambles grazing him gently as if refusing to hurt him any more than he has already been hurt. A strange bird follows him overhead, directing him as it flits from tree to tree. On the ground, a spry raccoon hurries him along, turning to look at him as if to say "keep up." His breath comes in rapid gusts, but he is not winded. He feels as if he can run forever.

Up ahead, he can see the light of a house. Glowing with the promise of help. The bird cheers him along, congratulating him on his success, and the raccoon reminds him that his pursuers aren't far behind. He is almost there.

He sees the man and the woman before they see him. The man is standing on his porch in his underwear, peering into the forest. She is illuminated in the doorway, a vision in white.

"Who's out there?" the man yells into the night.

The calls of the posse behind Octavius grow louder and more distinct. They are no longer wasting ammunition by shooting aimlessly, but the man on the porch seems to sense that there is danger coming. He goes into the house and returns with a shotgun, shoving the woman inside.

The bird prods Octavius on, and he runs out of the darkness into the man's line of sight. He cannot form the word, so he just thinks it. *Help.*

He believes that he feels the burning sensation in his shoulder before he hears the sound of the gun. But he keeps going in the direction of the man and the home. Surely they will help. Surely.

"Get back, now. Get back off my property I say." He cocks his rifle.

Octavius slows, but keeps going.

The gun cracks again and Octavius feels the pain surge through his leg. He falls to the ground, clutching his knee, crying for the first time that night.

Just before the posse reaches him, Octavius looks up and sees the man pull the white-faced woman away from the window. She looks right down at him, and he is close enough to the house to believe that he sees pity in her eyes. The lights in the house dim.

This time, as they drag him back into the woods, rougher and angrier than before, Octavius cannot even remember who he is. And he wonders how he got there.

[VOL. XXIX, NO. 3 / SUMMER 2007]

LORI WHITE

Postcards from the Road

1.

Tahoe hasn't changed much. The Golden Spike still has that wooden statue of Sitting Bull out front. Where'd that picture go? I thought Mom used to keep it on her dresser: you and me and the Sioux Indian chief. The finds haven't been too good. Picked up a carom board like the one we used to play with that summer at Cottontail. Thought you might like to have it. Lost a couple hundred at the Shores, but I met a guy at the table who says he can turn me on to a few estate sales. Good stuff. Swap meet rats love that shit. Things go quick, so I gotta get there early. I'll make my way south 'til the U-Haul's full, then home. Are you close to settling the probate? I could use the trailer to move everything into the house before turning it in. I'll try to call when I get to Stockton.

2.

Not much happening in the Central Valley, so I drove out to Bridgeport. Never understood why Mom was always bugging Dad to retire in Phoenix; California's got plenty of desert right here in the Mojave. After estate sales, alley drags have been paying off most. Found a dinette set like the one in the kitchen. Did Aunt Linda give that to us or was it Gram's? I'm headed north again to San Luis. Left a message for you with your secretary while you were in court. Don't forget: I need to be out of those storage spaces by the fifth. I just read the fine print on the copy you gave me. Guess Mom's still looking out for you with that 15 percent executor's fee. Fine, take it, no hard feelings. Somebody's got to be the favorite. We always worked best as a Smothers Brothers act. Maybe we can go fishing up at Castaic when I get back. I think our old rods are in the shed, but wait for me to go through everything, OK?

3.

Pismo turned out to be a jackpot. I went down to Ventura for three days; they've got a flea market there that draws from as far away as L.A. Sold most everything; sorry about the carom board. Almost called to have you come up for the day. They restored the old pier and I spent a night at the Blue Dolphin, for old time's sake. Mom used to say we stayed there because I liked the pool, but I bet a room like Gram's at the Biltmore was more than Dad could fork out. I'm headed back up to Salinas for one more sweep. Figure I can use the garage to store whatever's left. Been thinking about Mom's Pontiac. Maybe we shouldn't sell it so quick. I could use it to get around town when the truck's full.

4.

Walt gave me your message. Guess you knew I'd end up here eventually. Not surprised she'd pull this. Mom always had to have the last say, even in the afterlife. I'll sign whatever you need. "Keeping up the property" is open to interpretation, isn't it? I've learned that much about the law from you, little brother. San Francisco is full of secondhand shops, offering me three times what I paid for what she's calling junk. Ran into Karen downtown; looks as good as she did when we were in college. Seems she didn't know about you and Denise. Told her the divorce is final—hope I'm not jumping the gun. She might buy a coffee table from me so I'm springing for dinner tonight at Antonio's. Maybe even have a bottle of wine to seal the deal.

5.

I'm on my way home tomorrow, should be back by Thursday. Eureka was totally worth the trip. Got enough inventory now to set myself up at the Pasadena meet, if you include what's in the storage spaces. Perhaps I should call you "Counselor" from now on? I know you think Mom had her reasons, but try it from where I'm sitting. Even though I'm crazy Nate, maybe she gave me the house 'cause I didn't wreck a marriage. Cheating on your wife's got to be a step or two below having a drifter for a son. Leave the key in the usual place, will you? Dinner with Karen went well, by the way. I'll come by your office once I unload.

[VOL. XXIX, NO. 3 / SUMMER 2007]

The Writer's Wife

Look at him, my active man. Sometimes he sits and turns to the left. Sometimes, to the right. I wouldn't think of disturbing him. He is dreaming his writer's dreams, and his dreams are inviolable. I have the privilege of serving him, and of watching him.

Did you say something, dear? Nothing yet? Still dreaming? Well, while you're at it, I'd better get to my chores. No, don't get up. I can handle it: Fix the engine on the Prius; recondition the Steinway; point up the bricks on the west wall; build a bathroom in the basement, from scratch. Busy, busy is the writer's wife.

And please, don't even think of lowering yourself to the details of bill paying, dry cleaning, shopping, cooking, dishwashing, trash toting. May I get the door for you? May I get two?

Am I complaining about my lot? Never, sweetheart. The intellectual challenges alone make it worthwhile. How many ways can I invent to assure you that you're not losing your touch? Our topics of conversation: Your obligation to your gift. My obligation to your obligation. Were you born before your time, or after your time, or just in time? I forget.

Then there's our social life. The dinner parties, where everyone speaks in quotations. The book parties, where everyone says, "*There* he is." Or variously: "*There* she is!"

Do I want to go to Elaine's? Are you kidding? I want to live there!

And don't worry. I've laid out your uniform. Dark suit, dark shirt, dark tie. Your special look.

Do you think you might speak to me this month? It was so nice last month, or was it the month before that, when you asked me how I was. For a moment there, I thought you'd asked *who* I was. That's just a little joke. Nothing to upset yourself about. But what am I saying? Why would you be upset? Why would you—sitting there in your dreamscape—why would you even look up?

My folks, having met you but once, suggested I marry an actuary or a mortgage broker. Or a wife beater. Hell, what do parents know about the life of the mind—yours. The precious moments we share—

Such as the times you ask me to read something you've written, and if I say "I love it!" you say I'm blowing you off, and if I appear disappointed or confused, you go into a clinical depression, and if I say, "Then, please don't ask me, if you don't want my opinion," you go into a clinical depression.

Oh, dear. Did I say, "That was the best thing you ever wrote"? Of course, what I meant to say was, "Everything you write is a masterpiece. And this latest masterpiece just proves it." That's what I meant to say. You're right. I must learn to say what I mean. Forgive me?

But soon we make up, and you'll say, "Let's go to so-and-so's poetry reading." And I'll say, "Oh, darling! Let's! Just give me a minute to freshen up and hang myself from the hall chandelier"—which, by the way, I repaired last week.

Memories? Say, rather, treasures! The day your agent returned your call. The day your editor returned your call. The day you found your name in the papers. In the phone book. Remember the time we saw your first novel on sale in the Strand for one dollar? How we laughed! The night you awoke with an inspiration for a story, and in the morning it sounded so silly?

Remember when I tried to write something myself, and you said it was "interesting"?

You know? I used to *like* books.

Ah. You've turned to the left again. I'm pooped, just watching you. Watching you in your dreams. I dream, too. Here's mine: Lord, please let him find a younger woman.

[VOL. XXIX, NO. 4 / FALL 2007]

COLLEEN KINDER

One Bright Case of Idiopathic Cranofacial Erythema

I blamed the malady on my Irish side: the relatives who stared out from baby pictures like porcelain dolls. My mom's parents were immigrants, effortfully proper in that just-hoping-to-blend-in-and-prosper kind of way, not to mention Catholic. Severely Catholic. When I read about "lace curtain Irish" in an American Studies course in college, my ancestors provided an instant visual.

My father's side, on the contrary, is a long line of American mutts, California-based for too many decades to trace back across the Atlantic. Dad grew up in a house with sandals, TV dinners, various pets, no religiously coded conduct rules. The paternal genes were more loosely bound: less Mass, more beach. I never considered them as carriers.

Until the night the loud speaker called my Dad.

"Would the parents of the players please come out . . ."

He and I were high in the bleachers, slumped against the wall, waiting for the Holy Angels basketball game to begin. We were not expecting a voice.

"Oh, geez." Dad obeyed the voice, rising to his feet.

I consider my father a self-assured man. He started a business; he gives a fine toast; he'll make small talk with a corn farmer as easily as a senator. But standing at half court, amidst the other parents, my dad turned the color of a pig roasted on charcoals. The blush spanned from shirt collar to balding spot. It dimmed none as Sister Kristen thanked the parents for their support, brownies, carpools—nothing remotely mortifying.

I looked down court, baffled. I'd have to revise my inheritances. Mom was the reason I wore SPF 45. Dad: why I sat in last rows.

＊＊

"*Blushing*, though a fleeting episode, is experienced as an unwelcome public revelation of one's most private thoughts," wrote Angela Simon about a study at Morehead State University. "By 'blushing,' we specifically mean the transient feeling of warmth and/or skin color change associated with the occurrence of acute self-consciousness."

＊＊

Blushers remember a first time.

Sixth grade. Mrs. Mikulec had us keep journals in Language Arts class. I took the assignment further—on a plane to California.

Somewhere between Buffalo and San Francisco, a fleecy patch of clouds passed my oval window. Listening to the *Aladdin* sound track for about the seventeenth time, I was stirred by the coinciding songs of nature and Disney, and I opened my journal. There, I composed something that felt like true language art: my first metaphor.

Back at Christ the King, during a routine moment when boys shuffled through backpacks, girls clicked pens, Mrs. Mikulec called on me. She wanted me to share my latest journal entry with the class.

"No," I said.

"Yes, Colleen, it's lovely. Just read the plane part."

"No."

"C'mon, Colleen. They'll appreciate it."
"No way."
I had likened Delta flight 404 to a magic carpet ride.
"Yes. Get up here."
"No way."
"Colleen—"
One week had passed since the plane ride. One week, in the sixth grade scheme of growth, is enough to change your mind about everything. To forget your sanitary crush on Aladdin and start lusting after Jared Leto. A week is enough to decide you hate your own words. To regret language art.
"I *can't.*"
There was a podium in the front of the room.

••

Science explains it in this order:
    1. Situation causes shame or awkwardness.
    2. Adrenaline is released.
    3. Heart rate climbs.
    4. Breathing quickens.
    5. Facial blood vessels dilate.
    6. Blood flows to face.
    7. More blood flows to face.
    8. Face turns noticeably red.
    1-7, in a word, as heard from the inside: *Foooosh.*

••

It wasn't Aladdin. It wasn't the language art. It was her siege, multiplied by my resistance. A declaration to the public—the sixth grade class of Christ the King School—that reading in front of them was the last thing I desired to do. Then doing it.
    I watched the rest happen from the back row. I watched over Peter's head, over Ellen's, over Brian's, watching them watch the color bloom, billow, spread to the outer reaches of my face,

quitting only at the hairline. People think blushing is the fear of public attention. There's a difference between picking up the microphone, and the microphone plucking your name. The difference is a drastic crimson.

· ·

Participants in a study reported that it takes one to four seconds for a blush to occur.

Or longer. Or five to ten seconds.

It depends on the subject. It depends on how the subject defines his or her blush. How he or she visualizes the color advancing across the cheeks — in a poof? as a streak? like the reindeer's nose? Imagination colors the blush, clocks the blush. Imagination reads panic, or shame, or both. That first flicker, or its aftermath? Which supplies the color, which the heat?

I wonder about this blush of the imagination. When the test participants paused, their number two pencils hanging above the multiple choice options — 1-4 seconds, 5-10 seconds, 11-25 seconds, half minute or more — what public shaming dislodged from memory? Was it any quicker in the reliving?

· ·

Sister Karen Marie made a sport of calling on her most mortifyable pupils. There were three Colleens in my class of fifty. Two-thirds of these Colleens had the middle name Ann(e), two-thirds were redheaded, and three-thirds were prone to full-face blushes. I remember with pain the day "SKM" called Colleen McCarthy up to the chalkboard for some fill-in-the-blank-with-Bible-writers exercise. Colleen McCarthy did not know the Bible writer. SKM would not let her sit back down.

"Look," SKM said, alerting us to the sight of Colleen, fuming panic against the green chalkboard. "It's Christmas."

· ·

When Angela Simon asked blushers how other people respond to their facial coloration, the most common response was: "They tease and try to get me to blush more."

· ·

Willpower accomplished nothing. In fact, willpower like mine just stoked the fire. So I tried avoidance. I steered clear of any situation that might give my skin occasion to flare. I wore shorts under my plaid uniform skirt. I locked my journal in a small box under my bed and hid the key inside an unassuming stuffed animal beaver whose tail region I had slit open with a scissors. I did not raise my hand.

· ·

Erythrophobia refers to a pathological fear of blushing. It means "fear of redness."

· ·

Invisibility gets boring, particularly once puberty begins. I tried a new strategy. I set out to convince my public that they were rude to point out a blush. "That's the *worst* thing you can do," I'd chastise, on behalf of blushers everywhere. The problem was less in my cheeks, I'd realized, more in their eyes. So if they could just be a tad less *explicit* about their observations, notify me on a less frequent basis, in a less public fashion, then I might just see it was a breeze passing through my complexion. Passing. Breeze. Might. Just.

· ·

Peter Drummond put fifty-six college women in a lab room in Murdoch University in Perth, Australia, and told them to sing aloud to "I Will Survive" by Gloria Gaynor for twenty seconds. After each woman sang, the experimenter entered the lab room to inform her whether or not she had blushed. At random, half of the women were told they blushed; the rest told they had not.

Each woman was then left alone for four minutes. After these four minutes, the experimenter returned and played a recording of "I Will Survive" with the subject's voice in the background. Her voice was louder than Gloria Gaynor's.

As hypothesized, Peter Drummond found that having given blushing feedback to those who scored high on the Blushing Propensity Scale increased blood flow to the face, progressively.

"These findings suggest that expecting to blush may become a self-fulfilling prophecy."

· ·

You could boil my early development down to two traits. The first: ambition. Its underbelly: fear. Not raw fear, but the anticipatory sort.

$F^2 =$

Fear of my fear of not catching baseballs.

Fear of my fear of singing like a seagull.

Fear of my fear of holding babies too stiffly.

Then I grew up. I sophisticated. I specialized the ambition, got distance on the fear. By "got distance," I mean multiplied it out.

$F^3 =$ Fear of flare-up.

Fear of my fear of my fear of forgetting names.

Fear of my fear of my fear of my fear of sounding insincere.

Fear of my fear of my fear of clicking "*no*" when asked "*Save Changes?*"

What keeps all formulas intact is the blush—the awareness that I'm transparent. Faced with a public, for better or worse, I run the risk of lucidity. In the event of a falter, a curve ball, an unexpected, I have no place to handle it deeper than the plane of my skin.

· ·

The awareness-raising campaign proved problematic. I was *telling* people they had the power to hike up the hue of my cheeks, learning, meanwhile, that even friends—even fellow Colleens—will lord such power. So why not deny it? I could accuse my audience of blush illiteracy. A *blush is not a blush is not a blush*. But rather:

a) Amusement. Church giggles smothered in a sleeve.

s) Surprise. Spider in the shower.

p) Panic. Wallet not in your pocket. Wallet not in your purse.

e) Empathy. Colleen McCarthy kept at the blackboard, called Christmas.

d) Deluge of Emotion X. The end of *Ghost*.

A blush can manifest anything. A blush can manifest something *good*. Hilarious! Something you don't know about. Even though roughly 87% of my blushes were born of raw humiliation, I prattled on about the spectrum. Not only because 13% was substantial, but because adolescence was teaching me things about self-esteem. About mine, it's quirks. That what I needed, for the time being, was a placebo.

· ·

The Maybelline Blush Scale:
Flushed.Blush.Peach.Punch.Roseberry.Flame.Cherry.Wine.

· ·

How do I know I blush?

I do. I know, because that much heat can't be white. How could it stay porcelain white? I know I blush because I've laid a hand against my cheek, afterwards, felt it calm like a light bulb. I know because my skin's thin and colorless; I've peeled it off after sunburns—sunburns that made strangers suck back their breath, sunburns I relished, under which I could smolder to high heaven. Only on sunburn days did I have room to imagine what it's like in another's pigment. With my skin scorched, I considered how I might act, given a guest pass to a Greek. How I could pull off just about anything, both cheeks dressed up. How, if all those F's got reciprocated, even for a couple hours, the base might be snuffed right out.

．．

- *Flushed*: The windowless office of my teaching assistant Angus, who wore kilts and never sat down when discussing a work of Shakespeare.
- *Blush*: "It says 'Card Rejected, ma'am. Insufficient funds?'"
- *Peach*: Saying good-bye, to anyone—but men especially—on elevators.
- *Punch*: Realizing, mid-afternoon, March 9, that I had not written a rent check since people were remarking "Happy New Year."
- *Roseberry*: Fielding a nun's question—what religion are you?
- *Flame*: At the table of the MFA workshop, hearing this essay's narrator critiqued.
- *Cherry*: The subway car where I spilled a bag of plastic hangers, moving my belongings from Manhattan to Brooklyn by F trains.
- *Wine*: The backdoor of a man who held eye contact too long, as he placed the *Collected Works of Hunter S. Thompson* into my hands. Fumble. Thump. *Fooosh.*

．．

How do I know I blush? Actually *color*? Peach then punch then flame, skipping cherry, to wine? I know because I've caught the aftermath in bathroom mirrors. I know I blush because there's a yearbook photo of my Dad and me dancing "The Twist" in the Holy Angels Father-Daughter Dance Competition. A long rash stretches from cheekbone to jaw.

I know I blush because there are precedents, photo evidence, physical heat. I know I blush by my audience. Because people do the favor of lowering their eyes. Because other people don't. Other people let you know what they see. Like I didn't feel the spike in temperature. Like I wasn't the furnace.

How do I know I blush? Pink, red, scarlet? Because that's a preposterous question. Because I've never entertained that I don't: it's that forcible. That visual. Each skin cell, an eye.

• •

Some claim that blushing is purposeful, from an evolutionary standpoint. Had it no purpose, humankind's red-faced would have been eliminated from the gene pool long ago — as, were, perhaps, a freak purple-faced people who never got their pale counterparts into bed.

Blushing clues onlookers in that the looked-upon person is suffering. The onlookers, then, have the prerogative to alleviate that suffering. Their options are many: crack joke, digress, flatter, point. You might call blushing involuntary communication — a tacit apology for a moment, a secret, a fumble, a fart. One individual feels the heat; the clan gleans the meaning; society is less contentious for all.

This evolutionary compromise must have been hammered out before language was. With a few words, a sensitive soul might have raised her hand and explained that there's pain in it for the spectator, too — even from the back row, the top bleacher. If evolution could come up with empathy, it should have done away with the blush. And when humans began chatting, their skin could have stopped saying so much.

• •

I didn't know any Koreans until college. The first Korean I made friends with didn't drink. "The Asian flush," he said, regretfully. I didn't know what that was, but doubted it could trump my blush.

He explained that his face could flare up after a single drink. *Funny*, I thought. My people drink to cancel out the blush — to enable what would, in sober hours, stain the skin a guilty scarlet.

For my first three years of college, I kissed no one without a half-quart of alcohol in my bloodstream. I spent my Sundays hung-over, reminded over brunch what was comedic about my Saturday night. It wasn't until my senior year that a nice young man stopped by my dorm room — on a Tuesday — and we ended up horizontal on the futon.

"*Stay*," I told his ear, surprising myself.

"I should go," Chris said, sounding pliable.

He and I would quarrel about the conditions of our inaugural kiss for the next two years. I remembered this: me on top of Chris, playing predator — sober predator — for the first time in my life. Chris objects, having full memory of the previous Saturday evening, when he escorted me home from a toga party, to make out, until I got up to throw up.

. .

Studies of blushing have aimed to identify the personality traits of people with high "blushing propensity scores." In 1991, Leary and Meadows published a list of these traits.

The first was "embarassibility."

Then "interaction anxiousness."

Followed by "self esteem."

And finally "refinement."

Leary and Meadows explain that by "refinement," they mean "the degree to which one enjoys or is repulsed by crass, uncouth, and vulgar behavior."

. .

Early morning. Planned Parenthood. I'm excessively early, having applied the caution to "beat the line" too earnestly. I nap in the cabin of the car, hearing others pull up: women, girls, their friends. I hope this will be quick. I just need birth control.

But birth control requires an exam, my nurse tells me. I expected a warm woman; she is not warm. "We can't prescribe a pill without testing for herpes." I pause—then realize this is not a choice she's presenting. She gets tools. At the sight of these tools, my hands begin rubbing one another, rubbing hard. I wasn't expecting a test. My fingers knead my knuckles. Then knead palms. The talking stops. She doesn't give fair warning. The metal's cold.

"You need to relax."

My fingers knead my palms. "OK." My fingers knead my eyebrows. They knead into eyeballs. I try gripping the paper gown.

"You're *pushing*," my nurse sighs. "Relax."

I am told about pushing and am supposed to relax.

"Take a breath." I take a breath, as my nurse observes, no patience in her body language, no placing aside tools. I'm doing that thing that complicates her job: working myself up.

"*Relax.*"

Chris would know. He could read the braiding tension. He knew how to melt my resistance and pace us just behind it. This is what first love meant: a man literate in the exponential fears, patient enough to wait them out, saying nothing but what helped. Sweet-nothing placebos.

"You're crying." That's not a concern. That's the accusation of my nurse.

Sex was an obvious fear. It fell on the same side of the line as singing solos and driving go-carts and spelling aloud at bees. Performance—with audience; not work I could master alone. I learned about sex among Catholics, girls who aspired to bring virginity on their honeymoons. F had years to multiply, and did.

"I won't do this with you pushing," the nurse protested, tool down.

These are the moments I don't get people. These are the moments when not getting people feels like tightness just behind the eyebrows, an ice-cream headache, a tear pen. *Relax*. As if self-command were that simple, a linear path — brain to cheeks, brain to legs, brain to belief.

··

Hypothesis: Since previous research has proven that blushing phobics do not have a particularly low threshold for blushing or especially intense coloration, then fear of blushing may be fueled by mechanisms other than facial color, such as a biased interpretation of the communicative value of the blush.

Participants: Forty female undergraduates at Maastricht University

Method: Females presented with vignettes of awkwardness (e.g. spilling wine, mistakenly picking up someone else's backpack and getting accosted by that person, spilling coffee).

Remuneration for participants: Chocolate bars.

Title of study: "Do Blushing Phobics Overestimate the Undesirable Communicative Effects of Their Blushing?"

Summary of conclusions: No.

··

How I know I blush: Chris.

I just e-mailed, saying hey, writing about blushing, starting to wonder, as out of control as I think?

"When you blush, it's slow, steady and complete," replies Chris. "Pretty much the entire face to your ears."

He continues, "When you're trying to control it, when you're in a public situation, you usually stick your neck out and nod a little, with a bit of an 'oh my' smile on your mouth. Or you do a little nod and cough, your lips tight."

About here, I had to look away from the monitor.

• •

The most common strategy that participants of Angela Simon's study used to conceal a blush was: "try not to act embarrassed."

• •

"When it's a complete surprise, you say 'Whoah,' kind of laugh to cover up the blush, and sort of stumble a few steps back, your left hand on the crook of your right arm, and the right arm kind of fanning the air to get the embarrassing thing away."

About here, I wished I hadn't asked.

• •

Last try: humor.

" . . . Then I turned BRI-ght red," my sister and I say when recounting our episodes. Molly not only shares my tendency to turn BRI-ght red, but she has BRI-ght red hair. Moreover, she is gorgeous. Molly has grown up with eyes on her, questions peppering her commute: if not "*You play basketball?*" then, "*Do you model?*" At my sister's six-feet two altitude, there's no place to hide a burst of color.

Self-deprecation she has made her art. Molly has dinner party guests rolling on the floor with first-date catastrophe tales. She digs up photos of herself in fanny packs, visors, braces, and attaches them to group e-mails. I can't tell if this is an entrenched defense mechanism, or if this is a swan, reveling in the ugly duckling days.

Regardless, I've adopted Molly's tactic. I've learned to make fun of my blush before anyone can pity it. To lean on the *BRI* in bright. To mime a facial explosion, using all ten fingers. *Foosh.* Watching Molly lets me imagine that the blush is an element of my charm—sweet, bizarre, old-fashioned, BRI-ight. I try hard to believe that any one inclined to like or love me would like or love me for bleeding emotion through my skin. That the blush is the flourish of an idiosyncratic voice. One that apologizes, but doesn't. That self-loathes as readily as it self-loves. That can't dwell on any gradation of self-perception in between.

"Of course then I turned *BRI-ght* red," I hear myself working into my stories, particularly around people I've recently met. New, uncalibrated audiences. If they think I'm OK with the color storms—or if *I* think *they* think I'm OK—then the flash flood moment is less disarming—to me first, then them, though by them, it doesn't matter. It's my defense mechanism come full circle. I've taken the audience out of the equation. Now: it's a question of charming myself. How convincingly? Can't tell you.

• •

Sister Karen Marie showed us what Christmas looked like, but left it to her Holy Angels pupils to learn about the postcoital blush for themselves.

Before I knew there was such a term, I stood before the wall-to-wall mirror of my dorm room bathroom, one hand raised to one cheek. The cuts of rouge stunned me—how brazenly, how beautifully, the red clashed against the lace-curtain white expanse of chest. Here was a blush in full bloom, no freckle of shame visible beneath it.

Science claims that the facial coloration of sexual climax has no relation to erythrophobia. What I know science neglects to consider is how much a woman has to let go in order to reach her peak.

• •

In 1990, Shields, Mallory, and Simon discovered a correlation between blushing and age. As subjects grew older, they blushed less—with less *frequency*. No note on the intensity of the facial coloration.

. .

All three sisters are together—Katie, Molly, and I—on vacation, riding in a taxi cab in southern India. Molly lives here now, New Dehli's token six-foot redhead. Just the other day, outside the Taj Mahal, I watched her get mauled by no less than fifty giggle-frenzied school girls and short middle-aged men. *"One snap!"* the strangers chimed, holding up cameras, beckoning family members to join in. The whole crew forsaking the white fortress at our backs. The most photographed site in the world.

On our taxi ride through the mountains, Molly and I begin exchanging mortifying moments, one-upping each other's crimson climaxes. Molly at Pakistani customs, the intimate contents of her suitcase yanked out. Me: bungling dance lessons in Havana, claiming *"tengo un problema con los pies."* Molly: fidgeting with PowerPoint, ten quiet coworkers waiting. Me fumbling for my cell phone, a noise-free writer's colony tisking. Stains here, burps there—

"God, you guys," Katie says with disdain. Katie, sitting shotgun, holding her place as oldest child, looks out the cab window. Katie has never been a blusher. She sunburns like an albino, but no rashes of shame. I attribute this to confidence—confidence she grew up *with,* not into. There are no microscopic eyes camping out in Katie's skin.

"Stop," she commands us. "This is painful."

We ignore Katie. We keep going. *"Then I turned BRI-ght red . . ."* We pile blush upon blush, until our faces bloom with vicarious shame. "I'm talking BRI-ght red."

Molly fans her face, the laughter asphyxiating her. *"You DIDN'T . . ."*

I notice pink blotches at the base of Molly's neck. I've never had neck blotches. Have I?

Katie is shaking her head. Without seeing her face, I know Katie's lips are parted, displeased and uncomprehending. *"Jesus . . ."* she says, wishing her last name was Tomasseli.

I can think of no better use of a reunion of Kinder's than this. A mutual roasting, remembering that when I turn the color of Pinot Noir, I'm in beloved company.

I do the honors. Dredge up the latest blush. For old times' sake, I make Katie and Molly squirm and glow, respectively . . .

. .

"I don't like meeting people's eyes so I focus on eyebrows instead." I read this admission aloud to a freshman Rhetoric class at the University of Iowa. I'm leaning against the edge of the front desk. It has taken me two and a half months to hazard such a lean, fearing that the fold-up desk would collapse upon meeting the rookie teacher's buttock. Today: so far, so good.

I've just had my students write on a piece of paper:

1) What they find hardest about public speaking

2) What mental trick they use to overcome their fears

Now, after collecting the twenty-three scraps of folded paper, shuffling them for anonymity, I'm sharing with the class.

"I practice my speech in front of a mirror in my dorm. . . ."

The University of Iowa requires all freshmen to give three speeches for this Gen-Ed class. The University of Iowa does not give its Rhetoric teaching assistants any guidance on how to teach public speaking. My pedagogy is about as sophisticated as the plastic grin of a soccer mom. I coax; I nod; I'm always the first to clap.

I figure it might behoove them to know that few phobias are unique. And since it's the gimmicks, the mental ploys, the placebos that tide us over until our confidence finds a way to solidify, then I can at least give my students' confessions a safe, faceless forum.

"I hold my hands in my pockets so no one sees them shake. . . ."

I interject supportive commentary as I read: "Yup, that's hard for all of us," or "Not a bad idea."

"I don't think public speaking is that hard so please—"

My voice slows. It's too late to censor the sentence. I feel twin bull's-eyes emerging on my cheeks. Forty-six silent eyes have me.

"— *stop making such a big deal about it.*"

[KR ONLINE / SUMMER 2008]

No

The most honest rejection letter I ever received for a piece of writing was from *Oregon Coast Magazine*, to which I had sent a piece that was half bucolic travelogue and half blistering attack on the tendencies of hamlets along the coast to seek the ugliest and most lurid neon signage for their bumper-car emporia, myrtlewood lawn-ornament shops, used-car lots, auto-wrecking concerns, terra-cotta nightmares, and sad moist flyblown restaurants.

"Thanks for your submission," came the handwritten reply from the managing editor. "But if we published it we would be sued by half our advertisers."

This was a straightforward remark and I admire it, partly for its honesty, a rare shout in a world of whispers, and partly because I have, in thirty years as a writer and editor, become a close student of the rejection note. The shape, the color, the prose, the tone, the subtext, the speed or lack thereof with which it arrives, even the typeface or scrawl used to stomp gently on the writer's heart — of these things I sing.

. .

One of the very best: a rejection note sent by the writer Stefan Merken to an editor who had rejected one of his short stories. "Please forgive me for not accepting your rejection letter," wrote Merken. "At this time I cannot accept a rejection of my short story. I accept more than 99 percent of the rejections I receive. Many I don't agree with, but I realize that accepting a piece of fiction for publication is a very subjective judgment call. My acceptance of your rejection letter is also a subjective process and therefore I am returning your letter to you. I did read your letter. I read every letter I receive. Your letter was well-written, but due to time constraints from my own writing schedule, I am unable to make editorial comments. I do make mistakes. Don't you, as an editor, be disheartened by this role reversal. The road of publishing is long and tedious. You need successful publications and I need for successful publications to print my stories. I will expect to see my story in your next publication. Good luck in the future."

     • •

The range and scope are astonishing. I have twice received two-page rejection letters from magazines, one an epic and courageous deconstruction of my essay and its many flaws and few virtues, and the other an adventure in sophistry that I still marvel at, in the way you admire a deft bank robber from afar—such astounding creativity, turned to such empty enterprise. In the early days of my own career as an editor I took rejecting pieces very seriously, and tried, as much as possible, to write a thoughtful note explaining why the piece was not quite something for me to accept and pay for. But as all new editors learn, such earnest letters from editors very often are taken by writers as invitations to amend and resubmit pieces, or worse, to argue and debate, and most editors come round eventually to terse generalities simply to defend their working hours and shreds of sanity. Plus I learned that debating poets in particular was painful, although it did give me the chance to daydream about a series of rejection notes designed specifically for poems, which would fault rhythm, meter, cadence, swing, image, line-breaks, verb choice, elusiveness, allusiveness, self-indulgence, self-absorption, liability to lust, and too much muck about love. I nearly had the card printed up that way, with little boxes you could check, like Edmund Wilson's famous *EDMUND WILSON REGRETS THAT HE CANNOT . . .*, or the lovely form letter that Ursula Le Guin sends to this day, but

I got sidetracked by a torrent of devotional poetry that I had to reject posthaste, and never got around to it.

＊＊

Many magazines lean on a form letter, a printed note, a card, and I study them happily. *The New Yorker*, under the gentle and peculiar William Shawn, sent a gentle yellow slip of paper with the magazine's logo and a couple of gentle sentences saying, gently, no. Under the brisker Robert Gottlieb, the magazine sent a similar note, this one courteously mentioning the "evident quality" of your submission even as the submission is declined. *Harper's* and the *Atlantic* lean on the traditional Thank You But; *Grand Street*, among other sniffy literary quarterlies, icily declines to read your submission if it has not been solicited; the *Sun* responds some months later with a long friendly note from the editor in which he mentions that he is not accepting your piece even as he vigorously commends the writing of it; the *Nation* thanks you for thinking of the *Nation*; and the *Virginia Quarterly Review* sends, or used to send, a lovely engraved card, which is worth the price of rejection. The only rejection notice I keep in plain view is that one, for the clean lines of its limbs and the grace with which it delivers its blow to the groin.

I am no poet, as friends of mine who are poets are quick to remind me, darkly, but here and there I have inflicted poems on various and sundry small quarterlies, and I have come to love the bristle and bustle with which they reject work. I mean, it takes brass balls, as my brothers say, to reject a batch of poems with a curt note while including a *subscription form to the review in the same envelope in which the rejection huddles.* You have to admire the defiant energy there, the passion for persistence. The sheer relentless drive of the small to stay alive is more remarkable, in the end, than the grandeur of the great, no?

＊＊

Sometimes I daydream of having rejection slips made up for all sorts of things in life, like for moments when I sense a silly argument brewing with my lovely and mysterious spouse, and instead of foolishly trying to lay out my sensible points which have been skewed or miscommunicated, I simply hold up a card (*BRIAN DOYLE REGRETS THAT HE IS UNABLE TO PURSUE THIS MATTER*), or for when my children ask me to drive them half a block to the park (*GET A GRIP*), or when I am invited to a meeting at work I know will drone and moan for hours (*I WOULD PREFER TO HAVE MY SPLEEN REMOVED WITH A BUTTER KNIFE*), or for overpious sermons (*GET A GRIP!*), for oleaginous politicians and other mountebanks (*IF YOU TELL ONE MORE LIE I WILL COME UP THERE AND PUMMEL YOU WITH A MAMMAL*), etc.

On the other hand, what if my lovely and mysterious spouse issued me a rejection slip on the wind-whipped afternoon when I knelt, creaky even then, on a high hill over the wine-dark sea, and stammered *would would would will will will you you marry me*? What if she had leaned down (well, not quite leaned down, she's the size of a heron) and handed me a lovely engraved card that said *WE REGRET TO INFORM YOU THAT WE CANNOT ACCEPT YOUR PROPOSAL, DESPITE ITS OBVIOUS MERITS*? But she didn't. She did say *yeah*, or I thought she said *yeah*, the wind was really blowing, and then she slapped her forehead and went off on a long monologue about how she couldn't *believe* she said *yeah* when she wanted to say *yes*, her mom had always warned her that if she kept saying *yeah* instead of *yes* there would come a day when she would say *yeah* instead of *yes* and really regret it, and indeed this very day had come to pass, one of those rare moments when your mom was exactly right and prescient, which I often think my mom was when she said to me darkly many years ago *I hope you have kids exactly like you*, the ancient Irish curse. Anyway, there I was on my knees for a while, wondering if my lovely and mysterious paramour had actually said yes, while she railed and wailed into the wind, and finally I said, um, is that an affirmative? because my knees are killing me here, and she said, clearly, yes.

.   .

I suppose the whole concept of the editorial Yes is properly the bailiwick of another essay altogether, but I cannot help pondering the positive for a moment, for there are so very many ways to say yes, more than there are to say no, which is interesting on a philosophical and cultural level as well as an editorial one. You can say yes with glee and astonishment, you can say yes with the proviso that you anticipate changing this bit or that, you can say yes while also saying we'll need to sail toward one more draft, you can say yes to a piece of the piece, you can say yes to the idea but not to the piece, or you can, in a sense, say yes to the writer but not to the piece — this isn't quite for us, but we're interested in the verve and bone of your work, call me. The best advice for saying yes I've heard came from a friend of mine who edits a nature magazine. *Use the phone,* he says. *It matters that a voice says yes.* This is the same guy who says you should always envision a writer as your mom when you say no, so as to avoid being snotty, and that you should overpay a young writer on principle once a year, just to mess with the universe.

.   .

My friend James and I have for years now plotted a vast essay about editing, an essay we may never write because we have children and paramours and jobs and books to write, but we take great glee in sketching it out, because there are hundreds of subtle joys and crimes of editing, and editing is hardly ever what the non-inky world thinks it is, which is copyediting, which is merely the very last and easiest piece of editing — rather like a crossword puzzle, something you can do near-naked and beer in hand. *Real* editing means staying in touch with lots of writers, and poking them on a fairly regular basis about what they are writing and reading and thinking and obsessing about and what they have always wanted to write but haven't, and also it means sending brief friendly notes to lots of writers you have never worked with yet in hopes that you will, and also it means listening to lots and lots of people about lots and lots of ideas, some or all of which might wend their way into your pages, and it means being hip to the zeitgeist enough to mostly ignore it, and it means reading your brains out, and it means always having your antennae up for what you might excerpt or borrow or steal, and it means tinkering with pieces of writing to make them lean and taut and clear, and always having a small room open in the back of your head where you mix and match pieces to see if they have any zest or magnetism together, and it means developing a third eye for cool paintings and photographs and drawings and sculptures and carvings that might elevate your pages, and writing captions and credits and titles and subheads and contents pages, and negotiating with and calming the publisher, and fawning at the feet of the mailing manager, and wheedling assistants and associates, and paying essayists more than poets on principle, and soliciting letters to the editor, and avoiding conferences and seminars, and sending the printer excellent bottles of wine on every holiday, including Ramadan and Kwanzaa, just in case.

..

And dickering with photographers, battling in general on behalf of the serial comma, making a stand on behalf of saddle-stitching against the evil tide of perfect-bound publications, halving the number of witticisms in any piece of prose, reading galleys backwards to catch any stupid line breaks or egregious typos, battling on behalf of the semicolon, throwing away all business cards that say *PROFESSIONAL WRITER*, trying to read over-the-transom submissions within a week of their arrival, deleting the word *unique* on general principle and sending anonymous hate mail to anyone who writes the words *fairly unique*, snarling at writers who write *We must* or *We should* or, God help us all, the word *shan't*, searching with mounting desperation for a scrap or shard or snippet of humor in this bruised and blessed world, reminding male writers that it's OK to acknowledge that there are other people on the planet, halving the number of times any writer says *me* or *I*, checking page numbers maniacally, throwing away cover letters, checking the budget twice a day, and trying to read not most but all of your direct competitors, on the off-chance that there might be something delicious to steal.

And then away to lunch.

· ·

My friend James has a lovely phrase for the joy of actually editing a piece: mechanic's delight, he calls it, and I know whereof he speaks, for I have sipped of that cup with a deep and inarticulate pleasure. I have been down in the engine room of very fine writers' minds, my fingers following the snick and slide of their ideas into sentences. I have worked like hercules to clean and repair a flawed piece and bring out the song fenced round by muddle. I have distilled vast wanderings into brief journeys. I have snarled with delight to discover a writer deliberately leaving a fat paragraph for me to cut, a gift he confessed with a grin. I have said no to the great when they were fulsome and yes to the unknown when they were stunning. Many times I have said yes when I should have said no, for all sorts of reasons, some of them good, and more times than I know I said no when I should have said yes.

· ·

I have rejected essays but turned them into letters to the editor. I have rejected essays but asked to borrow one or two of their paragraphs for class notes in the back of my magazine. I have rejected essays but recommended submission to another magazine, which is a polite service to the writer, but I have also rejected essays and inflicted the submission on another magazine, which is a venial sin. I have rejected essays by pleading space concerns, which is not always a lie. I have rejected essays I admired for inchoate reasons that can only be caught in the tiny thimble of the word *fit*, about which another essay could be written. *It doesn't quite fit*, could there be any wider and blanker phrase in the language, a phrase that fits all sorts of things?

· ·

I was lucky to train under wonderful and testy editors, a long brawling line of them, starting with my dad, who edited a small trade newspaper, laying it out in the basement of our house with redolent rubber cement and long strips of galleys and galley shears the size of your head. He was and is a man of immense dignity and kindness, and no editor or writer ever had a better first editor than my dad, to whom I would show my early awful overwritten overlyrical self-absorbed stories, which he would read slowly and carefully, and then hand them back, saying gently *beginning, middle, end.* I thought he was going nuts early, the old man, but he was telling me, in his gentle way, that my pieces were shallow, and that no amount of lovely prose matters unless it tells a tale — a lesson I have tried to remember daily since.

On my first day as an editor, in Chicago many years ago, beneath the roar and rattle of the elevated train, the first great editor I worked for gave me a gnomic speech about how *we do not use the word hopefully to begin a sentence here*, another remark I never forgot. Later, in Boston, I worked for a very good editor whose mantra was *elevate the reader*, and then I worked, again in Boston, for a genius editor who actually had a bottle of whiskey in his desk and a green eyeshade in his office. He cursed beautifully, in great rushes and torrents, and wrote like a roaring angel, and had been in a rabbinical seminary, and had shoveled shit in an Australian circus, and driven a cab in Brooklyn, and much else. As testy and generous a man as I ever met, and a glorious editor, whose driving theme was *say something real, write true things, cut to the chase.* More advice I have not forgotten (hope-fully).

• •

Some of the best yesses I have issued over the years: yes to a sixty-year-old minister in Texas who had never published an essay in his life or even sent one to an editor but he finally wrote down (very slowly, he told me later) a brief piece about the two times in his life, many years apart, a Voice spoke to him out of the air clear as a bell and to his eternal credit he did not in the essay try to ex-plain or comment on these speakings for which refusal to opine I would have kissed him, given the chance. Yes to a twenty-year-old woman who wrote a lean perfect piece about her job run-ning the ancient wooden-horse carousel in a shopping mall. Yes to a sixty-year-old woman who wrote the greatest two-line poem I have ever seen to date. Yes to a thirty-year-old Mormon man who wrote an absolutely haunting essay about laughter (which was also funny). Yes to a twenty-year-old woman who was a waitress in a bar in a rotten part of town and wrote a haunting brief piece about the quiet people who sat at the bar every night when it closed. Yes to a sixty-year-old man who drives a bus and wrote a piece about a six-year-old girl who was so broken and so hilarious and so brave that when I finished reading the essay I put my face in my hands and wept and wept. Yes to a fifty-year-old doctor who had sent me arch essay after arch essay but finally sent me a perfect essay about the best teacher she ever had, to which I said yes so fast I nearly broke a finger. Yes to half of an essay by Andre Dubus, an essay we were cheerfully arguing about when he died of a heart attack, and I asked his oldest son if I could print the good half and not the mediocre half, and he said yes, which made me smile, for I could almost hear Andre cursing at me happily from the afterworld, in that dark amused growly drawly rumble he had when alive.

• •

When my own essays are rejected I immediately inflict them on another editor, whereas I am always mindful of my dad's advice that a piece isn't really finished unless it is off your desk and onto another's, and I am that lesser species of writer who can never stay focused on One Important Project but always has four or five pieces bubbling at once, so my writing life is a sort of juggling act, with pieces flying here and there, some slumping home through the mailbox and others sailing sprightly away in their Sunday best, eager and open-faced. When one slouches home, weary and dusty, I spruce him up and pop him into the mail and lose track until either he comes home again riddled with arrows or I get a postcard from another desk, sometimes in another country, *I've found a home!*

And then every few years I gather some thirty or forty together again, actually printing them out and spreading them out on the floor, a motley reunion, so as to make a collection of essays, and I have often thought that there is an essay even in this small odd act, their jostling for position, my kneeling over them attentively, worrying again about their health, listening to their changed and seasoned voices, listening for who wants to stand by whom, putting them in parade order like kindergartners bounding off on a field trip, two by two like braces of birds. No one ever talks about the paternal aspect of being a writer, the sending of your children off into the world, where they make their own way, go to work, enter homes, end up in the beds of strangers, and only occasionally do I hear news from the frontier. But such is the wage of age.

. .

Why *do* editors say no, anyway? Well, I cannot, of course, speak for All Editors, and I cannot even properly speak for myself, because I reject some pieces from a murky inarticulate intuitive conviction that they're just not our speed, but there are some general truths to note. We say no because we don't print that sort of material. We say no because the topic is too far afield. We say no because we have printed eleven pieces of just that sort in the past year alone. We say no because the writing is poor, muddled, shallow, shrill, incoherent, solipsistic, or insane. We say no because we have once before dealt with the writer and still shiver to remember the agony which we swore to high heaven on stacks of squirrel skulls never to experience again come hell or high water. We say no sometimes because we have said yes too much and there are more than twenty pieces in the hopper and none of them will see the light of day for months and the last of the ones waiting may be in the hopper for more than two years, which will lead to wailing and the gnashing of teeth. We say no because if we published it we would be sued by half our advertisers. We say no because we know full well that this is one of the publisher's two howling bugabears, the other one being restoring American currency to the silver standard. We say no because we are grumpy and have not slept properly and are having dense and complex bladder problems. We say no because our daughters came home yesterday with Mohawk haircuts and boyfriends named Slash. We say no because Britney Spears has sold more records worldwide than Bruce Springsteen. We say no for more reasons than we know.

••

Even now, after nearly thirty years as an editor, years during which I have rejected thousands of essays and articles and poems and profiles and ideas (even once a play, *I have rejected a play*, there's the phrase of the day), I still, even now, often feel a little sadness when I say no. Not always—I feel nothing but cold professionalism when I reject a submission from someone who clearly hasn't the slightest idea or interest in the magazine itself, and is just using the magazine as a generic target for his or her work; for example, people who submit fiction, which we have never published—or never published knowingly, let's say.

But far more often the writers *have* looked at the magazine, and *are* submitting something we might publish, and *did* make it with all their hearts, and it just doesn't make it over the amorphous and inexplicable bar set in my head, and I decline their work with a twinge of regret, for I would so like to say yes, to reward their labor and creativity, the way in which they have opened their hearts and souls, the courage they have shown in bleeding on the page and sending it to a man they do not know, for judgment, for acceptance, for rejection. So very often I find myself admiring grace and effort and craftsmanship, honesty and skill, piercing and penetrating work, even as I turn to my computer to type a rejection note, or reach for one of our own printed rejection slips, to scrawl something encouraging atop my illegible signature. So very many people working so very hard to connect, and here I am, slamming doors day after day.

..

After lo these many years as a magazine editor I have settled on a single flat sentence for my own use ("Thanks for letting me read your work, but it's not quite right for this magazine," a sentence I have come to love for the vast country of *not quite right*, into which you could cram an awful lot of sins), but I still have enduring affection for the creative no, such as this gem sent to a writer by a Chinese publication: "We have read your manuscript with boundless delight, and if we were to publish your paper, it would be impossible for us to publish any work of a lower standard. And, as it is unthinkable that in the next thousand years we shall see its equal, we are, to our regret, compelled to return your divine composition and beg you a thousand times to overlook our short sight and timidity."

I have been an editor for thirty years, and in those dark and inky years during which my eyesight has gone and my fingertips have been hammered into blunt squares, my patience evaporated and my posture shot to hell, I have never seen, given, or received anything to top that as a rejection notice, and so I conclude as once did that noted editor Henry Louis Mencken, of Baltimore, who once finished a harangue aimed at newspaper editors (whom he called "a gang of pecksniffs") by noting that "no one has asked me for my views, and moreover, my experience in the past has not convinced me that they are desired. So perhaps I had better shut up and sit down," which I do.

[VOL. XXX, NO. 2 / SPRING 2008]

A Life in Pods

"You push a button. You count to thirty. You have a sensational cup of coffee, as fresh as it is frothy." So says the instruction sheet for my new coffeemaker, a gift from my husband, who, it might be noted, has never been a coffee drinker. When questioned about the gift, he confesses to having picked it up for free at some promotional event at the mall. Upon reading the fine print, I understand why the company is giving the machines away: "Our coffee pods are specially designed and premeasured with our coffee blends. One pod makes one sensational cup of coffee." It's not the machine they make the money on: it's the pod.

Because I am not averse to the occasional new experience, I decide to give the machine a whirl. As promised, there is no labor and mess involved. All I have to do is add the water, drop in the pod, and wait. Within thirty seconds, the coffee is dispensed directly into the cup, not unlike those vending machines one finds at auto body shops and in the lobbies of highway motels. If I were making a cup of coffee by the antiquated method to which I've become accustomed, I'd still be measuring the beans at this point.

But already, I am disappointed. I miss the rough texture and heady fragrance of the beans, the noisy whir of the grinder, the slow gurgle of water making its way through the filter basket. I take a sip and am unsurprised to find that the prepackaged concoction, Vanilla Bistro, resembles the instant coffee I subsisted on in college. Instead of the complex, layered flavors of a well-roasted coffee bean, there is a cloying chemical taste, sugary but not truly sweet, with a vanilla-ish tang that is to real vanilla what a McDonald's apple turnover is to a homemade apple pie.

.   .

I recently spotted one of my graduate students outside the university where I teach, sitting alone on the stoop, eyes closed, head tilted to the side. A thin white cord stretched from each ear to her open palm, on which rested a rectangular white disk, narrower than a business card and not much thicker, bearing the telltale pome. I half expected to see a professional camera crew rounding the corner, for Apple could not have designed a finer advertisement for the iPod shuffle. Or rather, Apple *had* designed this image almost verbatim (it towers over 101 on a billboard drivers can't miss), and my student—attractively slim, fashionably dreadlocked, trendily oblivious to everyone around her—had, intentionally or not, mimicked the ad with precision.

The iPod, like the coffee pod, offers not the experience of the thing itself but instead a simulation of such, neatly packaged and conveniently sized. Both pods promise a tidy, singular experience: just enough coffee for one, thank you very much, just enough music for me. Gone is the chaotic café, the boisterous concert hall. Gone are the coffee grounds littering the kitchen counter, the friends gathered around the living room stereo. What remains is a pared-down product from which the soul—and the society—has been neatly extracted.

.   .

My earliest experience with the pod was as a young child, sitting on my grandmother's porch in rural Mississippi, shelling peas. My grandmother and I occupied identical wooden rocking chairs, three metal bowls arranged on the small table in front of us. One contained pea pods, green and fragrant and plump; one held the shelled peas, which plinked pleasingly against the sides of the bowl; another was reserved for the empty pods, ripped open at the seams. We were accompanied by my sister, my mother, and a few aunts and cousins.

The front door of my grandmother's house stood open, a screen in place to keep out the flies. Added to the green scent of peas was the smell of coffee percolating in the kitchen just a few yards away. The percolator was a ceramic affair, big enough to serve all the adult women who had gathered for the shelling. Every half hour or so, I would take a break from the monotony of peas to help my mother with the coffee. What anticipation I felt, watching the dark liquid bubbling up into the little glass dome. Upon removing the lid, my mother would lower her face to the urn and breathe deeply, blissfully, before pouring the coffee into an eclectic assortment of mugs, which I would then deliver to the adults. The endless peas that needed shelling, combined with endless mugs of coffee, made the conditions just right for socializing.

The term *kaffeeklatsch* was coined in Germany in the early twentieth century, a derogatory reference to the way women gossiped during afternoon coffee. It is unlikely that the women of my family would have heard the phrase, but they could easily pass an afternoon talking about who had been saved and who had backslidden, who had married and who had died, what local girls or boys had run off to Jackson or joined the Army or taken up alcohol. Over a string of steamy summers, I gladly suffered the achy hands and blistered fingers that invariably resulted from an afternoon shelling peas in exchange for my seeming invisibility at these gatherings, when the women divulged all kinds of secrets they wouldn't ordinarily utter in front of the children.

• •

Chocolate, one of the most coveted natural elixirs known to man, has its origin in the pod. The cocoa pod looks nothing like the pea pod. It is large and tubular, generally yellow or light green; when fully ripe, it resembles a gourd. The cocoa tree, *Theobroma cacao*, is cauliflorous, which means that the pod grows directly from the trunk, giving the tree an oddly tumescent appearance, as if it is in the clutches of some exotic disease or the victim of some parasitic growth. Whereas pea pods are geographically widespread, cocoa trees, and thus their coveted pods, exist only within twenty degrees of the equator.

The inception of a cocoa pod is a delicate business: the flowers of the cocoa tree open at night and have only forty-eight hours to be pollinated. Among the insects that take part in this particular botanical waltz are midges, ants, aphids, wild bees, and thrips (the latter of which are known as "thunder bugs," because they are finicky flyers, preferring to remain at rest except during thunderstorms). Given this limited window for romance, it's not surprising that only about one out of every hundred flowers on the cocoa tree eventually yields a pod. By the time the pod has ripened, 150 to 180 days after pollination, it contains rows of white beans encased in a sweet, milky pulp. A split-open cocoa pod has an unmistakably sexual look, which is appropriate, given the cocoa bean's aphrodisiac quality. (The last time my husband wooed me with truffles from San Francisco's famed chocolatier Joseph Schmidt, we ended up with a pea, as they say, in the pod.)

..

A full pea pod of the inedible variety is seductively curvy, its miniature hills and valleys formed by the treasure hidden inside. The pod is covered with fine hairs suggestive of the lanugo that coats newborn human infants. The peas in a pod are arranged in a row, each pea touching the same seam.

Snow peas and snap peas have edible pods, so the pea need never be separated from its natural container, while garden peas or "English peas," those tender, round bits so popular in chicken pot pies and casseroles, are, in modern-day life, almost always divorced from the pod before we lay eyes on them. Garden peas were considered such a delicacy in France toward the end of the seventeenth century that one Madame de Maintenon wrote in

1696, "Some ladies, even after having supped at the Royal Table, and well supped too, returning to their own homes, at the risk of suffering from indigestion, will again eat peas before going to bed. It is both a fashion and a madness."

Might the small, boat-shaped pod—gorgeously curved, unexpectedly hairy—have contributed to this insatiable lust for peas? Or was it the thrill of ingesting a tiny, taut bit that had been divested of its protective shell? The uncontained thing enjoys a kind of sensual quality that the neatly ordered thing does not: a mound of rolling, plinking peas; loose coffee beans spilling through one's outstretched fingers; a riff emanating from an acoustic guitar inches from one's ears.

··

In the Wachowski brothers' 1999 film *The Matrix*, all of humankind is reduced to a podded existence. Human beings pass their lives in complete solitude, each trapped within his or her own pod. The pod system has been orchestrated by the computers that run the planet, and people are little more than expendable battery power for the bio-electrical energy on which the computers exist. The pod here is a symbol of imprisonment and isolation. One of the more interesting aspects of the movie is that, save for the messianic Neo, the prophetic Morpheus, and a few stylishly clad disciples, humans are oblivious to their enslaved condition. Within the darkened pods, entire lives unfold in rich Technicolor. A person's life is not actual, but virtual. He or she loves, suffers, bears children, ages, eats, plays sports, reads, makes love, composes music, commits acts of kindness or cruelty—everything that could possibly occur within the span of a life occurs also in the pods, as each individual slumbers alone and untouched through a lifelong dream of living. Only in death are the machines' unwitting victims, like Randall Jarrell's ball turret gunner, "loosed from the dream of life."

··

Should you find yourself near the Empire State Building during regular business hours, and should you be feeling sleepy or over-stimulated or simply at odds with the world, you might be tempted to take the elevator to the twenty-fourth floor, home of MetroNaps, where, for fourteen dollars per session, you can drift off to dreamland in the comfort of your own private sleep pod. The ad copy on the company Web site reads like something straight out of a futuristic horror flick. In the MetroNap pod, a glowing white, egg-like contraption in which one reclines for the prescribed twenty minutes — no more, no less — customers receive "the quick recharge needed so they can do more with their day, both professionally and personally."

Remember the infamous pea that kept the delicate princess from getting her beauty rest? In the sleep pod, whose "contours are perfect for napping" and whose "mechanical processes are perfect for waking," the urban professional prince or princess *becomes* the pea. In a small room lit by softly glowing sconces, the MetroNap customer listens to "tranquil, relaxation-inducing music," waiting to be awakened "with a gentle combination of light and vibration."

Unlike cocoa beans or peas, which nest in comfortable proximity to others of their ilk, the pod-bound urbanite is the very emblem of isolation. Gone is the passion of the illicitly shared bed, the side-by-side collusion of matrimonial slumber. Gone is the thrill of rubbing limb to limb, the delicious shiver of skin touching skin. To be a sleeper in a pod is to be both product and proponent of a flawed equation, a heartless modern mathematics which insists that to be relaxed is to be alone.

． ．

Whales, dolphins, and seals travel in groups called pods. The groupings are often matrilineal, although there are many variations on the composition of the pods. The stronger whales within a pod protect the sick, the young, and the injured. Pods comprised of females and their offspring allow a mother to dive deep for food while her calf is protected by the other adults. When one member of a whale pod seeks shallow water due to sickness, the other members follow along; marine biologists speculate that this may account for the fact that whales are often found stranded in groups, entire pods risking death to avoid abandoning a single member. Members of a dolphin pod play together and engage in sexual relations with one another. The size of dolphin pods tends to increase with water depth and openness of habitat — in other words, with proximity to danger. Sometimes several pods temporarily join together to form herds comprised of hundreds.

Far from the isolationist tendencies of the techno-pods which have become a part of our daily existence, these marine pods are the very emblem of sociability and fellow feeling.

• •

Whether synthetic or organic, biological or technological, all pods share the function of containment. The pod protects, holds together, creates symmetry; simultaneously, it excludes, isolates. In the case of marine mammals on the open sea, this exclusivity is key to survival. In the case of the land mammal *Homo sapiens*, its implications are far less elegant.

All across the United States, from major metropolitan centers like Los Angeles and Chicago to smaller, lesser-known cities, a dazed-looking populace shuttles frantically from pod to pod, activity to activity, along a discombobulated network of freeways and frontage roads, side streets, and subdivisions. Even our mode of transportation, the glassed-in automobile, which grows more pod-like with every concession to aerodynamics, serves as a sort of insulation, keeping the crowd at bay. In a document titled "Traditional Urban Design and the Municipal Zoning Ordinance," Demetri Baches, former planning director for Belmont, North Carolina, calls for a return to a traditional, integrative approach to urban design, lamenting the fact that "the city has been broken up into pods of identical product, each pod unrelated to the other."

It is this very unrelatedness that drives the current passion for pods. One may listen to one's iPod while sipping coffee brewed from a prepackaged, single-serving pod. One may do all of this in the confines of the office cubicle before racing off to nap in a gleaming white pod. It becomes less and less necessary to speak or be spoken to. The modern pod in all its permutations is designed to deliver the greatest amount of individual satisfaction with the least amount of social interaction. Our passion for the pod is symptomatic of our growing elevation of luxury over society, singularity over community. What matters is what you *have*, not whom you enjoy it with.

I know it is old-fashioned and painfully out of style to long for a lifestyle aesthetic in which the word "company" refers to the people you're with instead of the economic entity that produced your latest gadget. I am aware of the myriad arguments for how technology brings us together, and I don't deny that there are many ways in which technology makes human connection easier than it has historically been. But there is no question that it is also much easier these days to disconnect, to implant oneself for hours, days, even weeks at a time in a self-styled pod of personal convenience in which productivity may be increased, but *pleasure*—pleasure as it has been known for millennia, in every civilization—is exponentially decreased.

To be civilized is to live in harmony with other citizens, to accept one's place in the crowd, as part of a larger whole. The pod, of course, cannot eliminate the crowd, but it can and does make the crowd, for the purposes of the individual, temporarily disappear. It is a deceptive kind of magic. No matter how melodic the music, how frothy the coffee, how cozy the space where we prop up our feet to enter the world of our own dreaming, we must eventually emerge from the pod. Like Hanra, the accidental hero of Bohumil Hrabal's haunting meditation on literature and loneliness, we may wake one day to find that we have endured too loud a solitude.

Diablo Baby

Which one of you is my father?

I know what you, with the twitching lips, and you, and you — with the knotting eyebrows and bulging notebook — will say. The obvious thing. Ask your mother.

I have. She speaks to me (and sings to me and dances for me) just as a mother should. And I, Diablo Baby, talk to her. I never gooed and gaaed and gurgled like other mothers' babies. Why pretend to be ordinary when you are not?

But when I ask her the big question, all she can do is show me a tattered rag of a sari. It is bleached cotton, so old, frayed and grimy that it could be a strip of dry bark curling at the edges. But the picture on it glistens; white chalk flesh, yellow and red hibiscus of vegetable dye. There is a body in the picture, a body that has trapped the glint of silver in its bulges and ripples and folds. A piece of bloated moon that sits on a carpet of succulent forest flowers, on a sheet of smooth, fiery blood.

I have looked at this image many times. In it my reflection holds still. (When I look at myself in the stream, the water trembles, afraid of my steady gaze, my horns, my tattoos.)

My mother made the picture. She also made me. She thinks she had some help there, though she knows no names to name. When I ask her, Where is my father, she replies, In my head.

Then you came, she says, so we don't need him any more. And we have the picture, don't we? And the story in the picture?

So if I want a father, I must mine a story as strange and

raggedy as my mother. A story with a forest girl, a temple, a church, a baby. And a blue-white, horned, phantom lover.

On the edge of the forest was a village and in the heart of the village were two buildings, one on the right side of the dusty street, one on the left. The buildings could have been brothers, so alike were their mortared, whitewashed walls. But like many brothers, their heads were somewhat different. The building to the right, a temple, had a brick pyramid for a head. A tapering triangle of a *gopuram* sat like a stiff hat pulled down over its face. At the tip of this hat, a solitary red flag waved in the breeze. A piece of the flag was cut out of its right side so that what remained was a trembling, open mouth.

The building to the left, a church, had a more modest, flat head. But a huge bell filled up the balcony that jutted out of its forehead. Even bigger and more impressive was the cross crowning the roof. The cross was painted a dazzling white that sucked in the sunlight and threw a halo around itself.

Every morning at daybreak, a girl in a torn, dirty sari carrying a basket and a broom made her way to the temple. As usual there was a big brass tray waiting for her on the step nearest the open front door. She put down her broom and uncovered the basket that was covered with a piece of damp cloth. She emptied the basketful of blazing red and pink and orange hibiscus onto the brass plate. Then she picked up the broom and went around to the backyard where yesterday's flowers lay in a limp and fleshy pile along with everything else that had been swept out of the temple. She filled the basket with this rubbish, sorting it first to see what was there. Anything edible she pulled out and slipped into the little bundle tied to the end of her sari.

The temple-priest called out to her as he did every morning. Hey Sukhi, he said. The flowers are really fresh this morning. I don't know where you manage to find them. Do you want some pieces of coconut?

Sukhi nodded and he threw a large handful in her direction. She picked up the pieces and sat on her haunches, chewing.

He lingered at the back door while she ate. He was bald, with a tuft of hair at the back of his head. He was always bare-chested, and the jungle of dark hair on his chest made him look like a tame bear.

He frowned at the broom lying by her.

Still working for the foreign devil? he asked. Why do you go to the white man's temple?

Sukhi stopped chewing and considered this with puzzlement. Who is a devil? she asked. And why is he white?

He sniggered and threw her a few more pieces of coconut. You'll find out soon enough, he said, looking at her knowingly. You keep sweeping that church day after day and you'll meet the devil all right. A white devil with a blazing cross on his heart. Gray eyes shining out of his chalk face like a hungry cat.

Sukhi picked up her broom and basket. You stop working there if you know what's good for you, he called after her.

Sukhi swept the church with her broom; her basket was now filled to the brim with junk from both temple and church. Then she dusted and polished the silver cup at the altar.

The church-priest gave her a coin. He also gave her something to eat. She liked sitting in the church's backyard, chewing and thinking her own thoughts. But neither the temple-priest nor the church-priest could leave her alone. Neither could do without her, so lovely and fresh were the flowers she brought every morning, and so well did she sweep and dust and polish.

Now the church-priest began his usual sermon as she ate. Still taking flowers to that temple? he asked, eyeing the wilted flowers in her basket.

My child, he said, his voice growing rich and sonorous. Come home to this church and be saved. Remember what I have told you. The devil is always watching you from where he sits burning in hell. He waits, the devious snake, to open his mouth and strike. He is horned; he is lecherous. When he sees the bare breasts under your sari, when he finds your untouched soul, do you think he will let you go?

Ah, the devil again, thought Sukhi, and she listened carefully. Though the temple-priest and the church-priest can't bear each other, they have this mysterious devil in common.

Her head was full of the devil as she made her way back into the forest. The forest was still, in a deep, stupefied sleep. In fact, the forest that afternoon was a fit place for the devil, if he really liked fire as much as the priests said he did. She could feel the relentless fire on her head and back and feet as she made her way, a single thought throbbing in her head, never pausing till she reached the pool. The watering hole was deserted except for a few thirsty birds that took wing as she neared the water.

She was hot, so hot. She pulled the filthy sari off her body and went naked into the water. The world outside her closed eyes was a furious blur of orange.

She thought she felt something cool slither up her leg. It could have been a water snake, but she did not move. Instead she heard herself whispering playfully, teasingly, Devil, are you here? Are you watching me?

She floated. She must have floated for hours, or floated into sleep, or into a dream. In this place where she had drifted, a lost and empty boat looking for its moorings, the fiery world waiting outside her eyelids had vanished. The heat had dissolved, so had the priests, and her hungry sunburnt body in the muddy forest pool. The cool-tongued intruder making his way up her leg lived in this place where there was no thirst, no drudge of filling the belly. The fire on her skin was being put out. The anger and bewilderment in her heart were dying. And at the very last moment, just before the coolness slipped out of her and left her, she saw, though her eyes were still shut, an image she could capture again in meticulous, three-dimensional detail. She need never be alone again. She saw a baby plump with her desire, sharp-horned, self-possessed. On his body he flaunted all the caste marks of his paternity, or the lack of it.

[VOL. XXX, NO. 4 / FALL 2008]

I Met Loss the Other Day

I met Loss the other day. I took his measurements. My yellow tape looped around my arm, pins held tight between my pursed lips, I circled him. I measured his thin wrists, his frail neck, his elegantly sloped shoulders. Inseam, sleeve length, the stretch of his forearm, I marked them down in pencil.

He was small. He stood very still as I worked.

His entourage, six thick-necked men, boisterous despite their size, pale handkerchiefs peeking from their dark suits' breast pockets, poked in the nooks and crannies of my shop. They hula-hooped with my skirt wires, nudged one another with my dead mother's ornate wood-handled umbrella, tossed fabric bolts back and forth. Loss looked straight ahead, glancing over only when a crash erupted or someone called to him affectionately.

No one used his name. To them, he was Oss, Lossie, Bone-daddy.

Loss wanted a single-breasted suit, standard issue, merino wool and cashmere with a peaked lapel, but also a prayer robe and a felt cloak. He was going on holiday, he told me. Where, he didn't say.

He produced a tailor's pattern book from 1589. I turned the dry pages. Cutting patterns for clerical robes, silk kirtles, ropa de letrado, all given in ells. One ell equals forty-five inches: this is ancestral knowledge, parceled with the family Bible and shears, passed down the years from grandfather to father, father to son. Loss didn't know this. He handed me a conversion table.

"A Savile Row tailor threw me out," he told me.

I told Loss I could give him what he wanted. Ducking the pincushions that whizzed by my head, I flipped through my notebook to a blank page and noted his figuration and posture. I asked him to stand relaxed. He nodded but remained stiff.

As I sketched, I asked Loss about his operation.

Hundreds of people were in his employ, Loss told me. Cataloguing, mostly. Rows of dark heads with neat parts bent over typewriters, clacking away.

"You can't imagine the clamor," he said. "Eventually it numbs you."

Worse, Loss said, were the administrative meetings. The ceaseless bickering over what constituted loss. Keys, located after four panicky minutes: lost or just misplaced? A silver dollar stolen from an aunt's purse and tossed down a wishing well, a swallowed tooth, an uncle in the grasp of dementia. How are we to gauge? The problems of classification were endless and unyielding.

As he spoke, I saw the warehouses. Each person's losses filed in long skinny drawers. The cavernous echo of clerks' footsteps as they pushed ladders to the far reaches. Each birth a long span of empty drawer that filled. Slow or quick, it always filled.

Each time someone died, Loss told me, the records were purged. In the night, bonfires dotted the perimeter.

I finished. We discussed drape and cut, scheduled a second fitting. Loss offered to pay in cash. Half up front, half after the skeleton baste. His money roll was enormous. He peeled away crisp hundreds like onion skins.

"No need to pay the second half," I told him. Loss raised an eyebrow.

"Have a clerk pull my note cards," I said. "I'll take those instead."

Loss shook his head. Beneath his eyes were tiny plum veins.

"They'd fill a wheelbarrow. Take the money. Buy something. Only in Vegas can you trade with your losses."

I hefted the heavy felt in my hands. Loss reached out and stroked it. I waited. He said nothing.

I waited some more.

"Okay," Loss said finally, "but just a sampling. And duplicates only." We shook.

After he left, I oiled my shears. I marked the thin brown-speckled pattern paper with Loss's measurements. Scotch-taped to the window, the paper shone like stained glass. In my hands, the fabric came apart and then together again in Loss's shape. Not alchemy, but close, I thought. Close.

At the appointed hour, Loss returned. His entourage waited outside, kicking empty cans into the gutter. In the gray light they looked at once thuggish and impossibly young.

During the fitting, Loss was patient. He stretched out his arms like a child playing airplane, reached for the sky, ducked and feinted. A few minor adjustments were agreed upon, but everything fit him beautifully.

I promised him the finished garments sewn up tight as a shroud in ten days' time. Loss nodded, said his assistant would collect them, and then reached inside his jacket and handed me three manila cards.

Each card was annotated in an old-fashioned typeface. My name appeared at the top left, the series number at the top right. Dead center was the list. *Gold filling*, the first card began. *Train schedule. Yellow slicker just before the sky opened. Bearings (ball). Bearings (sense of). Orange rind. Tax forms.*

Things I couldn't remember losing. Things I'd missed all my life.

"Sure you don't want the money?" Loss asked. "You could buy another slicker."

"No thanks," I said.

Loss shrugged. I had the sense he'd seen it before: people unwilling to let go of what was gone.

Before he let himself out, Loss brushed my cheek lightly with the back of his knuckles—just the way you always would. Just the way I know you will again, after you walk barefoot down the dirt drive to your mailbox, slit open my envelope and find these cards, after you finally hold in your hand what for all those years I could never bring myself to show you.

[VOL. XXXI, NO. 1 / WINTER 2009]